RISE

Leave What Holds You Down

AND

SOAR

Live In What Lifts You High

By Paul C. Buechel, M.D.

© 2020 by Paul C. Buechel

All rights reserved. No portion of this book may be reproduced, stored in a retrieval system, or transmitted in any form or by any means—electronic, mechanical, photocopy, recording, scanning, or other—except for brief quotations in critical reviews or articles, without the prior written permission of the publisher.

Published by Fitting Words LLC

www.fittingwords.net

Unless otherwise footnoted, all Scripture quotations are taken from THE LIVING BIBLE, copyright 1971, 1972, 1977 by Tyndale House Publishers, Wheaton, IL, 60187. All rights reserved. Used by permission.

Scripture quotations marked [ESV] are taken from the Holy Bible, English Standard Version, copyright 2001 by Crossway Bibles, a division of Good News Publishers. Used by permission. All rights reserved.

Scripture quotations marked [HCSB] are taken from the Holman Christian Standard Bible, copyright 1999, 2000, 2002, 2003 by Holman Bible Publishers, Nashville, TN. All rights reserved. Reprinted and used by permission. HOLY BIBLE: NEW INTERNATIONAL VERSION®. © 1973, 1978, 1984 by International Bible Society. Used by permission of Zondervan Publishing House. All rights reserved.

Scripture quotations marked [NKJV] are taken from the THE NEW KING JAMES VERSION. © 1982 by Thomas Nelson, Inc. Used by permission. All rights reserved.

Scripture quotations marked [KJV] are taken from The King James Version of the Bible (public domain).

John MacArthur. *Twelve Ordinary Men*. Nashville, TN: Harper Collins Christian. 2002. Used by permission.

ISBN-13: 978-1-7331023-3-9

Table of Contents

PART II

Acknowledgements

I must thank my loving and ever-supportive wife, Victoria, and my amazing daughter, Lexie, as well as my parents, Paul and Marlene, and my five siblings, Bruce, Laura, Ellen, Dan, and Marcy. God has used my life experiences and relationships with them all to forge me into what he needs me to be. Thus, I am ever grateful for their influences and love.

I also need to thank all those of other faith systems who have patiently listened and debated faith issues, as well as those who have helped me in discussions of my questions regarding their respective beliefs. My prayer for them is, if such has not occurred yet, that they and their families would ultimately have their eyes, ears, minds, and souls opened and fully enlightened by their true God and Father, allowing them to finally see the real truth of the gospel of Jesus their Christ.

I ultimately and most importantly need to thank God my Father for his inspiration to me more than three years ago for this work and, of course, for his great assistance in compiling this text. May his kingdom be furthered by the words that have been penned here!

PART I

Introduction:
Tales of Beasts and the Fire

"Those who trust in the Lord will renew their strength; they will soar on wings like eagles; they will run and not grow weary; they will walk and not faint." (Isaiah 40:31 HCSB)

Zzzzzzzzzzzzzzzzzzzzzzzzzziiinngggg! The hair stood straight up on the back of my neck. It was not quite dawn and -60° F, with a -90° F wind chill. I turned and looked around: nothing. It must be the cold.

I turned back once more to gaze upon the icy landscape before me, purple and silent in the early light. Then it happened again: zzzzzzzzzzzzzzzzzzzzzzzzzziiinngggg!

I suddenly realized that this sensation definitively was not from the bitter cold but was a warning, that primeval instinct that prey animals have possessed for millennia. Spinning around, I saw the great ice bear, a polar bear or *Nanuq*, as the Inuit call him, fifty yards away and running straight at me.

Only three hours before, I shot a nearly two-thousand-pound, nine-and-a-half-foot-tall ice bear outside my tent in the Arctic darkness as he charged into camp to make a meal out of one of us or one of our sled dogs. There wasn't time for me to even put on my boots. I stepped out onto the ice pack in thin liner socks (my feet stayed numb for days thereafter). A miracle shot at close range in the darkness ended that behemoth's threat, just as the northern lights began to dance in pinks and greens.

Now, that first bear's corpse was nearby, and my rifle was still leaning against the outer tent, one hundred long yards away. I reached down and realized I did not even have my sheath knife on my belt! I'd made a fatal mistake.

My friends warned me earlier, saying, "Even if you go behind the tent to use the bathroom, always take your rifle. Nanuq will come. You will not hear him. You will not see him. He will take you."

Whenever we three would go out to do activities such as chopping ice for a dogsled trail, only two of us axed ice. The other was assigned bear watch, holding a rifle and doing nothing but constantly scanning our perimeter for this perfect predator, one that can truly appear out of nowhere in the Arctic maze of water holes, ice blocks, and frozen towers.

My blunder was based upon my false reliance on what I had observed while spending more than seventy days in the field with brown, grizzly, and black bears in Alaska and the Lower 48. Man and dog scent contaminating an area would always drive these other bears far away. But this great white predator was a different bruin altogether. The ice bear, given the extreme cold as well as its massive size and weight, requires astronomical caloric intake to survive in this unforgiving region. So, it is a ravenous and unceasing hunter. And it fears nothing.

Unlike brown, grizzly, and black bears, the polar bear never has a chance to develop fear of man, nor any subsequent avoidance techniques. They live on the ice cap, and when the ice freezes, they come down into contact with man's hunting and whaling parties, as well as into his villages, looking for their next meal.

Their sense of smell is amazing. They regularly scent game (seal, walrus, the occasional arctic fox or ice-locked whale, man and his dogs, and even other polar bears) up to twenty miles away and once documented even sixty!

The local Inuit say, "When man and Nanuq meet on the ice, one lives and one dies." Thus, the polar bear never learns avoidance behavior. It either takes the man, or the man takes the bear.

The natives also quote an age-old Eskimo proverb in speaking to Nanuq: "Someday we shall meet in this world of ice. When that happens, it does not matter whether it is I who dies or you." These men tell me that in their village, they have to kill twenty to thirty bears yearly in self-defense. And they estimate losing eight people per year to bear attacks.

Getting back to my predicament on this particular Arctic dawn, I was unable to run given the deep snow and my heavy arctic clothes and boots. I also knew that running would kick-start the bear's predator instinct, in which case he would chase me down before I could reach the weapon; polar bears can hit speeds of thirty-five miles per hour! Again, I had made a fatal mistake.

I quickly asked for God's help and then felt his peace. I could not run, so instead I moved toward the bear, arms up, throwing ice at him, and shouting. My two Inuit friends and our ten sled dogs all lay fast asleep. The strong wind carried my voice away from them.

The bear slowed down, stalking me between ice blocks. I had a camera and snapped a few photos to document my demise while slowly backing up, keeping my eyes on him and getting ever closer to my .375 H&H. As much as he could, he instinctively kept his large black nose and mouth behind ice blocks, peering at me over the ice pieces with piercingly cold black eyes. Mother bears teach their cubs this stealth technique at an early age, making them nearly invisible amongst the ice.

Nanuq then went over to the dead bear and put his nose into the very boot tracks where I had been standing when I had received God's warning. Then his massive head came up. He was huffing and snorting, impressively blowing snow from his nostrils in an unforgettable and amazing display of power and defiance.

Then this nine-and-a-half-foot, two-thousand-pound ultimate predator decided the dead bear was an easier breakfast. He began ripping off big chunks of the frozen meat, wolfing these down for five minutes. He then stood up and looked straight at me before turning and walking off. The Lord had saved me once again. It was the second of what would soon be three times withn several days.

***

In the Arctic you are required to fly in full cold-weather gear in the event of an emergency landing. My pilot and my guide said it was the coldest winter there in fifty years. Our single-engine plane's two-hour flight north from Tuktoyaktuk was ending. I recall seeing the sun dip below the horizon on our descent. The engine sputtered. Then both it and the propeller stopped!

The pilot let out a prolonged five-second yell, pulling on the stick and trying to get our nose back up. I remember looking behind me where my friend, a pilot himself, sat wide-eyed, sandwiched between two of our sled dogs.

Rise and Soar

To both the pilot's and our own amazement, as he pulled up and drifted, trying to regain some altitude, that engine somehow miraculously restarted, thus avoiding a crash either onto, or perhaps even through, the arctic icepack.

Further, I later became lost in an Arctic storm. I was going on just two hours' sleep when I became separated in a blinding ground blizzard, with temperatures at -60° F and wind chills at -90° F to -100° F. I sometimes resorted to driving perpendicularly to try to pick up the track of the snowmobile somewhere in front of me, which I was supposed to be following.

What was supposed to be an eight-hour trip turned into a grueling seventeen-and-a-half-hour snow machine ride back to an Eskimo village. Visibility was near zero. Fatigue and the snowstorm so slowed my reflexes that I fell off my machine twice upon hitting large ice blocks, badly jarring my neck and hip.

Then my sleep-deprived mind, with hours of nothing but white fuzzies filling my vision, began to make up sensory stimuli to fill the void. I saw caribou, stop signs, trees, fences, bridges. They seemed real, but I soon learned to ignore them—so much so that I nearly ran my machine straight through the first real pine tree I encountered at dawn as I finally neared the village.

My numbed mind upon this overnight odyssey grew so tired that all I wanted to do was dismount and lie down in a snowbank for a nap. Doing so would have likely been fatal, yet the urge was amazingly strong. I even once fell asleep on the machine while driving, arousing a brief time later at a dead stop with my head bowed to the dash!

Later, upon catching up to James, one of my normally stoical and reserved, yet now wide-eyed, Eskimo friends, I was told, "We aren't going to make it!"

Nevertheless, it was an amazing feeling to ultimately pull into that Eskimo village as the sun peeked over the horizon. Finally catching up to James, as I pulled my machine onto his homestead, he flatly said, "Paul, you are one tough hombre." I am not so sure about myself, but I do know who was and is truly the Strong One, and my God fortunately had his own plans!

***

Let us consider these verses:

> "The Lord is my light and my salvation; he protects me from danger—whom shall I fear? When evil men come to destroy me, they will stumble and fall! Yes, though a mighty army marches against me, my heart shall know no fear! I am confident that God will save me." (Psalms 27:1–3)

> "You are my Rock and my fortress; honor your name by leading me out of this peril. Pull me from the trap my enemies have set for me. For you alone are strong enough. Into your hand I commit my spirit." (Psalms 31:3–5)

> "Defend your people, Lord; defend and bless your chosen ones. Lead them like a shepherd and carry them forever in your arms." (Psalms 28:9)

I also recall his protection in another significant hunting adventure west of the Pecos River in far West Texas. It had been a multiple-hour chase at elevations up to twelve thousand feet. I finally caught up to and now faced down, at just one yard, a monstrous, one-hundred-ninety-two-pound, stock-killing mountain lion. It had killed seven horses on one ranch in just the past week. While my dogs distracted him through a flurry of claws and fangs, I held my .45 revolver right against his side and ended this threat to ranch survival. I came out amazingly unscathed.

***

"The Lord who saved me from the claws and teeth of the lion and the bear will save me from this Philistine!" (1 Samuel 17:37a)

So, I now ask of you, what are your own personal bear and lion stories? What are those beasts of your life that God has helped to sustain and to preserve you through thus far? What have you faced down, to this point, over your lifetime? Think back on how many times he has either brought you through the fire or delivered you from the fire.

I can think of many other personal examples of car accidents, falls, stupid things I did in younger days, injuries, illnesses, and multiple other missteps. Now looking back, I can clearly see how he was definitively with me, keeping me intact and molding me for his exact purposes. He protected me through each event, using each one to shape me, gradually, more and more into his instrument, albeit as imperfect and unworthy as I am. He in truth tries to do so with all of us, if we will only let him!

***

A few years back, I started a list of these saving events, those times when, in retrospect, God was either bringing me through the fireor delivering me from it. It is helpful for me to review this every so often. And this also helps our discussions of his interventions with children, grandchildren, and even younger adults who may not have such a clear grasp of his assistance and intervention in their still-early lives.

Showing God's providence to future generations can indeed be a very positive thing for a family!

Some of my life's most significant through-the-fire events include the following:

1) As a ten-year-old out walking alone in our northern winter woods after school one January day, I failed to see the bank of the iced-over river that I played and fished in each summer, as it was covered with a foot of snow atop the ice. I did not know where I was as I stepped into the snowy depression, which unbeknownst to me was actually out onto the river ice. I instantly realized my mistake as I heard a loud crack and then plunged through the ice! Immersed to my waist, I leaned quickly backward, my palms behind my back. I had somehow caught on the brittle ice edge, keeping the rest of me thus far out of the deep, raging river below, which tugged and tore at my boots and legs, trying to pull me in and underneath the ice. No water flow was visible atop the river's snow cover. To go underneath would probably have been my ultimate demise, as the entire river was iced over and covered with deep snow. For some reason, the frail ice behind my lower back, upon which my palms were clinging, did not break, and I was eventually able to worm my way, upon my back, out onto the more solid ice and then, gradually, to the bank. The temperature was about $10°$ F, with a brutally severe below-zero wind chill. My jeans froze into cast-iron leggings, and it took me well over an hour to walk the two-plus miles home given my very small steps, as I was so restricted by my now metallic pants. Looking back, there was certainly a divine intervention here!

2) A winter later, while walking through deep snow, I was once again far from my house, despite the warnings my mother would always give me. I looked up on a high hill and saw a large black shape peering down at me—a black bear! The snow was at least two feet

deep, and the monster started lumbering toward me. I ran as fast as I could down through a valley, up a hill, then down into another valley, following my tracks back toward home. Yet I knew well that little boys in deep snow cannot hope to outrun a black bear. I could hear the creature's footfalls behind me as it closed in, and soon I could even hear its panting. Suddenly, I tripped over a log hidden in the snow, landing facedown. I felt the earth-pounding steps behind me draw nearer. I covered my head and awaited the attack I expected to come. The huge creature stood right next to me, its hot breath upon my face. Then I felt something licking my cheek, and I turned over to see a huge Newfoundland, friendly as could be, simply wanting to play and give chase to this running boy. His owner came up behind me, apologizing profusely for the scare. Ever since, I have wanted one of these dogs for my own but have yet to achieve this goal!

3) At twenty years of age, while driving my 1967 Chevelle down a big hill late one summer night, the van in front of me stopped short without any turn signal, just at the bottom. We had both been going extremely fast, so there was no time to attempt to veer off the road or to get around him. Tires and metal shrieked and glass shattered as my car buried its nose and engine beneath his bumper, coming to an abrupt stop and then starting to smoke profusely. The driver's door was jammed as I tried to get out. Undoing my seatbelt, I managed to crawl across to the passenger door. It miraculously opened, despite the severe damage to the vehicle frame. I crawled out and walked around to the back of the vehicle, stumbling into the crowd that had formed. As flames appeared, the crowd became hysterical and screamed, "The driver is still in the car!" I reassured them that I was he and indeed was out. I believe this too was a miraculously divine rescue!

4) Just as a deep pre-storm darkness fell off the southeast Alaskan ABC Islands, we left the brown bear haven of salmon streams that we

had been scouting all day. We got into our small two-man skiff and headed out toward the larger boat we had come in on. Suddenly, a major storm hit. It was so severe that our craft was launched vertically up into the waves as if on a swing going to the maximum length of the chain straight upwards and then back down into the frigid black waters. The seasoned guide I was with appeared frightened—a bad sign, as he had decades of experience. I had hip waders on, so my plan was that whenever we capsized or were thrown into the sea (as appeared imminent), I would pull these off and roll down the tops. Using them as balloon floats, I would then try to make my way through the freezing water and the major waves of the bow for the shore of a nearby island. Nevertheless, we were able to get the skiff to the temporary safety of our large boat, although it too was dragging anchor in the gale and had to be moved to a safe haven around to the back of another island, away from the wind and storm. It was a treacherous trip, but we were divinely spared.

5) In 2012, a family member became mentally ill after a significant psychosocial stressor. He felt that he had sinned so greatly over his lifetime that God would never forgive him. He recounted minor yet in his view unforgivable acts, such as sending his son to school without a coat one day. He failed multiple psychiatric treatments and sessions. I had many, many discussions with him via telephone and sent him books and other scriptural references that discussed and reaffirmed God's true forgiveness and grace. But he was simply not able to accept these given his mental illness. After I had flown into his city, I was blessed to have a two-hour discussion with him, face-to-face, the very night before he passed away. I reviewed multiple scriptures on forgiveness and grace, as well as discussed his own situation. After our talk he went to bed. But I once more spoke to him before I left, telling him that I loved him and putting my papers of the scripture references that we

had discussed into his Bible on the table next to his bed. I was struck by how he was simply and completely unable to comprehend or process what I had repeatedly discussed with him, due to his mental illness. I went back in later that night and again told him that I loved him and would see him in the morning. This was the last time that we spoke, as he died early the next morning of natural causes. While his passing was extremely difficult for all of us, it taught me many lessons, and I am certain, especially after speaking with him that night, that he is indeed with Christ in paradise now!

6) In 2014, I was putting up a tree stand high in a curved tree. Just before I could secure the chain around the upper trunk, the stand shifted a bit, pitching me off from about twenty feet up. There were multiple large rocks sticking out of the ground around the base of the stand. I reflexively flapped my arms like a little bird but was unable to avoid the fall. Both knees struck the ground, but fortunately, they landed in soft mud on either side of a large rock. I still had a significant degree of soreness for a week or so, but the outcome could certainly have been much worse!

7) In 2015, after a sudden onset of severe neck pain, my right arm went dead. I could not move it much at all. It was completely numb. I was certain that surgery was needed, having suffered multiple neck injuries previously over my lifetime. Nevertheless, tests and neurosurgical evaluation revealed that, while there was a floating disc piece that had compressed nerves (as well as some other disc problems), surgery could be put off for the time being at least, as my arm miraculously improved quite dramatically within just one day. This disabling issue has not recurred since.

8) In 2016 on a Florida vacation, my young daughter along with my wife and I were stuck in a riptide. We went out on a particularly bad day, one day after a woman drowned from the rip in that same surf. We

were caught along a pier in a significant rip, and my young daughter, being on a small float, could not be pulled in easily by my wife, who was out farther than I. So, I swam against it toward the shore, trying to get a noodle float or something else to pull them in with. My wife is an excellent swimmer and has been caught in rips before, so she knew what to do, that is swim parallel to shore. The problem was my daughter. She was hysterical at being pulled out so far. Her eyes were wide, not because she could not swim, as she too was an excellent swimmer, but because she was terrified. She was certain that a giant man-eating shark was about to come up from beneath and chomp her. I swam to shore, got a noodle, and began the trip back out. Then I saw an elderly woman also caught in the riptide. Her husband was not able to adequately help her, and she was so tired that she could no longer swim for herself. The two of us managed to get her in to shore, and fatigued as I was, I headed back into the surf. I was nearly spent but was praying I could make it out to help my wife bring our daughter back in. I thought about trying to find a Jet Ski, but there seemed little time for this. My wife was trying to calm my daughter yet unfortunately could not get her in past the rip, nor had she swum out of it yet, as it was quite wide and strong at this point. As I reached them, my wife grabbed my float while holding onto our daughter's. Fighting the surf, the two of us finally managed to get her in after an extremely tiring effort. We spent the rest of that day at the pool and avoided the rip areas for the rest of that trip!

9) One summer night in my college days, I began climbing out of the window of my friend's muscle car rather than using the door as any normal and rational person would do. With my feet resting on the windowsill of his door, he began driving his jacked-up ride over fifty miles an hour through an empty mall parking lot, spinning out and swerving and refusing my requests to stop and let me off. The car hit a

Rise and Soar

pothole, and my feet slipped down the door. Feeling I was going to be run over and likely have my legs crushed, I pushed off with my feet and jumped as far from the car as I could. We all feel bulletproof at that age, so I somehow thought I could run as fast as the car had been going and remain on my feet. Ha! The force was so great that it slammed me down and then spun me across the pavement. It was a true blessing that my arm hit first, as I put it out reflexively to break my fall. Both long bones of the forearm snapped and shattered between the wrist and the elbow. My hand wound up where my elbow should have been, and I saw little in between. I remember looking at what was left of my arm and seeing gravel in the marrow cavities of the bones. My arm was a mess of bloody pulp with bones sticking out, yet I felt little pain. Strangely enough, my first thought was that I would probably miss the championship softball game my team was playing the following night. I was trying to figure out a way to still be able to play—maybe as a pinch-runner? Fortunately, after the arm's impact, my heel hit second as I rolled, and my head hit third. Had the head hit first or even second, I doubt I would have survived. A few weeks later, a boy similarly goofing around in a local high school parking lot fell off the hood of a car going only ten miles an hour. He struck his head and died. Despite my stupidity, God's divine intervention interceded once again. The initial orthopedist in the ER shook his head, saying, "I don't know that we can save that arm, but we will try to see if the bone grafts take." He laid the bone chips side by side as in a mosaic and told me, "Sometimes they take but other times they do not." The only other option would be amputating my arm at the elbow. What followed was two weeks in the hospital, with five surgeries to ultimately reconstruct the arm. By miraculous intervention, the bone grafting took, and my arm in time recovered to nearly normal function.

***

Okay, how about the times I've been saved from the fire? There are multiple stories as well, including:

1) My daughter required a CT scan of her head at a very young age. Because of its radiation effect on developing tissue, a CT at such age gives an approximate one in two hundred fifty risk of brain cancer in later childhood. Then in 2016, she began to have signs and symptoms of a brain tumor, namely an intermittently enlarged pupil with severe and constant headaches, which often awakened her from sleep. These are common warning signs of increased intracranial pressure, most often from a tumor in this age group. Being myself a neurologist and my wife a neurosurgical nurse and neuroscience clinical nurse specialist, we of course noticed these warning signs in her history and exam, so we were nearly convinced that there had to be a mass lesion ongoing, most likely a malignant brain tumor. All the medications we tried were not successful. She then underwent an MRI of the brain, and God's providence as well as the prayers of many fortunately gave us normal brain scan results. The headaches were found to be secondary to severe allergies, despite the atypical history and exam that had been so highly suggestive of a structural mass lesion in the brain.

2) In the 1980s, I worked in a coal unloading zone, emptying train cars coming from the mines. It was extremely loud down there. After each train was backed in, I would unload the coal. Then as the cars were pulled back out, I would broom the tracks clean for the next train coming in, sweeping all residual coal down through the grates into the boiler system below. Typically, there was a set period after one train was pulled out before the next was backed in. One day, however, as the empty train was pulled out and I turned my back as usual to work upon the tracks, the next train was backed in early. With all the noise, I could

not hear it. I turned around to see it only yards away from me and coming on! While not moving extremely quickly, it still would have been a likely fatal hit or, at least, a severely disabling one. I was just able to get out of the way as the big line of coal cars backed in past me. I then saw several coworkers running my way who had been shouting and jumping, trying to get my attention, whom I had not heard over the din.

At this same job, while working on the side of a coal car, I would unlatch the three chutes at the bottom with a crowbar and then use a sledgehammer or air hammer to beat the sides of the chute and train car, loosening the coal enough to get the flow going down through the grates into the boiler system. There was also a huge, two-ton blade about six inches thick and just wide and tall enough to fit into each car, which was run by an operator in a ceiling control box. With wet or frozen coal especially, the blade would be released from above and brought down inside the car as we worked from outside. This smashed and loosened the coal from above. Once, as I worked beside a particularly rusty old car, the blade that was banging around inside suddenly broke straight through the rusty wall and missed my head by perhaps a foot. I was looking down and never saw it come through. But I felt the wind part my hair as it spun by me. The man in the blade house up above shut it down and came running, amazed that I was not injured or worse. I vividly recall several wide-eyed and open-mouthed coworkers telling me what a close call it was. It was another heavenly intervention.

3) I worked another industrial job for the film industry. I stripped asbestos, sandblasted, pipefitted, and maintained boilers and chemical machines. I would also change out parts in the pits below these machines. This meant climbing into dark and deep holes that went far beneath these devices. Then I would change out filters, fittings, and pipes and clean the machines as required. The protocol was to have

the operator turn the apparatus off up above and then notify us when it was safe to go down into the pits, which were often still rank with the fumes of rough-smelling chemicals, including some that contained damaging particles. One of my coworkers suffered severe hemorrhaging in his lungs after breathing in one such chemical.

Working alone one day, I was given the okay to descend, meaning that the machine had been turned off. I climbed down into the pit and removed a pipe to begin servicing it, when suddenly, I realized the machine was still on and the chemicals were still flowing! An extremely strong vapor was coming off the chemical in the now-open line. The fumes were so bad I felt I could not stay conscious. I remember feeling that I wanted to lie down and sleep right there in that black hole, which would have been disastrous for me.

It was a long way up the ladder and out of the pit to the floor above—at least a forty-foot climb. I knew I needed to get out of there, and my last memory here is of grabbing on to the bottom of that ladder and starting my way up. I remember nothing else until awakening twenty minutes later on the lawn outside the door by that machine. Somehow, I had managed to get up the ladder, onto the main floor, and then through the nearby door that led outside. As I came to, a coworker found me. I told him to shut down the machine, as fumes had by now filled a significant part of that area. I have no other way of explaining how I climbed up there by myself, nor how I got out into the fresh air. This was definitively an act of divine intervention.

4) In my internal medicine internship in early 1991, my resident and I were caring for a critically ill patient with AIDS, hepatitis B, and kidney failure. It was a life-or-death ICU situation. He needed blood and fluid volume, *stat*. He was not breathing well. He was about to die right there in our intensive care unit. We needed to put a large line called a Quinton catheter into the subclavian artery under the collarbone. It

would allow for adequate access so that he could be rehydrated, transfused, and have dialysis to filter kidney wastes enough to give him a chance to survive.

Because his blood pressure was minimally low, we were working on him with his head tilted downward, a position the medical community calls Trendelenburg. The field I was working in was extremely bloodied, causing poor visibility as, with my fingers in a pool of his blood, I made the chest incision for the large catheter to be placed. But the scalpel cut right through my glove and deeply into one digit, intermixing our blood significantly. I knew his history, but at that point, there was nothing else to do but keep working. I remember my resident being wide-eyed and exclaiming, "Do you know what this man has!"

My reply was, "Jim, we have no time. Let's finish up here!" We were able to help that day, and the man survived for another week or so before passing away.

I'd had a hepatitis B vaccination, so I fortunately did not contract that illness. And miraculously, I did not contract the HIV virus either, although I was tested yearly for AIDS for a decade.

5) On a 2002 trip high in the Alaska Range, near the Little Susitna River, I was snowmobiling on a grizzly hunt. No bears were dumb enough to be out, as there were extremely deep snow levels and brutally cold single- to negative-digit temperatures with additional wind chills of -25° F, even at this mid-April time of year. Upon many high passes in these mountains, I would hit white-light conditions where basically everything looks about the same in its whitish-gray hue, making it difficult to judge depth, drop-offs, and angles. As all in the Arctic know, whether dog sledding, skiing, snowmobiling, or even just hiking, crevasses are often covered with snow, making them fully invisible until the moment one steps upon them. As I rode my machine across

what I thought was the top ridge of a tall mountain, I unknowingly was on a snow bridge, a large drift between two mountaintops.

Suddenly, everything beneath me gave way. I was in freefall beneath the machine, no longer holding on, uncertain of how far I was going to fall. I have never had another sensation such as that: a complete loss of control with no idea how far the descent would continue. I was cognizant of avoiding the six-hundred-pound Arctic Cat above me that would crush me were it to land upon me. As I fell down, down, down, my only thought was rolling as soon as I hit bottom to scoot out of its way. When I finally struck ground, which was padded with a large degree of remaining snowpack, I immediately rolled out of the way as the machine slammed down next to me. Amazingly, I was completely intact! And there was a visible path out of the abyss. I was able to roll the machine upright, and it started, allowing my escape. This event could easily have had devastating consequences. Had it been a deeper or steeper crevasse or had it initiated an avalanche, I might not have been able to escape. Yet I skated away, once again truly blessed!

6) In 2004, I not only had close-quarters contact with the above-noted Canadian Arctic's duo of hungry polar bears but with a Texas mountain lion as well. In the Arctic event, I again was divinely blessed to have further avoided any injury when my plane engine stalled over the icepack or when I became lost during the seventeen-and-a-half-hour snow machine ride back to the native village.

Now, that Texas lion was a huge male. And it was killing horses and cattle at an alarming rate. It killed seven horses in only one week on one West Texas ranch. Even worse, it was killing mainly for sport or just plain meanness; the cat was not eating its victims. The ranchers were desperate to have it eliminated. So, a friend, his four dogs, and I struck out after the big tom.

After being out several hours, our dogs struck the cat's trail and began chasing him. We tied our mounts at nine thousand feet and climbed up to a twelve-thousand-foot elevation, never quite getting close enough for a good shot. I remember pulling back the bushes once at just three yards and seeing this monster tom lion, which was much bigger than the typically smaller West Texas cougar. (It ultimately weighed more than one hundred ninety pounds and was seven feet long, nose to tail.) I had a Colt .45 revolver, and my friend had a .22 pistol—we were certainly undergunned for this cat.

Anyone who has been to West Texas knows that there are not many tall trees, mostly scrub oaks. It was thus difficult to get the lion to go up a tree, which any hound hunter knows is always the goal. We chased this giant for hours. A lion has an eighteen-foot vertical leap from a standstill, so it would often jump to a higher ledge we could not access, forcing us and the dogs to find another way around. Somehow, we managed to continue the chase for many hours until he finally treed, right at my eye level, in a small oak.

Staring him in the face, less than one yard separated us as I put a six-gun round into his chest. Yet, as big as that cat was, he still had plenty of fight left. In an instant, he was down on the ground at my feet. The four dogs jumped upon him. What ensued was a cartoon-like blur of fangs, dust, claws, and scrapping. I tried to make out the lion. Holding my revolver directly against his side, I finished the fight and saved what remained of the dogs. (One had a crushed snout, and another needed several hundred sutures to close multiple gashes.)

7) In 2005 near Glacier Bay, Alaska, the waters were extremely stormy. In the many gales that I have experienced at sea, this was the only time in which I almost got seasick. The boat pitched and rolled, at times going nearly vertical, with great waves incessantly breaking over the deck. I and the owner of our eighteen-foot boat were trying to

maneuver a rocky coastline amidst series of straits and narrows, when the engine suddenly poured black smoke and died. We were then at the mercy of the mighty blow, trying to maneuver using only our small sail. Nevertheless, my friend is an excellent sailor. He told me what to do as we tried to maneuver through. Then the boom swung unexpectedly. He ducked too late and sustained a blow on the head almost hard enough to knock him overboard or incapacitate him. Fortunately, he was soon able to get up and continue giving me the best instructions on what to do. We were being pushed toward a rocky peninsula jutting out from the shoreline as well as multiple small islands. Had he gone into the water or been knocked unconscious, as had nearly occurred, I almost certainly would have been unable to keep the boat from breaking up on the rocks.

8) On the infamous Route 81 in the mountains of upstate New York on a wintry and icy January day, I lost control of my Gran Fury, spinning out and then sliding toward the edge of a steep drop-off. I was smack in the middle of a large snowstorm. The wipers could not get the big flakes off the windshield quickly enough to allow good visibility. So, I had even been forced to drive with my head out the window at times for better visibility! As I began to slide on this downhill curve toward the large drop with no guardrail directly in front of me, I said a quick prayer and threw the car into neutral, which stopped the wheels. It was a trick my father had taught me early on in my driving years up north. As the car slowly slid toward the edge, I pushed my seat back as far as I could to try to distribute weight posteriorly in what looked to be a futile effort. The front wheels went over the edge, and I looked at the long drop down into the chasm before me. Then the vehicle miraculously stopped. Its old rear-wheel drive came in handy at that time, and I was somehow able to back the vehicle off from the edge. I considered jumping out but was afraid the shift in weight would send the vehicle

Rise and Soar

headlong into the abyss. I was amazingly able to get the car back onto the road and complete my blustery day's journey safely.

9) Early one Thanksgiving morning in the 1990s, I drove into the middle of nowhere on a West Texas ranch. I parked in the darkness and walked two miles into the brush, looking for my tree stand. Nevertheless, as anyone who lives there knows, scrub brush and small trees all look the same in the dark, and on this day I was unable to find the stand.

As it began to get light, I needed to sit down or risk scaring off anything and everything from that area. I did so, then pulled out a pair of rattling antlers. Anyone who hunts West Texas knows rattling horns can bring in a significant number of bucks, and often they come at you extremely quickly. On another occasion, I had drawn in eight bucks beneath my stand simultaneously within several minutes of rattling—a truly amazing phenomenon that seems to occur regularly in that part of the country (but, in my experience, only rarely elsewhere). I sat with my back against a large holly bush and rattled once and then twice, mimicking two bucks fighting. Suddenly, from directly behind I heard very loud hoof steps. I leaned forward from the waist and turned around to see a large buck shoving both antlers through the bush, directly at my back. They came within six inches of me. Had I not leaned forward, those horns would have punctured my lungs. I'm sure my eyes were as wide as his as we stared at each other for that single second. He then ran off just a short distance yet did not leave completely. He stayed about fifteen yards away, snorting and stomping at me for twenty minutes. I was unable to get a shot with my bow but felt blessed to have avoided critical injury or worse. I am certain that without divine protection, I would not have made it back to my vehicle that day.

10) Our country road ends at a T. It turns out onto the top of a large hill where a nasty blind curve obscures oncoming traffic. Unfortunately, some drive this much too quickly, and severe accidents have occurred. As you pull out, your best bet is to make certain that nothing is coming. But since you cannot see far enough down the hill to rule out oncoming traffic, the goal instead is to pull out quickly, stay on the narrow right shoulder, and gun it, hoping to be able to either outrun any oncoming vehicle or give it room to get around you. In 2016, while taking my daughter to school one morning, I stopped my truck at the intersection, looked both ways, and seeing nothing, was about to pull out when something told me to hesitate. My foot hovered above the gas pedal. In that split second, from my side a big pickup careened over the two-lane hilltop with only two wheels on the road. It was directly in the center of the road and was completely out of control, traveling at about eighty miles per hour. Had I stepped on the gas pedal, I am certain that I and that driver would not be here today. My daughter would likely have been severely harmed as well. There is simply no way that vehicle could have stopped, let alone slow down or go around me, as he came over that hilltop on those two wheels, fully out of control. I am convinced that this too was a divine intervention!

11) Ascending a hilltop on a two-lane, North Carolina country highway with my wife, we saw a car stopped and signaling. It was waiting for us to pass so that it could turn left across our lane. Then it suddenly sped along past us without turning. In an instant I knew why. As we crested the hill's summit, a tractor trailer was bearing down on us unable to stop (due to failed brakes, we later learned). All the big rig's driver could do was try to turn sideways. Yet his trailer was skidding right at us, leaning as if to tip onto us, tires spewing thick black smoke as it slid directly at us while occupying both lanes. It came on so fast that all I could do was slam the wheel to the right. We flew off the road

Rise and Soar

and down a hill, miraculously missing several large trees and ultimately going up the hill's opposite side. We came to rest in a stand of mailboxes. The truck driver came running to us, exclaiming, "How did you get away? I had you—you were dead!" He had come within mere feet of sliding his rig into us and either decapitating our car (and perhaps us) or crushing us underneath it.

12) Another time, a less dramatic yet still miraculous intervention on a roadway occurred. My daughter and I were going down a steep curve on a wet road, on a big hill to boot. Somehow the truck began to spin. I lost control, and there was no shoulder. Going off the road would likely have resulted in it overturning and rolling several times. I said a quick prayer out loud for help from Jesus, and miraculously, as my daughter can attest, the truck simply righted itself, sliding into the appropriate lane and continuing smoothly down the rest of the hill and through the curve. We both looked at each other, realizing what had just happened. There was simply no other explanation. Total control of the vehicle had been lost; this was not something I myself had achieved by optimal maneuvering, braking, or steering!

13) My wife and I sat upstairs having soup and watching the brewing severe weather reports, our three-year-old asleep just down the hall. We heard the tornado warnings but foolishly were giving her a few more minutes to rest before taking her to the basement. Unbeknownst to us, a huge soon-to-be killer EF4 tornado formed in the cow field two hundred yards across the road. It roared up, sounding like an express train and, fortunately, went high over we fools still sitting upstairs. I watched it touch down over the hill behind us, where it grew up to one-and-a-half miles wide and started a twenty-three-mile path of destruction and death. It was one of the worst tornados in Tennessee history. Certainly, God's mighty hand protected us on that Good Friday 2010!

14) While roofing recently, I twice had footholds pull out of steeply angled roof surfaces I was working on. Luckily, I had pre-thought that, if such occurred, I should direct my momentum toward the gable to stop my slide, rather than zooming the other way, which would have been off the roof. Both would only have been one-story falls, but they remind me of a near three-story fall a few years ago back when I was miraculously spared by the Lord's hand and a flimsy gutter pipe.

A large piece of steel roofing had blown loose in an overnight storm, resulting in a persistently loud banging in the wind, which kept us awake all night, especially the baby in the room just below. I got on the roof at dawn to bolt it back down, with my wife holding the ladder. But I lost traction on the slick, wet steel and almost slid off that side of the house. As it sits on our hill, it is a near three-story fall onto gravel below, so there is no good outcome no matter how I fall. Yet somehow my foot caught, and I inexplicably stopped sliding at the gutter's edge. Even more surprising, the gutter held to its flimsy attachments. And I, amazingly unscathed, was able to clamber off to safety.

15) In 1981 while doing landscape work, a coworker Mike and I were planting large trees with six-hundred-pound tree balls (the roots with soil wrapped in burlap after being dug from the nursery). We moved them in the bucket of a large tractor. One of us would sit up high in the tractor bucket on the tree ball, straddling the trunk and holding it away from the metal edge to avoid bark and trunk damage. On this day, as I rode fifteen feet off the ground with a big oak, the driver hit the wrong lever. Rather than lowering the bucket to ground, he tipped it downward! I fell backward out of the bucket, the tree just above me, and then hit the earth and rolled as fast as I could, the six-hundred-pound ball narrowly missing me. Mike looked pale and could barely speak, stuttering, "I-I-I . . . almost . . . k-k-killed . . . y-y-you!" What a blessing there was a more reliable someone looking out for me that day!

***

I now want to ask you this question: how many instances of divine rescue such as these can you recall in your own life and list for your posterity? Also, how often do you feel in danger? Or lost? Or alone? Or confused about what to do next, about where your life is going, or why you are here, or whether there is any purpose at all to your life upon this planet?

Yet, we must not worry unnecessarily, because God is continually preserving us for all that and forging us into exactly what he desires us to be! Our human heart is eternally restless, as Saint Augustine penned, until it comes to know our loving heavenly Father. He is always with us. We are truly never alone.

Do you know him? Really and truly know him? Have you had a personal and committing experience with him in which you have given your life to him, realizing him as the truly loving God that he is? This is so very much more than simply a knowledge of him, a mere belief in a good God above. He is again always with us, staying actively involved in our lives, and is ever trying to reach us and to bring us closer to him. His hand is actively involved in all that happens to us, both good and bad.

What! Does he cause bad things to happen to us? We will look at this in detail later in this volume. Suffice it to say at this point that all that happens to each of us is definitively in keeping with his will and is in his timing and is ultimately for his glory. However, he does not deliver us from our own poor choices, nor does he pull us from every single fire that we jump into or put ourselves through due to our human hearts' stupidities, lusts, greed, and pride.

Once again, he is actively involved with each of us. The question is whether we truly know him as our personal Father. He is loving, yes, but is also holy, meaning that he is a fully just God, one who cannot tolerate sin—a concept that can make him seem aloof and unattainable for us and, to some, even likely a mere myth. Yet, he stays immanently involved and thus is always there with us throughout our lives, every step of the way, constantly trying to turn our heart toward him if we do not yet know him or, alternately, attempting to keep our heart on his wavelength if we already do truly know him as our Father.

***

Let us think for a moment about the effect of fatherlessness on young people. I have personally seen this in our prison systems. Extremely few of the young men I meet in these facilities had true fathers who could have been examples for them of what manhood is supposed to be—that is, a strong and protective, yet also gentle and loving, character example. They almost always have either no paternal example or a false one. I have taught in impoverished ghetto schools as well. I recall one sixth grade class in which not even one of those minority students had a father in their home!

We, too, regularly see examples around us, in our schools, at work, and in our society, where the lack of an appropriate father figure as a beacon to guide us into adulthood has led to devastating effects. Now, magnify this from the individual level to society itself—and even to the world. In this way it is easy to see the effects of not having God as our eternal Father!

We see this daily in what is clearly a world of ever-worsening crime, hopelessness, absolute lack of caring about other human beings and their situations, and a complete lack of direction. People seek gratification through multiple different harmful channels, all of which will leave them lost after a useless chase and often with dire consequences, physically and emotionally, in this world. And in addition, they, too, face the great tragedy of being a lost and hopeless soul in the world to come.

Open your mind right now. I understand there are doubts. Perhaps you have run into people who call themselves Christians but are extremely hateful and judgmental. They may have even hurt you mentally or physically. They are people whom you would never wish to be like. This is very unfortunate. Yet let me start by saying that such pseudo-Christians are not God, nor are they Jesus Christ! They are not a true representation of him, nor of what he desires for you. They misrepresent him. And unfortunately, because there are no perfect and divine people, but because all have mere human hearts and minds, this does repeatedly happen in our imperfect world. Nevertheless, do not allow yourself to be dragged under the bus with them—to throw your own life away.

Again, open your mind to think logically about this amazing world of creation all around us. Did this truly happen by accident? Did we really form from mere amoebae, from a few primordial cells that, by astronomically extreme chance, happened to line up into the right configuration? We will look at this in more detail later in this text. For the present time, I again ask you to approach this question, and thus this book, with an open mind. Does it truly seem, in the greatest probability and likelihood, that this life is really all there is? Do we live in this beautiful world of creation, as super complex beings with amazing minds superimposed upon the complex physical creatures that we are, only to be here for a few decades and then to simply cease to exist?

As a neurological physician who has treated both the mental and physical aspects of brain disease for over thirty years, I cannot believe that this world is the final bottom line and that our worldly life here is the end-all at our death. I have studied the brain, mind, psyche, and body through school and onward for many years, including my three-plus decades spent practicing medicine. As a result, as the years pass, I become more and more convinced of the absolute existence of a divine creator, one who takes an active role in our lives! I have witnessed too many events and outcomes that could never be explained physically, especially things that I have seen occur in the healing of situations and illnesses for which even modern scientific medicine has no answer and provides no hope. I will discuss this further in more detail later in this text.

Now, I understand doubting. I, too, have been there. I understand the perception that no human could ever give you a definitively absolute and convincing answer, and I agree that, indeed, none can. Only the Lord God can do this. And that is exactly why you need to investigate him for yourself, not merely by listening to what parents or other family members, friends, religious teachers of any faith, or other mentors tell you. Believe me, you need to have this correct! This is not merely a stock purchase, a pickup basketball game, or a fishing tournament in which you can afford to be incorrect!

You must initiate your own investigational period in your life (which I pray you will extend beyond the scope of this mere book) with that same open mind in order to appropriately seek the truth. As Jesus said, his followers will find the truth, that of his word, and this truth, he stated, "will set you free."

***

I have dedicated this work to the Lord Jesus Christ and intend this literary effort to help all of us, myself included, to get to know him either for the first time or, if we already do know and trust him, then to do so to a better degree, realizing that he indeed is the only God, our only savior.

Without him, we will never be satisfied, and we will never have true direction. There is nothing else that can take his place in our hearts, in our souls, or in our minds. Being without him is like being lost in a dense and darkened forest without a compass or a functional GPS. Yet with him, we indeed can rise above the trees. That is, we can transcend, or get above, the craziness of this world as if on eagle's wings, and then we will soar while still on earth. That is what he so wishes for us to do, until we ultimately move on into a beautiful eternity with him.

I can see many, many personal examples, as almost all of us can (especially the longer we live) if we will look back over our lifetimes at those times when the Lord either took us through the fire or carried us around the fire. He was there with me through my many trials and tests. In these, he truly was my light and my salvation. He did save me, and he will continue to do so!

He does all of this for his purposes, shaping us for a specific role, a life's work that is individualized for each one of us. Each was born for one purpose in this world, and if we do not know him, we will never know what this is. We will thus remain unfulfilled, unsafe, and alone, constantly grasping for fulfillment as well as for true joy and true peace and, ultimately, for rescue, all of which we will never be able to attain solely through our own human efforts.

As you move further into this book, I believe the most important thing is to ask the Lord your God to reveal his true self to you. As the Bible (which is in fact God's living, breathing, and holy Word) states, if you seek him, you will find him. Ask him to show himself to you fully so that you can now leave behind all misconceptions and misrepre-sentations. To do this, you will need to set aside your prideful, worldly, doubting, analytical, and self-reliant human mind. Are you so arrogant that you would presume to know everything?

Please understand that I am not asking you to simply, from the start, have a blind faith. Nevertheless, you must investigate this for yourself. If you do so, he will grant you wisdom to form a true and strong faith, as he promises in his Word.

Your search can never truly be a valid and completely unbiased investigation unless you are willing to remain cognitively open to the possibility of the existence of a true and loving God, one who is your own heavenly Father, the very one who loves you so much that he gave his only Son to bear the burden of *all* of your lifetime of sins. By his blood they are taken completely away. In doing so, he restores you to the God who wants to rescue you in this life and, then thereafter, to welcome you into a lifetime of eternal happiness with him! What is the alternative? Consider the sobering yet hope-providing proclamations in God's own Word here:

"Rich man! Proud man! Wise man! You must die like all the rest! You have no greater lease on life than foolish, stupid men. You must leave your wealth to others. You name your estates after yourselves as though your lands could be forever yours and you could live on them eternally. But man with all his pomp must die like any animal. Such is the folly of these men, though after they die they will be quoted as having great wisdom. . . . For the power of their wealth is gone when they die; they cannot take it with them. But as for me, God will redeem my soul from the power of death, for he will receive me. So do not be dismayed when evil men grow rich and build their lovely homes. For when they die, they carry nothing with them! Their honors will not follow them. Though a man calls himself happy all through his life—and the world loudly applauds success—yet in the end he dies like everyone else and enters eternal darkness. For man with all his pomp must die like any animal." (Psalm 49:10–13, 14b–20)

***

Please keep in mind that the Lord our Father, our very God, has planned and even desires something much better for you than your current situation. It is with God's intent to demonstrate this to you that I have put together this volume, a multiyear work that he inspired me to undertake. I have prayed and continue to pray that the printed words and his scriptures employed here will truly help to enlighten all who read them and also that my heart's thoughts and meditations upon them will be acceptable to him, such that these will be exactly what he needs to convey to each reader. Consider the following:

> "Come to me with your ears wide open. Listen, for the life of your soul is at stake. I am ready to make an everlasting covenant with you, to give you all the unfailing mercies and love." (Isaiah 55:3)

> "See, I have put my words in your mouth! Today your work begins, to warn the nations and the kingdoms of the world." (Jeremiah 1:9–10a)

> "The Lord God has given me his words of wisdom so that I may know what I should say to all these weary ones. Morning by morning he wakens me and opens my understanding to his will. The Lord God has spoken to me, and I have listened; I do not rebel nor turn away. I give my back to the whip, and

my cheeks to those who pull out the beard. I do not hide from shame—they spit in my face. Because the Lord God helps me, I will not be dismayed; therefore, I have set my face like flint to do his will, and I know that I will triumph. He who gives me justice is near. Who will dare to fight against me now? Where are my enemies? Let them appear! See, the Lord God is for me! Who shall declare me guilty? All my enemies shall be destroyed like old clothes eaten up by moths!" (Isaiah 50:4–9)

"I waited patiently for God to help me; then he listened and heard my cry. He lifted me out of the pit of despair, out from the bog and the mire, and set my feet on a hard, firm path, and steadied me as I walked along. He has given me a new song to sing, of praises to our God. Now many will hear of the glorious things he did for me, and stand in awe before the Lord, and put their trust in him." (Psalm 40:1–3)

***

I write this text without pride or hubris. It is not simply a mere man's story or legacy but rather is a strong testament of demonstration to others about what our great God can do in your life, if you will only let him bestow his gifts upon you!

I am not trying to fill a book with mere words or information. Rather, I pray that this message will be life-changing for all who encounter it. This effort is done in Jesus's great name alone. The goal of this book is to share our Creator God's message. In so doing, I have asked him to open my mind, allowing mine to be in touch with his and thus to have my writings declare exactly what he would have me reveal to this modern world.

We must not hide the light of his truth! Rather, we must share it for others' sakes and for the kingdom's sake! If I had the cure for cancer, why would I keep it to myself? Would you not, if able, pull to safety that person clinging to the cliff edge or the one who was about to fall into an abyss? Or, had you the skills, would you not correctly pilot the falling airplane in which you and others were about to crash? Yes, of course, we all would!

***

Each of us is in fact writing our own book, the story of our life. Our books have past closed chapters, a current ongoing chapter, and the future ones yet to come. God is continuing to influence us and thus is writing our stories, with or without us! All that he asks us to do, in order to have ours written as a magnificent story, is for us to stay on the correct path—that is, to stay with him and in him on our journeys, thus keeping him in us as well. He then will write our stories as he has all along intended to do, from here on, to their gloriously beautiful conclusions! He has great plans for every one of us if we will only stay the course and submit to him and his will.

Ask him to show you your own true course. Find out his specific will for you. Most of our lives' trials do not make sense to us now. We do not grasp why we need to go through such. Yet at our story's end, we will fully see and be able to understand.

So, let us begin to write extraordinarily superb future chapters going forward, without looking at past bad chapters. Keep such closed from here onward and stay upon his road! Seek him. Find him. And dwell in him for the rest of your days. He will indeed make these the very best days of your life! Remember his promise given in Mark 6:56: "and as many as touched him were healed."

I. Rise Above the Trees

"I am recording this so that future generations will also praise the Lord for all that he has done. And a people that shall be created shall praise the Lord." (Psalm 102:18)

Running trails in a dark and dense pine forest at the dawn of a crisp and clear winter morn, I was struck how, when upon higher ground or beneath openings in the tree canopy above, I could see an amazingly beautiful sunrise. Its red, orange, yellow, and pink hues were etched upon a deep blue sky as the sun peeked over the distant mountain. Yet when down in the bottoms, those low-elevation, thickly treed zones, I could not see much at all. In fact, it was still very dark and gloomy down there. I considered how, if I were a hawk, I could ascend to fly above these dense woods, thereby gaining a clearer and more accurate view of the entire situation.

In a similar way, we too must get above the trees in each of our lives in order to be able to clearly see who God actually is and to learn what he wants for us, as well as to understand how we should follow him. We each need to transcend our dark woods and our trees, those distractions that darken our paths and make our vision gloomy. They adversely color and alter our days as well as our future destinations and, in doing so, steal our joy, our peace, and our fulfillment along life's course. And even more importantly, they threaten to keep us from our ultimate rescue by God.

***

I will never forget my many experiences in the high Arctic and the great northwestern wildernesses of Alaska and Canada. I was often alone and out walking for hours, deep within primeval, misty mountains and dark rainforests, fog and blinding rain and snowstorms, and dense swamp-grass thickets, the domains of the brown bear, the grizzly bear, the polar bear, the black bear, and the wolf.

At times I was very close to these magnificent creatures. We would commonly surprise each other with close encounters. Walking alone through the wilderness with senses on high alert, rifle at the hip and ready, listening keenly to every sound, head on a swivel, always scanning the perimeter around and behind you, including smelling for the cached carcasses these predators protect like royal treasure (or even catching the scent of the bruin itself) is, while exciting, also very hard work. And you must be ever-vigilant to keep yourself safe. While God certainly did guide and assist me in these adventures, as he always does with those who truly know him, I compare these experiences to the many storms and dark forests we each go through during our lifetimes.

We are all searching for something to fill us, and we look for answers to this life's big questions: Why are we here? How did we get here? What is the meaning of this life?

Have you ever been lost, either in the deep woods or in life itself, feeling confused on where to go, how to go, and when or whom to go with? Does your world seem a disjointed, discombobulated mess of seemingly hopeless issues, conflicts, hopes, and dreams? Are you unsure about how to attack and achieve? How does one try to deal with, let alone resolve, so many unknowns? The good news is that there absolutely is an answer. In fact, there is only one answer.

Join me now on an inspiring journey that leads not only to joy, that is, to true happiness, but also to peace, fulfillment, and even rescue from the craziness of our world!

***

One spring day, while hiking a winding river flowing through a dark and dense mountain forest, I realized that, given all the meanderings I had done, I was unsure of the exact way home. However, despite being down in a dark morass of confusion, I was finally able to find a clearing where the mid-morning sun was visible.

Now, I have followed that sun many a day while out in the wild, having learned what a truly great direction-giver it is. We all know the sun rises in the east and sets to the west. Knowing such allows one to easily tell north and south directions as well. If you face directly east, north will always be to your direct left, your nine o'clock, while south is always to your right, your three o'clock as these are termed. Discerning these directions early and late in the daytime is easy (as long as there are no clouds)! Midday gets harder. It takes a bit more time to watch how the sun is moving, by either visualizing its arc through the sky or by improvising a sundial with a rock and stick. With the latter, you watch an upright stick's shadow movement by first placing a rock at its shadow's start and then placing another at the shadow's new site about twenty minutes later. This lets you determine the east-west line, as the shadow will move to the east as the sun goes on its westward course throughout the day. So, the second rock placed points east, while the first points west.

God likewise desires to give us his map, his compass, and his direction. Consider this verse:

> "Open my eyes to see wonderful things in your Word. I am but a pilgrim here on earth: how I need a map—and your commands are my chart and guide. I long for your instructions more than I can tell." (Psalm 119:18–20)

Getting back to my walk on this day, I was fortunate to have habitually done what I call checking the sun, as I was about to dip under the forest canopy. I noted where it was, relative to my position, and also how its course would be from my familiar starting point. (I learned this early on and taught my daughter to also do it each time she enters a forest, beginning when she was three.) This knowledge then makes it fast and easy, when in directional trouble, to look at the sun to show me my true direction home.

In the same way, we are best able to move through our lives with proper and optimal directions if we keep our sights, our compass headings, fixed directly upon our Lord Jesus Christ. This fulfills our plans and goals without our feeling lost and will even let us feel rescued when in these difficult states.

Whether we know him or not, our lives will have many dark forests to traverse, fraught with foggy mists, dead falls, sheer cliffs, deep water, grasping muck, and even some tough insects and predators. Such will occur in all our lives, whether we know God or not. Nevertheless, as Proverbs 3:6 tells us, if we in all we do "put God first," he will direct us and crown our efforts with success. But if we do not, the opposite is true. Consider:

Rise and Soar

"The steps of good men are directed by the Lord. He delights in each step they take. If they fall, it isn't fatal, for the Lord holds them with his hand." (Psalm 37:23–24)

"He fills me with strength and protects me wherever I go. He gives me the surefootedness of a mountain goat upon the crags. He leads me safely along the top of the cliffs. He prepares me for battle and gives me strength to draw an iron bow!" (Psalm 18:32–34).

God then gives us direction, if we will only stay fixed upon him and stay in his holy Word. His word becomes the perfect guidebook for our journey. Consider how knowing the physical sun in the above example makes it so much easier to keep one's true course. Similarly, knowing God and his true Son makes it much easier for us when we lose our way in desperate times, those dark valleys in life. We can quickly and readily sail through such all the sooner and all the easier, putting them behind us—so different than if we did not know him.

Taking time to begin to seek him and his guiding light is never a useless act. It will take you a bit of time to get to know him and to learn that you can always trust him to carry and deliver you, as he sees you through each dark wood that you encounter. Nevertheless, you will still receive his help and blessings.

And soon, as he helps you through your current darkness or storm, you are eventually guided to the correct and saving course. You can now clearly see his guiding light through the trees, leading you home to the perfect place. He will show you how to get out of, and then to get above, their dark canopy.

Even as the trees lessen, as you are coming out of the denser forest, you already will begin to see many new things. Your eyes being opened, you will then see things in the light of the true Son, as Jesus grants you his many blessings along the way.

Eventually, you will be able to soar on wings (as in Isaiah 40:31) and see the end of the trees lying just ahead. That then opens into the beautiful panoramic vista of what now lies before you, not just in this life, now being lived with Christ as your guide, but also in the everafter, namely that glorious, eternal paradise with him!

We must all realize that Christ's cross, his sacrifice for us, is the one and only solid and reliable rock. It is the one that transcends all else, rising higher than any mere mountain or forest, no matter how tall and overwhelming such may seem.

> "He himself gives life and breath to everything, and satisfies every need there is. . . . His purpose in all of this is that they should seek after God, and perhaps feel their way toward him and find him—though he is not far from any one of us. For in him we live and move and are!" (Acts 17:25b, 27–28a)

***

On many forest walks, you will see what I like to call mega-trees, that is, three- to four-hundred-year-old giants. I always question, "How did they get so big and live for so long?" How indeed! They were rooted in good soil and received plenty of proper nourishment, water, and sunlight.

In the same way, those of us who find in Jesus the true living water and the true light, that is, the real son, will receive optimal sustenance, grace, and blessings. These will allow us to grow to our full potential, becoming glorious and mighty oaks that tower over all those other much more numerous (yet more easily uprooted and blown over) smaller trees!

I also question that if ten-plus generations of people, in the case of three- to four-hundred-year-old trees (or even thirty-plus generations with redwoods or sequoias), lived and passed on during that one solitary tree's existence, then how insignificant are human beings with all of our strivings, our anxieties, our victories and losses, all of our dramas, and our meager gains? Look at what God says:

"Lord, help me to realize how brief my time on earth will be. Help me to know that I am here for but a moment more. My life is no longer than my hand! My whole lifetime is but a moment to you. Proud man! Frail as breath! A shadow! And all his busy rushing ends in nothing. He heaps up riches for someone else to spend. And so, Lord, my only hope is in you." (Psalm 39:4-7)

Next, we will look at a series of important doctrines and beliefs that the true God, our heavenly Father, wants us to understand and to incorporate into our very being so that we will have a full relationship with him.

II. Sin and Forgiveness

Sin. We feel like we hear this term all the time. Does it grate on your nerves a bit—or even a lot? Does it aggravate you? If so, good! That is the true message that your conscience is trying to get through to you about sin. This is what that inner conscience, your very soul, is doing: it is convicting you, pointing a finger at you. Consider this story:

"No, sir," I told my angry patient. "As we discussed before, I cannot give you narcotic pain medication any longer. The rules have changed. The VA will no longer let me do that, and as we discussed last time, that was to be your last prescription."

It was late in the evening, and I was at the back end of a long hallway. I was usually the last doctor to leave. Even the nurses had left the clinic before me. My patient looked down and, reaching behind his back, pulled out a .38 caliber revolver. He did not point it at me but turned it over in his hands, mumbling, "You know, driving up here, the police pulled me over. The officer asked if I had a gun, and I told him yes. He asked where it was, and I said it was in the glove compartment. He said, 'Leave it there.' Then he let me go."

My patient continued to finger the gun, looking at it intently. He then looked up at me with determined eyes, eyes that had done their sworn duty protecting our country during a tour in Vietnam. We had discussed this multiple times before. Now he was once again in a desperate state. Over two years of visits, I had learned that his present job involved twelve-hour shifts in a marijuana patch in the national forest. He was paid with a twenty-dollar bill and a twelve-pack of beer. He was handed a shotgun and told to shoot on sight without asking any questions should anyone other than the growers appear.

To this day, I still do not believe he would have used the weapon. But all alone at this late hour, I wanted us both to be able to go home without incident. So, I gave him a small prescription and concluded by saying that this would be the last time. I never saw him again.

I use this as an example for all of us of things that we all do, perhaps not quite as graphic, yet sometimes, much worse. We repeat bad habits, desiring things we know to be inappropriate or harmful, perhaps even illegal. Why do we do this? The answer lies within our hearts and minds. Our desires are of this world and about only ourselves, not the welfare of others.

Sin is not good. It is like a deep, dark wilderness valley nestled between big mountains. Its high tree cover is so dense that we cannot see the sun, nor find our directions easily. Just as such a dark valley would keep us from our destinations and our loved ones or from our goals, sin similarly separates and keeps us from the One who made us: our heavenly Father.

But oh yes, sin can sound fun, exciting, and enticing. Yet, almost always the outcome is utter disaster, either to us physically or to our minds, to our families, in our jobs, or in our other multitudes of blessings. We throw our human folly against the protection that God is trying to provide for us.

So, why does God always ask and encourage and plead with us not to sin? Does he not want us to have fun? This is absolutely the wrong way to view this. Look at it in this way: he is not keeping you from the imagined fun but is trying to preserve you for the truly good things in this life! Indeed, he wants us all to have fun, enjoyment, and happiness to the maximal degree that one can have in this world. But he also, above all, wants to protect us. Remember, he is our loving Father. He knows what the outcome will be from that lie, that affair, that greed, that lust, that theft. While we realize something bad could happen if we choose to sin, we all too often feel like we may be able to get away with it. No one will ever know, and we will be happier having done or not done whatever the sin is.

This is exactly how sin, the tool of the evil one, the devil, wants us to think. If you think about God's rules from the viewpoint of an autonomous, individualistic person, one set upon achieving self-oriented goals and pleasures, these rules seem highly restrictive. But if you think about his rules from the viewpoint of a true Father who loves and cares for you, you will see them in a different light. Consider:

> "God's laws are perfect. They protect us, make us wise, and give us joy and light. God's laws are pure, eternal, just. They are more desirable than gold. They are sweeter than honey dripping from a honeycomb. For they warn us away from harm and give success to those who obey them." (Psalm 19:7–11)

These protective laws are meant to help us! If you had a supportive, earthly father, think back upon the rules he applied—or at least attempted to apply—to you while you were growing up. Did he not have your best interests at heart? You may not have seen it or felt that way when you were young and being denied things you thought would be more fun and exciting. Yet looking back, we can recall those times when we chose and did things we had been warned or counseled not to do. And now, in retrospect, we can see the poor results that occurred.

While unfortunately these poor consequences from sinful activities cannot always be undone and may leave permanent scars, the good news is we can have full and complete forgiveness from sins because our heavenly Father sent his Son, out of his love for us, to take the blame for us and thus to take all sins away from our souls! In a truly amazing act of his great grace and love for us, he allowed his Son to exchange his royal, heavenly clothes for our tattered, sinful rags. So, when we die, if we have believed in and have a personal relationship with our Lord, God then will count us worthy, as one of his own children, as much as he does his own Son, Jesus.

Jesus Christ also mediates for us at the time of our death and judgment. The evil one will be there listing our wrongdoings and accusing us before God. Nevertheless, if we know God and his Son, they will draw a protective circle around us, saying, "No, this one is ours." They will bring us into eternal paradise with them. Listen to God's own reassuring promise given directly in his own Word:

> "Let me tell you how happy God has made me! For he has clothed me with garments of salvation and draped about me the robe of righteousness. I am like a bridegroom in his wedding suit or a bride with her jewels." (Isaiah 61:10)

You might say: "What? Can all my sins be forgiven? No way. Maybe others' sins, but not mine. You do not understand what I have done, how bad I have been." This is another trick of Satan. He tries to keep you in this thought pattern, separated from knowing God until you die and are judged for your sins. He tries to keep you from achieving the eternal benefit of God's great grace. Yet, time after time in his Word, the Holy Bible, our Father assures us of his forgiveness:

> "This is the LORD's declaration. 'For I will forgive their wrongdoing and never again remember their sin.'" (Jeremiah 31:34b HCSB)

> "Once again you will have compassion on us. You will tread our sins beneath your feet; you will throw them into the depths of the ocean!" (Micah 7:19)

> "They will be my people, and I will be their God, just and true and yet forgiving them their sins." (Zechariah 8:8b)

Many also say, "I am not ready to go to God yet. I first have to get myself cleaned up before I do!" This is another delaying tactic of Satan. He is striving to delay you to the point where you put off God for long enough that either your heart hardens, such that you stop seeking him, or until your death. At either point, Satan then has you! Isaiah 59:2 references this final endpoint from which there is no return: "Your sins have cut you off from God. Because of sin he has turned his face away from you and will not listen anymore."

Instead, do not worry about where you are now in terms of what God sees. He knows your thoughts and your heart already. Remember—he made you! He wants you to come to him as you are. He will clean you up. If you come humbly to him, admitting that you are a sinner who needs his help and wants a personal relationship with him and his Son, Jesus Christ, he absolutely will fully forgive all your sins! What better news could we ever hear?

And how do we know this for sure? We are certain of his promise because there are many, many references to this throughout Scripture.

God reiterates time and again his solemn oath, his never-changing plan. For instance, in Isaiah 44:22, he states that he blows away your sins, like the clouds. In Micah 7:19, your sins are listed as being sunk to the depths of the ocean. And in Psalm 103:12, they are "moved as far away from God as the East is from the West." They are "remembered by God no more" (Hebrews 8:12) and even erased from the Book of Life, which is the scorebook kept in heaven. It lists all that we have done and will do in this world. I find the best example here is all-inclusive, as Paul in Colossians 2:14 wrote: our sins have been nailed to the cross of Jesus Christ. If we have that firm, personal relationship with him and believe his promises, he covers every error and misdeed we have done. Consider these further references:

> "You were dead in sins, and your sinful desires were not yet cut away. Then he gave you a share in the very life of Christ, for he forgave all your sins, and blotted out the charges proved against you, the list of his commandments which you had not obeyed. He took this list of sins and destroyed it by nailing it to Christ's cross." (Colossians 2:13–14)

> "I will be merciful to them in their wrongdoings, and I will remember their sins no more." (Hebrews 8:12)

> "Let us go right in to God himself, with true hearts fully trusting him to receive us because we have been sprinkled with Christ's blood to make us clean and because our bodies have been washed with pure water. Now we can look forward to the salvation God has promised us. There is no longer any room for doubt, and we can tell others that salvation is ours, for there is no question that he will do what he says." (Hebrews 10:22–23)

"'Though you have scorned my laws from earliest time, yet you may still return to me,' says the Lord Almighty. 'Come and I will forgive you.'" (Malachi 3:7a)

"Though sins fill our hearts, you forgive them all." (Psalm 65:3)

"I bless the holy name of God with all my heart. Yes, I will bless the Lord and not forget the glorious things he does for me. He forgives all my sins. He heals me. He ransoms me from hell. He surrounds me with loving-kindness and tender mercies. He fills my life with good things! My youth is renewed like the eagle's! He gives justice to all who are treated unfairly. He revealed his will and nature to Moses and the people of Israel. He is merciful and tender toward those who don't deserve it; he is slow to get angry and full of kindness and love. He never bears a grudge, nor remains angry forever. He has not punished us as we deserve for all our sins, for his mercy toward those who fear and honor him is as great as the height of the heavens above the earth. He has removed our sins as far away from us as the east is from the west. He is like a father to us, tender and sympathetic to those who reverence him. For he knows we are but dust and that our days are few and brief, like grass, like flowers, blown by the wind and gone forever." (Psalm 103:1–16)

"Sprinkle me with the cleansing blood and I shall be clean again. Wash me and I shall be whiter than snow. . . . Don't keep looking at my sins—erase them from your sight. Create in me a new, clean heart, O God, filled with clean thoughts and right desires. . . . O my God, you alone can rescue me. Then I will sing of your forgiveness." (Psalm 51:7, 9–10, 15a)

Okay, you may think, but what about *big* sins? I have ministered in prisons and had this question raised many times by men who had killed someone or done other terrible things. The answer is the same for these sins also. God's promise is that if we will only repent, return to him, and believe in his forgiveness and salvation, all will be forgiven!

When we sin, we grieve our caring Father greatly, as is demonstrated by his obviously pained response in Micah 6:3, "O my people, what have I done that makes you turn away from me?" We must realize our sins' effects and not allow them to keep us separated from God! Look at what God says about this:

"For how can we walk together with your sins between us?" (Amos 3:3)

"That is why the Lord says, 'Turn to me now, while there is time. Give me all your hearts. Come with fasting, weeping, mourning. Let your remorse tear at your hearts and not your garments.' Return to the Lord your God, for he is gracious and merciful. He is not easily angered; he is full of kindness and anxious not to punish you." (Joel 2:12–13)

"Everyone who calls upon the name of the Lord will be saved." (Joel 2:32a)

"For God was in Christ, restoring the world to himself, no longer counting men's sins against them but blotting them out. . . . For God took the sinless Christ and poured into him our sins. Then, in exchange, he poured God's goodness into us!" (2 Corinthians 5:19a, 21)

***

As an example, let us examine one type of sin, one that is a prominent, contemporary controversy, namely the LGBTQ (lesbian-gay-bi-sexual-transgender-queer/questioning) issue. I have spoken to people who identify as LGBTQ, including personal friends. Many say they were "made this way," implying that they cannot change. And unfortunately, most feel Christianity is against them.

Their feelings are understandable. Some of those I've spoken with feel they have been put down and abused by Christians who claim to speak for God. Some in our society, whether Christian or not, believe that this sin is worse than others. Perhaps this is because so many of us cannot relate to it or do not struggle with it. The best way I find for someone not in this sin pattern to relate to and to empathize with same-sex attraction is a change in mindset.

For instance, replace in your mind the practice of same-sex attraction with opposite-sex attraction of an abnormal or excessive nature, or with lust or greed or stealing or some other sin. Clearly, we each have different sin patterns. We will have no problems at all with some sins over our entire lives. Yet, others become our daily mighty battles. These struggles will never end until we arrive home with Christ. Yet with his help, we can fight and conquer these each day by putting nails into these sins, nails that hold them to his cross.

Picture your biggest sin, the hardest one that you struggle with. If you cannot imagine or do not know your sins, then you are already buried deeply in a very problematic situation. The healthiest situation you can be in is to be aware of your personal sins and the triggers and temptations you need to avoid. We each have a set. We are born with these. This is the original sin that all of humankind has incurred because of the first sin committed in the garden by Adam and Eve. As stated above in Psalms 65:3, "sins fill our hearts."

Let's further contemplate this concept of original sin. Many have told me, "I have felt this way ever since I was a child, for as long as I can remember." This makes sense too, therefore, if viewed as each of us being born with an individual sin pattern, due to that original sin within every man's heart. While we realize that psychological trauma, abuse, and other bad things can certainly cause this choice to be made as well, one's sin pattern still is quite often a part of the original sin constitution with which he was born.

Further, whether your sin is heterosexual adultery, lust, greed, murder, theft, gossip, lying, cheating, or any of the host of sins out there, if you are trapped by such, you cannot blame your repeated sin performance on the Devil, as per the old saying, "the Devil made me do it." Such an excuse inappropriately shifts the responsibility away from oneself. Does it not seem crazy to be stuck in a situation where you continue to repeat the same error again and again and again? Unfortunately, however, we will forever continue in this never-ending cycle if we choose to fight it all by ourselves.

Oh, sure, sometimes you can change for a week, a few months, maybe even a few years. But it is extremely rare to be able to stay out of such a cycle permanently, if based completely on your own merit and solely by your own efforts. And why is this? Because our human hearts are wired that way. Without God, they are bent upon sinning. Consider Jeremiah 17:9–10: "The heart is the most deceitful thing there is and desperately wicked. No one can really know how bad it is! Only the Lord knows!"

Each person through original sin inherits an individual sin pattern that includes large and small sins. And patterns vary between persons. So, the statement, "I was born this way," does hold merit and makes sense. No, this was not how God intended it to be before the original sin of Adam and Eve in the garden. This is what happened as the result of mankind's first evil deed.

Should we become despondent and discouraged, we must remember God has given us an answer, or an out, through his Son, Jesus. What we repeating sinners all need, whether we are homosexuals, murderers, adulterers, liars, rapists, greedy misers, or whatever else, is this—Jesus!

Therefore, we need to lovingly present his Word to others, trying to help them see and compare its truth against their own thought positions. We might say, "I do not see it as you do, but please allow my concern to be expressed. And please open-mindedly consider that, according to God's Word, your position is not correct. It is not how God sees this issue."

No matter what the sin, we Christians must stand up to the offense, hating the sin but loving the sinner, while backing our loving, pleading words with God's own Word in a calm and noncritical manner. Despite an apparent lack of progress or understanding or even hostile persecution and threats, we must stay in the game for as long as possible. Be persistent. God's Word stands forever. It does not and will not ever change, not with any culture, a new societal more or norm, nor with the passage of time.

Regarding the same-sex issue, the Bible tells how God created men as men and women as women. Sexuality is his individual gift to all of us, and with it, he has given specific moral and ethical responsibilities and limitations he does not want us to cross nor to change for our own benefit. Therefore, when you meet a homosexual, a gay, a lesbian, or a transgender person, just as when you meet a murderer or a sex addict of opposite-sex attraction, the Christian view (that is, what Christ would have us do) is to bring his true self to them. We should be his voice, his hands, and his feet to every sinner.

Certainly, none of us will ever be perfect. God realizes this. What he does ask, therefore, is that we give our sin patterns up to him and return to him, getting to know him better and being truly sorry for these sins while also doing our best not to repeat them. Do we fall? Unfortunately, many times. Yet, if we use the powerful resource of God's Word, his Holy Bible, as our guide and our survival manual for the remainder of our lives in this world, he in turn sends us his Holy Spirit, and Jesus Christ remains with us throughout these battles, bringing us his grace, which then leads us to his peace, joy, fulfillment, and, ultimately, his rescue into eternal paradise with him.

***

When I witness to the lesbian/bisexual/gay/trangender community, I must show the compassion of our Lord Jesus. I like to ask people their stories so I understand them better. Then, I share that they do need Christ as the central point in their lives. They do not truly have him yet if they are in these relationships. They must have him as their main focus to be able to change and find real peace, his love, and ultimate healing.

I recommend emphasizing Scripture regarding this gender issue. The Bible says that God made male and female, two separate genders and each for a specific purpose: "So God created man in his own image; He created him in the image of God; He created them male and female" (Genesis 1:27 HCSB). God's big plan includes every person, as I like to say. Should I meet opposition, I reply, "Do not be mad or hate me because I am telling you his message. I do not hate you, but rather,

I love you. And is not true love a loving of others despite their differences?" Satan smartly continues to attack the gender issue. He wants to confuse God's purpose. God made sex, after all. Human sexuality is not meant to deviate from but to further his purposes and his glory alone. Satan hates this.

Some may ask, "What about the New Testament? Isn't homosexuality among the named detestable sins?" Look to:

> "Women turned against God's natural plan for them and indulged in sex sin with each other. And the men, instead of having normal sex relationships with women, burned with lust for each other, men doing shameful things with other men and, as a result, getting paid within their own souls with the penalty they so richly deserved." (Romans 1:26–27)

Again, remember that not just homosexuality but any sexual deviation from his plan of one man and one woman together in a marriage for life is sin.

> "Don't you know that those doing such things have no share in the Kingdom of God? Don't fool yourselves. Those who live immoral lives, who are idol worshipers, adulterers or homosexuals—will have no share in his Kingdom. Neither will thieves or greedy people, drunkards, slanderers, or robbers." (1 Corinthians 6:9–10)

Now, while it is often stated that Christ never spoke against same-sex marriage, let us read his statement here. Then ask yourself if you should hold to this position:

"'Don't you read the Scriptures?' he replied. 'In them it is written that at the beginning God created man and woman, and that a man should leave his father and mother, and be forever united to his wife. The two shall become one—no longer two, but one! And no man may divorce what God has joined together.'" (Matthew 19:4–6)

So, God has established one solitary, perfect, and nonchangeable plan for us to follow. Any sexual deviation from this plan, be it homosexuality, adultery, premarital sex, lust, masturbation, bestiality, and so on is sin and is wrong as much here today as it has always been since God's initial creation of mankind. No matter what any government, culture, or organization says, does, or rationalizes, God's Word stands forever fixed, true, and unchanging!

We need to give up our autonomous, worldly selves. We have been told and taught to do what feels good and to have all the sex partners we want as often as we like. Only look out for yourself. Get all that you can no matter how you do so. Those stuck in these repetitive sin patterns say, "This is me! This is what I am. I cannot help it, nor can I change." It is true that you cannot change, not as an individual all alone. Sin's enslaving hold is too great. However, you can be changed with Christ to help you!

If you have never tried, I strongly recommend this approach: Ask for Christ's help and understanding. Then, spend time in prayer as well as in the reading of his Word. Further, as you do so, be sure to take the time to listen as he speaks to you. He will help you!

***

In summary, you need to humble yourself. Put aside your pride, what you may feel to be your superhuman intelligence, your doubts, your fears of judgment or of losing out on fun, and so on. Set aside all these things that keep you from seeking God. You must admit to him that you are a sinner in need of his help to break this cycle, these chains of sin that enslave you and that you cannot break by yourself. Then, express your belief in God's only Son, the Lord Jesus Christ, who was given as a sacrifice for all your sins. Ask him into your life, into your heart and soul. What do you have to lose?

Ask God to show you who he is and to reveal how he wants to take care of you in his perfect plan for your life. Spend time in his Holy Word. Get to know him better. As we get to know him better and better over time through his Word, his Word becomes incorporated into our lives and does indeed change us. The important thing now is to start! Ask him to help you understand what you are reading. Adjunctive activities such as spending time in a small group of Christian people or in a Christian, Word-based church, as well as interacting with Christian media, music, and books, are all helpful here.

Refresh your relationship with Christ. Go back to his cross. There you see your sins crucified. Ask him to fill you with his presence and with his love, and ask that such would then overflow from you to others, helping lead them to him as well! Take the time to seek and to better know him, and it will be so! Consider these relevant scriptures:

"I have thought much about your words and stored them in my heart so that they would hold me back from sin. Blessed Lord, teach me your rules. . . . I will delight in them and not forget them." (Psalm 119:11–12, 16)

"Your laws are both my light and my counselors. . . . Revive me by your Word. . . . Now give me your instructions. Make me understand what you want; for then I shall see your miracles." (Psalm 119:24, 26–27)

"Keep me far from every wrong; help me, undeserving as I am, to obey your laws, for I have chosen to do right. I cling to your commands and follow them as closely as I can. Lord, don't let me make a mess of things. Just tell me what to do and I will do it, Lord. As long as I live I'll wholeheartedly obey. Make me walk along the right paths, for I know how delightful they really are. Turn me away from wanting any other plan than yours. Revive my heart toward you. Reassure me that your promises are for me, for I trust and revere you." (Psalm 119:29–30, 31–35, 37–38)

***

So, let's return to that big question: are all sins forgivable? The answer remains yes, they are—all except for blaspheming the Holy Spirit (Matthew 12:31–32). This sin is the ultimate and final decision to deny Christ, be it through speech or by blatantly ignoring and rejecting Christ and the Holy Spirit's godliness and by denying their work in this world. If carried throughout one's life until death, one receives his final, ultimate, and eternal judgment. Blaspheming the Holy Spirit is the only nonforgivable error that we can make.

Now, why is this so grave a sin? It is because Christ came to give you his forgiveness, the forgiveness of your almighty, loving Father. But if you refuse this until that time when you either pass away from this world or until Christ returns, this is the one error that God will never forgive. Thus, you will be condemned to eternal judgment, separation from God in a state of permanent misery and anguish. It will be so terrible because you will be permanently separated from the one true God and his goodness forever. Those who deny God and his saving work through Christ or those who scorn and scoff at this gift will not be forgiven because they refused to accept his forgiveness!

Consider a patient who has a potentially fatal, yet curable, disease, albeit curable only with treatment. If he will accept and take the prescribed treatment, he will be saved. Yet if he refuses it, he will die. In the same way, if you reject God's gift of forgiveness for your sins, you will die without eternal life.

This gift is, nevertheless, freely available to you. And it continues to work, blessing more and more of us sinners, bringing us into the fold of our good shepherd even in our world today, as crazy as this place seems. You must believe and truly accept it and then let it transform you, rather than refusing it and being ultimately condemned to your eternal death!

***

"The more we see our sinfulness, the more we see God's abounding grace forgiving us." (Romans 5:20b)

Not too many years ago, before spending enough time in God's Word to realize how lost and sinful each of us is, I remember thinking, "Well, yes, I may have a little problem with pride and maybe some anger, but I am not so bad as most people. I am actually doing pretty well in avoiding all of the sins I read about in the Bible!" This is a very dangerous viewpoint. If we believe that we are excellent, good people in God's view, it makes us feel smugly overconfident, maybe even nearly perfect. This view changes as we spend adequate time in God's scriptures, as he reveals to us how lost and how sinful we all are. This is a necessary step: recognizing our extreme sinfulness and our need for a savior and realizing we cannot ever achieve salvation alone!

Simply being good will not get any of us into heaven. As is often said, and correctly so, "Heaven is not for good people; it's for forgiven people." None of us can do it all by ourself. We must have Christ. He took God's punishment for us and gives us his blameless, clean clothes of righteousness. If we refuse to accept his gift, when we die, we are granted our life's choice by judgment and are forever separated from God and cast into hell!

Many ask, "How could a truly loving God send people to hell?" As we will look in further detail, we find God is not just loving but that he loves justice also! We need to be forgiven from our sins before we can come into his presence! He originally made hell solely for the devil and his bad angels. He did not want people to go there. That desire is exactly why he sent his Son, to give us an open door to heaven. Christ died in our place to keep us from being judged and sent to eternal punishment!

We cannot comprehend how great our sin is until we get to truly know Christ. Then we realize the magnitude of what his forgiving grace has done for us. Again, I use my own example of plugging along contentedly for many years without deep scripture reading or correct interpretation of such. Perhaps you also think, "I am really pretty good, unlike so many other bad people." I reviewed the Bible's list of sins, thinking, "Hey, I'm in great shape, a bit of pride, perhaps a bit of anger. But wow! Out of that big list, I'm doing well in God's eyes. He must be proud of me, as I'm earning my way to heaven!"

How wrong is such thinking! Such an attitude suggests that we can control (and implies that we do control) our sinful natures. That is a rationalization and an absolute lie. What blissfully ignorant, false comfort is the perception that we have the power to save ourselves, to earn our own salvation!

Such is an extremely dangerous path to be on—not seeing the reality about yourself. If this is you, you are not ascending to the desired pinnacle of salvation but, rather, are descending into the pit of the Valley of Death. How tragic it is that so many trek this path for their entire lives! We need to hear Christ speaking truth to us through the Scriptures instead:

> "I felt fine so long as I did not understand what the law really demanded. But when I learned the truth, I realized that I had broken the law and was a sinner, doomed to die." (Romans 7:9)

We want to do well and to be good. But given the sinful nature that twists every human heart, we cannot do either persistently, try as we might. We need Christ!

> "I don't understand myself at all, for I really want to do what is right, but I can't. I do what I don't want to—what I hate. But I can't help myself . . . No matter which way I turn I can't make myself do right. I want to but I can't. When I want to do good, I don't; and when I try not to do wrong, I do it anyway. Now if I am doing what I don't want to, it is plain where the trouble is: sin still has me in its evil grasp. I love to do God's will so far as my new nature is concerned; but there is something else deep within me, in my lower nature, that is at war with my mind and wins the fight and makes me a slave to the sin that is still within me. . . . my new life tells me to do right, but the old nature that is still inside me loves to sin. Oh, what a terrible predicament I'm in! Who will free me from my slavery to this deadly lower nature? Thank God! It has been done by Jesus Christ our Lord. He has set me free." (Romans 7:15, 17–20, 22–25)

Christ frees us from the mire of sin's swampy debacle, that abyss that we are unable to pull ourselves out of.

Paul C. Buechel, M.D.

"So there is now no condemnation awaiting those who belong to Christ Jesus. For the power of the life-giving Spirit—and this power is mine through Christ Jesus—has freed me from the vicious circle of sin and death. We aren't saved from sin's grasp by knowing the commandments of God because we can't and don't keep them, but God put into effect a different plan to save us. He sent his own Son in a human body like ours—except that ours are sinful—and destroyed sin's control over us by giving himself as a sacrifice for our sins. So now we can obey God's laws if we follow the Holy Spirit and no longer obey the old evil nature within us. Those who let themselves be controlled by their lower natures live only to please themselves, but those who follow after Holy Spirit find themselves doing those things that please God. Following after the Holy Spirit leads to life and peace, but following after the old nature leads to death because the old sinful nature within us is against God. It never did obey God's laws and it never will. . . . You are controlled by your new nature if you have the Spirit of God living in you. . . . Yet, even though Christ lives within you, your body will die because of sin; but your spirit will live, for Christ has pardoned it." (Romans 8:1–7, 9–10)

"If we say that we have no sin, we are only fooling ourselves and refusing to accept the truth. But if we confess our sins to him, he can be depended on to forgive us and to cleanse us from every wrong. And it is perfectly proper for God to do this for us because Christ died to wash away our sins. If we claim we have not sinned, we are lying and calling God a liar, *for he says we have sinned.*" (1 John 1:8–10)

Rise and Soar

Therefore, truly knowing God and his Son grants you a true knowledge of yourself. You can clearly see your utter sinfulness and how you must have Christ to save you. This wisdom makes it easy to let him in and to submit your life to him!

"But," one may ask, "such submission, committing my life to him, sounds hard and not at all fun. Is it difficult?"

If you will simply try it, you will find it to be a great and restful comfort, a divine reprieve unlike any this world can offer. With him, we do not have to fight so hard while trying to be good in our attempts to please God, nor do we further worry about our final destiny. In truth, our only hope is to submit ourselves entirely to his mercy!

***

What battles are you fighting right now? Do you have problems in relationships, finances, addictions, or sicknesses? These problems are all, ultimately, at their bottom line, the result of some degree of sin committed either by yourself or against yourself. They are derived from the world about you. You cannot fight these alone. Give your fight to your heavenly Father. He has already defeated sin by sending his Son. And this sin, which has already been beaten, is the strongest foe you will ever fight in this world. Therefore, ask for his help, and he will meet with you in both your prayers to him and in his Word. These two channels allow you easy and personal access to him!

He will take your burden, and he will rescue and lead you forward into and throughout your future. Why not accept Christ today? Drop your burdens and your battles at his feet, at the foot of his cross. An excellent visual symbol that graphically demonstrates this to me is the gravestone of *Pilgrim's Progress* writer, John Bunyan, which shows one unloading his heavy burdens at the cross's foot! If we will only do this, we will shed our own crosses and sins. Then we can model God's holiness to the best degree that we humanly can.

The big question is: do you believe Jesus is God's Son, the One who died for you, and have you committed your life to him fully by taking him as your Lord and Savior? If so, your sins are gone. If not, they are all retained by you, and you will ultimately be dealt with by a holy and a just God.

Even as you may look now at sins past, someday you will look back at your pending sins with immense disgust and regret. Then you will realize their cost: not only their consequences in this life but also how they deprived you of a relationship with God and all his intended blessings for you. Regarding such consequences are the following scriptures:

"They have sown the wind, and they will reap the whirlwind." (Hosea 8:7a)

"You can't ignore God and get away with it: a man will always reap just the kind of crop he sows!" (Galatians 6:7)

God will forgive if you repent and return to him. But sin's consequences will still occur. You will never completely get away with any continued, intentional sin. You can be certain it will become known, as Numbers 32:23 states, "You may be sure that your sin will catch up with you."

***

A bigger concern in the arena of serial and repetitive sin is the one who has sinned so much for so long that he has deadened his conscience and hardened his heart. Such people have a progressively harder time getting back to God. And this is you, if you can read this message or hear his good news without feeling conviction or remorse.

Once again, God is not here to ruin our happiness or to spoil our fun. his rules are there for our good, for our well-being, as set by our loving Father. Do not let your god be greed, sexual sin, power, or anything else. If you do allow such, it robs you and your family, friends, and associates of God's shower of blessings over your life!

As examples, think of Zacchaeus and Judas Iscariot in the Bible. Both committed monetary sins. Or recall the sexual sins of David and Samson. The consequences for each sinner were great. But one in each pair had a dramatically different outcome. Zacchaeus and David recognized their sin and repented, turning back to God by whom they were saved. Judas and Samson did not do so. They allowed their sins to destroy them!

Consider further the positive examples of Paul and Gideon. Both of whom, though described as physically weak men, performed amazing feats for God. The statement that God's light shines best through broken vessels (2 Corinthians 4:7) is indeed applicable here.

***

Now that we have contemplated the above points, we are in a better position to define sin. Sin is any type of deed or thought, or at times the absence of such, that is the opposite of a good and loving deed or thought. There are sins of commission and sins of omission. Romans 14:23 is an excellent way to think of sin:

> "Anyone who believes that something he wants to do is wrong shouldn't do it. He sins if he does, for he thinks it is wrong,

and so for him it is wrong. Anything that is done apart from what he feels is right is sin."

This definition brings in the necessity of a conscience and of wisdom. I feel both are very appropriately characterized by the Holy Spirit, he who is ever with us, convicting us when we are wrong and guiding us in the appropriate paths to take if we will remain open to him.

Let's look to God's own Word for more guidance regarding sin:

"Quit quarreling with God! Agree with him and you will have peace at last! His favor will surround you if you will only admit that you were wrong. Listen to his instructions and store them in your heart. If you return to God and put right all the wrong in your home, then you will be restored. Whatever you wish will happen! And the light of heaven will shine upon the road ahead of you." (Job 22:21–23, 28)

"Since we believe that Christ died for all of us, we should also believe that we have died to the old life we used to live. He died for all so that all who live—having received eternal life from him—might live no longer for themselves, to please themselves, but to spend their lives pleasing Christ who died and rose again for them." (2 Corinthians 5:14b–15)

"When someone becomes a Christian, he becomes a brand new person inside. He is not the same anymore. A new life has begun!" (v. 17)

"For God was in Christ, restoring the world to himself, no longer counting men's sins against them but blotting them out. . . . Receive the love he offers you—be reconciled to God.

For God took the sinless Christ and poured into him our sins. Then, in exchange, he poured God's goodness into us!" (vv. 19–21)

"Christ has brought you into the very presence of God, and you are standing there before him with nothing left against you—nothing left that he could even chide you for; the only condition is that you fully believe the Truth, standing in it steadfast and firm, strong in the Lord, convinced of the Good News that Jesus died for you, and never shifting from trusting him to save you. This is the wonderful news that came to each of you and is now spreading all over the world. And I, Paul, have the joy of telling it to others." (Colossians 1:22b–23a)

"You were dead in sins, and your sinful desires were not yet cut away. Then he gave you a share in the very life of Christ, for he forgave all your sins, and blotted out the charges proved against you, the list of his commandments which you had not obeyed. He took this list of sins and destroyed it by nailing it to Christ's cross." (Colossians 2:13–14)

"Under this new plan we have been forgiven and made clean by Christ's dying for us once and for all." (Hebrews 10:10)

These scriptures tell us we are saved by Christ once and for all, and there is no ritual of prayers, good works, offerings, or anything else we must do to gain God's favor other than to accept and believe his gift.

***

Every sinner ready to confess and to repent today (as was the case in the days of yore with Zacchaeus, Matthew, Paul, and the multitude of other sinners in Scripture) is one of those for whom Christ came to grant forgiveness. As Jesus said, it is the sick people who need a doctor. By this he meant he could not and cannot help the self-righteous, represented by the Pharisees and Sadducees of his day. They were like people in this modern world who think their traditions, rules, tithes, and other efforts can save them and earn God's favor. God states that only the humbled, self-realized, and repentant sinner can be redeemed and forgiven!

Regarding major sins, those sins we might feel God could never forgive, let us look at the examples of Peter and Judas Iscariot in the Gospels. Both men did very bad things. They denied and betrayed Christ, respectively. And both afterward were quite saddened, grieving deeply over their offenses. Nevertheless, after their failures, one sought Christ while the other did not. How each reacted to their deed is what made the difference. Their reactions were what dramatically affected the final outcomes. Peter became one of the top three apostles in the early church after the resurrection (alongside Paul and John), accomplishing great and amazing things for God's kingdom. Meanwhile, the self-absorbed Judas ended his misery by hanging himself. And more than two thousand years later, his name has such a negative connotation that no one names even their dog, let alone their child, after him.

So, as Peter, we must keep our eyes fixed on Christ despite our sins and through all our failures, and repent and then forget them. We must not live in regret. We instead must realize that our best, through Christ, is yet to come! We need to remain vigilant to minimize ongoing sins and be joyful and thankful for God's forgiveness. In so doing, we will get past our bad pasts!

This is exactly what Peter and Paul did, and it is exactly why the outcome was so vastly positive for these two grievously sinning men!

They chose wisely when presented with that most important question each of us must ask: what will be my relationship with Jesus?

Like them, we modern-day sinners must decide what position we are going to take with respect to Jesus. Or, put another way, we must choose our stance and our attitude with him. Our response is of the utmost importance for each of our lives, as we see demonstrated in these two disciples' lives, because this one thing, our relationship with Christ, determines our eternal destiny. Will you choose paradise with him forever, no matter what you have done, or will you choose eternal punishment?

Let's say you choose Jesus. How do you go about getting this good relationship with him? How does one get there? First, you must open your mind to him, asking him to come in, to teach, and to show you what he wants you to do for him in this world, to show you the exciting adventure he has planned out specifically for you. Second, you must pray frequently and regularly, staying in daily conversation with your loving Father. Third, you must daily read his living and breathing Word. This gets more of him into you, so you become more like him, gaining his wisdom in this crazy world, as well as his peace, joy, fulfillment, and rescue. Fourth, join a biblical church and be active in a small group of believers for support, accountability, and knowledge growth. Fifth, you should seek out and spend more time in Christian media, primarily Christian books, music, and movies and allow less of the worldly media to influence your brain. Last, you must cut off bad past relationships and any other things that have kept a wall between you and Jesus, whatever they may be—perhaps bad friends, a lover or affair, a gang, drugs, alcohol, bad relationships, greed and possessions, or selfishness.

In prisons, I use a metaphor that can apply to all of us. I describe our lives as a partially finished book. Past chapters are done, and the rest is still unwritten.

Past deeds and choices do not determine your book's conclusion. Refuse to let a bad past drag you down. Move on and forget prior bad times. Use these for wisdom and as guides to help you avoid bad choices in the future. Christ wants you to get up and to move on, always continuing to work for his kingdom! Doing so, you will achieve the fulfillment both you and he desire. And you will receive his joy, peace, and rescue, even a rescue from your past errors. Going forward, the rest of your volume is still unwritten. Its near future as well as its final outcome are up to you! This is the plan God has had for you ever since you were born. Finding it is what you have been made for. Fulfilling it will give you great peace.

***

As a negative example, let us consider Judas Iscariot once again. Could he have been forgiven had he asked? While we can never know for certain, I believe that, given Christ's message, even though Judas had betrayed God's Son, if he had done more than just realize what he had done was wrong—that is, if he had thrown himself on God's mercy—he may well have been forgiven. Nevertheless, he never placed his faith in Christ and had a heart change. He never had a transformation through Christ. When he felt bad, he killed himself to stop his pain. He did not deal correctly with the consequences of his sin. His story emphasizes our need to seek God while we still can before our hearts harden to a point where we can no longer hear God's message. Consider Isaiah 55:6–7:

> "Seek the Lord while you can find him. Call upon him now while he is near. Let men cast off their wicked deeds; let them banish from their minds the very thought of doing wrong!

Let them turn to the Lord that he may have mercy upon them, and to our God, for he will abundantly pardon!"

Also look at Joel 2:12: "The Lord says, 'Turn to me now, while there is time. Give me all your hearts.'" And consider Ezekiel 18:30–32: "'Turn from your sins while there is yet time. Put them behind you and receive a new heart and a new spirit. . . . I do not enjoy seeing you die,' the Lord God says. 'Turn, turn and live!'"

We need to realize there is a potential Judas in each of us. Even those of us who are near to Christ are not exempt. Judas communed with him in person daily for three years. We need to be certain that we, unlike Judas, are repentant and changed! We must be certain we are definitively progressing forward in our course, in our sanctification (which can be defined as our holiness pattern). We should change from the time that we accept Christ until our dying day. We must be absolutely determined that we will not go through the Christian motions while continuing in our sinful heart's natural paths! We cannot just say we devote our lives to Jesus. We must instead ask him in and allow him to change our hearts!

Do not waste your life as Judas did. Do not allow any sin, be it sexual immorality, impurity, lust, evil desire, greed, or something else, to block out your relationship with Christ! Be a true Christ follower, not a selfish individual. Ask him to show you any residual reservoirs of unholiness still remaining in your life. He can help you with these if you remain in close, daily contact with him, regularly reading and incorporating into yourself his Word and communicating with him daily, even constantly, in prayer.

***

Like Paul and Peter, there were many other men in the Bible who committed terrible deeds but still were forgiven. In Genesis, for example, Cain, after killing his brother Abel, cried out when God cursed and banished him from his farmland home: "My punishment is greater than I can bear. For you have banished me from my farm and from you" (Genesis 4:13–14). God heard his cries and mercifully promised that he would always protect Cain from avengers. God also gave him a son, Enoch, who became an amazingly great man of God. Enoch is the only other person in Scripture besides Elijah to be taken up to heaven without physically dying. And Enoch's descendants included the first cattlemen, the first musician (inventor of the flute and harp), and the first metal foundry worker (in bronze and iron).

Similarly, Manasseh (in 2 Chronicles and 2 Kings) performed all kinds of despicable evils. He sacrificed Israeli children in fires to demon-gods and committed enough murders that the streets of Jerusalem ran red with blood. God judged him and had him taken away to Babylon in chains. Nevertheless, while there he repented, and God restored him. Therefore, despite all those terrible evils he did as a younger king, Manasseh's life had a very good ending. He became a holy king of God!

A further example is King Ahab, whom 1 Kings 21:25 describes as: "No one else was so completely sold out the devil." Scripture calls Ahab the most evil king in Jewish history. God had mercy on him, however, at least temporarily, when Ahab humbled himself, despite all he had so evilly done (although he later reverted to his evil ways).

***

We must remember that despite all our technological and scientific advances, our vast accumulation of human knowledge, the human heart has not changed since the days of the Old Testament prophets. They called all to repent and to return to God. And their message from God to the world's populace continues today! Yet, our sins still lead us into confusion, sadness, and bad consequences, deforming our lives and distorting our world. We Christians live, for the present, in this sinful world, and therefore, we exist amidst its evils. We must, however, stay the good course. We know that final victory with Christ is our endpoint, a victory that has already been achieved! We also know he walks our paths with us. Knowing him, then, allows peace into our hearts as we work toward our final goal of eternal paradise with our lord!

FORGIVENESS

We cannot discuss sin without discussing forgiveness. Consider God's own Word to see his view on the subject: "For the Lord your God is full of kindness and mercy and will not continue to turn away his face from you if you return to him" (2 Chronicles 30:9b). The Bible tells us no sin is too great to be forgiven except the solitary sin of rejecting God and his gift of forgiveness and eternal life through Christ Jesus, his Son. Such broad and amazing forgiveness necessarily brings about in us a very positive change, as the full weight of our guilt and shame is completely lifted off our shoulders. Then our minds are cleared of all worries about being good enough or about pleasing God. Such worries are in fact all about what is going to happen to us in the hereafter.

Now, if you accept and receive his grace, you have a reciprocal duty. If you truly understand you have received his forgiveness, it is important that you naturally extend forgiveness to others who have wronged you. If you do not or cannot forgive others, you do not know God's forgiveness!

Developing a mindset of forgiveness is difficult, and the ability to forgive is even harder. Still, these are divine gifts, blessings that are not known to the heart alone in its own understanding. Through Christ, however, forgiveness is a divine gift we can give others. And in doing so, we likewise give ourselves a gift. We escape the caustic, bitter, self-destructive, self-enslaving effects of unforgiveness, that of chronically harboring bitter feelings toward others.

We must always remember that as God freely forgave us, we are asked by him to forgive those who have injured us! Likewise, when we injure others, we must be cognizant to express sorrow and to ask for forgiveness. By doing so, we are mirroring and extending Christ to others by doing what he has commanded. Anything short of this is disobedience to his teachings. Let's close this section with more of God's promises of forgiveness.

"I, yes, I alone am he who blots away your sins for my own sake and will never think of them again." (Isaiah 43:25)

"I made you, and I will not forget to help you. I've blotted out your sins; they are gone like morning mist at noon! Oh, return to me, for I have paid the price to set you free." (Isaiah 44:21b–22)

"What happiness for those whose guilt has been forgiven! What joys when sins are covered over! What relief for those who have confessed their sins and God has cleared their record. There was a time when I wouldn't admit what a sinner I was. But my dishonesty made me miserable and filled my days with frustration . . . until I finally admitted all my sins to you and stopped trying to hide them. I said to myself, 'I will confess them to the Lord.' And you forgave me! All my guilt is gone. Now I say that each believer should confess his sins to God when he is aware of them, while there is time to be forgiven. Judgment will not touch him if he does." (Psalm 32:1–3, 5–6)

"Come, let's talk this over, says the Lord; no matter how deep the stain of your sins, I can take it out and make you as clean as freshly fallen snow. Even if you are stained as red as crimson, I can make you white as wool!" (Isaiah 1:18)

III. His Promise and Salvation

"Praise the Lord! He was angry with me, but now he comforts me. See, God has come to save me! I will trust and not be afraid, for the Lord is my strength and song; he is my salvation."
(Isaiah 12:1–2)

"But as for me, I know that my Redeemer lives, and that he will stand upon the earth at last. And I know that after this body has decayed, this body shall see God! Then he will be on my side! Yes, I shall see him, not as a stranger, but as a friend! What a glorious hope!" (Job 19:25–27)

Two of the most important questions we will ever be asked and that we must answer are these: How do we gain salvation? And do we desire it enough to pursue it despite our pride and all of our smarts, our busyness, our worldly possessions, our fears of missing out on worldly fun, or our fear of judgment, or perhaps because we simply like the pain of living outside of him?

For an absolute rising above this world and a definitively guaranteed salvation, you must make Jesus Christ your own savior and lord. You must accept him and make the gospel's good news your own. You cannot simply be aware of it, thinking, "Yeah, it's cool," or "It's neat," or "Love it!"

Instead, you must learn and know for certain, without doubt, that you are saved and sealed in Christ forever. You need only accept him and begin a personal relationship with Jesus. He has paid all in order to buy you out from under the clutches of your slavery to sin. Accept his purchase and allow yourself to be brought to him.

His gift is wholly based upon your faith in him, anchored in the strong and firm belief that he is indeed God's Son and is also, thus, God himself, he who shed his blood to cover you, a sinner, exchanging his glory for your own dirty rags. You must realize there is nothing else that you can do on your own to redeem or save yourself. Only the power of Christ's blood can ever save us! If we could save ourselves by being righteous, then there was no need for Christ to die (Galatians 2:21). Saving grace is available to all. But to be eligible, each one of us must accept it before either:

a) Christ returns to judge at his Second Coming.

b) We die, at which point there is no hope left.

After Christ returns, God will give all left on earth one last chance, as noted in Revelation when his angel pronounces the gospel one final time (Revelation 14:6–13). Those still alive can either choose salvation or continue to deny and refuse it. Scripture tells us that many will then choose Christ, despite their poor prior choices. Many will finally be converted and brought into Jesus's fold on that, their very last chance. Those latter converts will, however, have to both witness and endure the great suffering of God's wrathful judgment in the Tribulation. That time will be so terrible that most believers will likely be martyred for their faith. Like so many of their brethren, they will enter eternal glory, but theirs will be a more difficult road.

Let's also extrapolate to our world today. There are still many who even now are waiting and thinking about making their choice for Christ. Unfortunately, some will wait too long and will die before making a choice—so few of us will ever know exactly when we are going to die. To quote Christ in Luke 12:20, "Fool! Tonight you die. Then who will get it all?"

So why wait? What do you have to lose? Very little, if anything at all. And in truth, you have everything to gain!

***

I received an urgent code call to the emergency room. A very large marine sergeant lay splayed out upon the trauma bay exam table, arms and legs limply hanging over the sides. His torso barely fit upon the table. One glance at the heart monitor showed asystole, a flat line meaning no heart rate or rhythm.

I immediately pounded his chest with a precordial fist thump, trying to restart his heart. There was no successful response. Grabbing the bedside defibrillator paddles, I held these onto his chest, shouted "clear" to warn the nurse to stay off the table, and pressed both buttons. ZZZAAAAPPPPP!!!!!

"Who hit me!" the marine bellowed loudly, sitting straight upright and swinging a haymaker right hook just over my head. I felt its breeze as I ducked out of the way. He meant to knock my block off. It was reflexive action, common in persons who resuscitate rapidly after an electrical shock to restart the heart. The marine gradually calmed down after I explained that his heart had stopped. And he was in great spirits two hours later when I next saw him in the intensive care unit. His heart resuscitation had returned his life for the moment, at least.

While his is a tale of a temporary earthly salvation delivered by electromechanical means, we can easily extrapolate this to the eternal salvation that God promises us, if we will only follow him, believe the good that he has in store for us, and do what he asks us to do!

***

You do not need to have an extremely dramatic conversion event in order to be saved. But you do need to be able to point to a specific and definitive time in your life when you said yes to God's gift of Christ's blood as coverage for all of your sins, thus saving you for all eternity. You must say "I do" to God. Make a wedding vow. Couples can go on dates and even be engaged, but they never fully commit themselves until they officially say, "I do." So, one cannot simply say, "I like God and Jesus," or "Christianity sounds good," or "I am a good person." You need to settle this once and for all, so why not do it now? In so doing, you will seal yourself to him for salvation permanently. It is a certain occurrence! He desires you to commit so he can shower blessings upon you and ease your burdens in this world. Then he will also gather you into his loving presence when you pass to the next.

So, believe him. Make him yours and yourself his—right now! You can pray something like this: "Dear God, my Father, I know that I am a sinner. I realize this now. And I understand that I cannot do anything to save myself. I am sorry for my sins, but I need your help to repent and to completely change my life. I believe in your Son, Jesus Christ, and that he came to save me by his blood and sacrifice. I know without doubt that he is your Son, and I ask him to come into my life as my friend, Lord, and Savior. I dedicate the rest of my life to becoming better and better acquainted with him. Please help me and show me the way. I ask this in the name of our dear Lord and Savior, Jesus Christ, amen!"

If you can say this prayer honestly, both believing it and meaning it, then congratulations! Be joyful! Prepare to reap his showers of many blessings upon you, as you have become a child of God, a Son or daughter to him, as is stated in John 1:12: "To all who received him, he gave the right to become children of God. All they needed to do was to trust him to save them."

One, therefore, must in good faith pray, "I receive you, Jesus. Please come into my life and save me." Then, even hundreds of thousands of years from now, this will be that single moment you can look back upon and point to exactly when your life, as well as your eternal destiny, were forever changed!

So if you are one who says, "Well, I think I am probably saved," or "I do not know, but I want to be saved," or if you are still a seeker or even a nonbeliever who wants to be sure you get it right, you need to ask yourself these three important questions: Do you believe that you are a sinner and cannot save yourself? Do you believe Jesus is God's Son and that he died to save you from that sin? And do you confess faith in him as your personal Savior and the Lord of your life?

If, with God's help, you achieve a firm belief and can thus answer these three statements affirmatively, then you can claim his gift of salvation. You are now a child of God. Again, if you are ready, pray right now: "God, I accept your gift of Christ's death as forgiveness for my sins and your reward of eternal life with you. Please come into my life, save me, and bless and show me, day by day, how to know you better and better."

Once again, innumerable centuries, even millennia, from now, this will be the moment in time you look back to, pointing it out as the turning point of your life. You can now absolutely, with no uncertainty whatsoever, know you are saved and sealed by him for guaranteed eternal life with God and our Lord, Jesus Christ!

***

Certainly, though, we all will continue to sin. Sin is so ingrained in our natures. Yet we must seek to be repentant and to always return to him while doing our very best to sin less. Such sin reduction will naturally begin to occur as we incorporate (by getting to know him more and more in his Word, in prayer, at church, and in Christian media and discussions with our fellow Christians) Christ's very being and character traits into our daily lives. This results in a progressive transformation of character toward more and more holiness over time, a sanctification (a purification process) that cannot help but naturally occur in all who truly accept and ask for his presence to enter their lives! Consider God's Word here:

> "I say emphatically that anyone who listens to my message and believes in God who sent me has eternal life, and will never be damned for his sins, but has already passed out of death into life." (John 5:24)

> "For it is my Father's will that everyone who sees his Son and believes on him should have eternal life—that I should raise him at the Last Day." (John 6:40)

> "My righteous Servant shall make many to be counted righteous before God, for he shall bear all their sins. . . . He was counted as a sinner, and he bore the sins of many, and he pled with God for sinners." (Isaiah 53:11b–12)

Indeed, Christ does still plead for us with God his Father!

> "Jesus told her, 'I am the one who raises the dead and gives them life again. Anyone who believes in me, even though he

dies like anyone else, shall live again. He is given eternal life for believing in me and shall never perish. Do you believe this?'" (John 11:25–26)

"Jesus told him, 'I am the Way—yes, and the Truth and the Life. No one can get to the Father except by means of me.'" (John 14:6)

"Anyone who believes in me already has eternal life! Yes, I am the Bread of Life!" (John 6:47–48a)

***

"But wait," one may ask. "Don't many sinners achieve great worldly success, power, fame, mansions, and riches?" Unfortunately, we all see the daily injustices in our world. Yet those crafty, sneaky people will not get away with their vices and misdeeds forever, as described in 2 Timothy 3:9, "They won't get away with all this forever. Someday their deceit will be well known to everyone."

God, however, is not willing that any should be lost. He wants all people to be forgiven. He desires to be your Savior and Lord as well as your friend. As your heavenly Father, he wants a real relationship with you. He wants to be a true friend, not your judge! You can know him and his will and therefore receive his peace, joy, fulfillment, and rescue. Always remember this common saying: he can turn your mess into his message. Yet, in being your loving Father, God is not going to force you to commit, just as you could never command another person to love you.

Unfortunately, some people will ultimately be lost. As discussed above, all have been born into sin. Therefore, all need to be born again into Christ in order to be saved!

***

This brings up another point that is often debated, that is whether Christians can lose their salvation, the eternal sealing by the Holy Spirit, once they have taken Christ as Lord and Savior. Several denominations, including the Roman Catholic Church and the Church of Christ, do believe it is possible.

Nevertheless, the good news is that, in looking at God's truth as the final measuring stick, one cannot lose their salvation. It is a misunderstanding, an incorrect view, on the part of those who believe such. By this belief, they appear to think they can save or unsave themselves.

Yet, if you know who God truly is, you realize your salvation comes from him alone and not from yourself. How then could you, as a mere person, ever change this?

"Okay, but then," one might ask, "are Christians with this belief about possible lost salvation unsaved or not?"

It seems most likely to me that God overrides their skewed views (according to Scripture, which always needs to be the final authority). I think God will save those who believe that Christ died to save them, all of those who are in a personal relationship with Him. This permanent sealing is noted in:

> "[The Holy Spirit's] presence within us is God's guarantee that he really will give us all that he promised; and the Spirit's seal upon us means that God has already purchased us and that he guarantees to bring us to himself." (Ephesians 1:14)

> "This is too glorious, too wonderful to believe! I can never be lost to your Spirit! I can never get away from my God! If I go up to heaven, you are there; if I go down to the place of the

dead, you are there. If I ride the morning winds to the farthest oceans, even there your hand will guide me, your strength will support me. If I try to hide in the darkness, the night becomes light around me." (Psalm 139:6–11)

There are many, many more scripture verses dealing with this amazing gift of God's salvation. Consider the following:

"This certain hope of being saved is a strong and trustworthy anchor for our souls, connecting us with God himself behind the sacred curtains of heaven, where Christ has gone ahead to plead for us." (Hebrews 6:19–20a)

"All are saved the same way, by the free gift of the Lord Jesus?" (Acts 15:11)

"Believe on the Lord Jesus and you will be saved, and your entire household." (Acts 16:31)

"No one can ever be made right in God's sight by doing what the law commands. For the more we know of God's laws, the clearer it becomes that we aren't obeying them; his laws serve only to make us see that we are sinners. But now God has shown us a different way to heaven—not by 'being good enough' and trying to keep his laws . . . Now God says he will accept and acquit us—declare us 'not guilty'—if we trust Jesus Christ to take away our sins. And we all can be saved in this same way, by coming to Christ, no matter who we are or what we have been like. Yes, all have sinned; all fall short of God's glorious ideal; yet now God declares us 'not guilty' of offending him if we trust in Jesus Christ, who in his kindness freely takes away our sins. For God sent Christ Jesus to take the punishment for our sins and to end all God's anger against us. He used Christ's blood and our faith as the means of saving us from his wrath." (Romans 3:20–25a)

"Our acquittal is not based on our good deeds; it is based on what Christ has done and our faith in him. So it is that we are saved by faith in Christ and not by the good things we do." (Romans 27b–28)

"Being saved is a gift; if a person could earn it by being good, then it wouldn't be free—but it is! It is given to those who do not work for it. For God declares sinners to be good in his sight if they have faith in Christ to save them from God's wrath." (Romans 4:4b–5)

"I could never find God's favor by trying—and failing—to obey the laws. I came to realize that acceptance with God comes by believing in Christ. I have been crucified with Christ: and I myself no longer live, but Christ lives in me. And the real life I now have within this body is a result of my trusting in the Son of God, who loved me and gave himself for me." (Galatians 2:19–20)

"For if you tell others with your own mouth that Jesus Christ is your Lord and believe in your own heart that God has raised him from the dead, you will be saved." (Romans 10:9)

"Right now God is ready to welcome you. Today he is ready to save you." (2 Corinthians 6:2b)

"No mere man has ever seen, heard, or even imagined what wonderful things God has ready for those who love the Lord." (1 Corinthians 2:9)

"He is able to save completely all who come to God through him. Since he will live forever, he will always be there to remind God that he has paid for their sins with his blood. . . . for he finished all sacrifices, once and for all, when he sacrificed himself on the cross." (Hebrews 7:25, 27b)

"My grace is sufficient for you." (2 Corinthians 12:9 HCSB)

***

Now some may think, "Okay, does this all mean that if I accept Christ's forgiveness, that I am then home free, no matter what I do, that I have a free license to sin, as long as I repent of it afterward?"

No! Absolutely not! This is your conniving, devious, and worldy human mind, always working its evil gears in trying to get you back, attempting to chain you even more as a slave onto its sin-wagon, once again.

A true Christian, while still a sinner until his dying day, will commit less and less sins in both frequency and degree as he progresses in his walk with God throughout life. He realizes how each added sin hurts his relationship with the Lord. (Each committed sin is a sin that Christ has died for, so one adds to the misery that he suffered for us on Calvary by sinning!) The sinner also hurts himself and others. So, he sins less, becoming more Christ-like with time as he notably reduces his offenses against God and mankind. This sin-reduction pattern, over time, is the mark of a true Christian!

***

So, what is heaven, the place that is the end goal of our salvation, going to be like? Jesus said, "I go to prepare a place for you." In this new place, God is always with you, and you with him. There is no sickness, no death, no sadness, nor any evil, as God is holy and wholly in control. He calls all the shots.

There he also, per Revelation, is making everything new. Heaven is not some boring place where we float around on clouds playing dull, repetitive tunes on our harps and having no real fun. Erroneous thoughts of eternal paradise in this manner are what I believe often keep many people from seeking God. They do not understand what an amazing place awaits them, nor how bad the alternative will be.

So, regarding heaven, they ask, "What! No football or basketball there? No video games? Do they have my comics and my chips there? Is it deep dish pizza or flat crust or even, shudder the thought, no pizza? We already have all we need to be happy right here and right now in this world! Why do we need to obey and seek a heavenly Father?"

This is an incorrect view of eternal paradise! Instead, try to imagine being constantly with our heavenly Father, he who loves us more than you can ever imagine. There in his eternal love for you, nothing will ever be the same! Day after day after day, new and exciting events will take place—forever. That is, from the moment you enter, to infinity! There will be no pain, no disabilities, and no gait assistance devices. No doctors or lawyers will be necessary. There will be no tax problems. Further, there will be no temptations, no wrongful things, no time schedules to meet, nor will there be any more disappointments or frustrations.

Such a place is so exponentially beyond even the best worldly comforts our human minds can imagine that I fear we rarely ponder it,

Rise and Soar

and perhaps may downplay or even doubt how truly amazing heaven will be!

Think of your absolute best days here in this world so far: perhaps your wedding day, your children being born, a great sports feat or some other victory, or an amazing vacation or adventure that you took. Then, as hard as it might seem, try to imagine how heaven will be dramatically better, exponentially far beyond any of those few great days you recalled. And it will be that way every day! How would and how could God ever make heaven some boring old place? No. Every new day in heaven will be completely exciting throughout each moment, becoming your best day ever and repeating onward for all eternity! We will also get answers to our many questions. Finally, everything will make sense to us.

***

Always remember God is faithful and his grace is enough. He leads us only to places where his great grace can help us. But he does not always miraculously free us from illness, pain, death, or persecution. Yet he is with us in all these storms with his supporting love and grace. He will never abandon us. While certainly difficult to believe at those rough times in our lives, we must remain faithful to this belief. As discussed above in this volume, he at times takes us through the trial and through the fire, while at other times, he keeps us from it.

Once again, salvation is in Christ alone by grace alone through faith alone. Through this, our faith we believe with our hearts and confess with our lips that Christ is the true lord, the One who died to redeem us from all sin. If you do so, then you are saved!

So, are you saved? If you died today, would you go to eternal paradise or not? How can you know for certain? The all-important questions here are: Do you believe that you are a sinner who cannot save your-self? Do you have a desire to repent and turn from your sinful ways? Do you believe that Jesus is God's Son who came here to die and rise again and who, in so doing, saves all who believe in him? And finally, do you believe in and accept him as your Savior and Lord?

We must remember, as Scripture states in James 2:19, that "even the demons believe." They, however, are certainly not among those destined to be saved! Therefore, beyond mere knowledge or belief, you must confess your faith in him, asking him into your heart and into your life to be your own Savior, your own Lord, and your guide through-out the rest of this life. He will give you his righteousness and take your sinful, dirty rags away. He places these upon himself while giving you his glorious royal robe! Then you will see your life change. So much that mattered so greatly to you prior will no longer be of importance or necessity.

You will receive his peace, his joy, his fulfillment, and his rescue, as you live to glorify him and to fulfill that special duty that he has ordained for you in this world. How do we know? Because God prom-ises all of this in his fully reliable Word! We are living without, that is, missing out, on all these blessings if we are out of his Spirit. Then he cannot fill us as he wishes to. Settling for anything other than him will leave you unsatisfied, feeling an empty hole inside.

Ask God to fill you with his Holy Spirit. Then yield to his purposes and plans for you. Ask him, "What do you want me to do, Lord?" Do not quench or put off his Spirit, but ask to be filled with him each day. Then believe it, and it will be so.

Truly, if we are Christians, those who have accepted Christ as Lord and Savior, the Spirit will never leave us, although he can be resisted, minimized, and muffled. Such actions deny us his benefits, his fruits in our lives. As he promised, the Lord will never leave nor forsake his own.

But if we continually tone down the Spirit, ever reducing his volume in our lives, we will miss out on all the good things that he gives! So do not resist. Let him in and see what you have been devoid of. Stop your losses, your bleeding, and your misery—right now!

Once we are sealed with the Spirit, he is always present with us. Yet we can still grieve him. Ephesians 4:30 says, "Do not grieve the Holy Spirit of God, by whom you were sealed for the day of redemption" (NKJV). Do not make him regret being with you. He loves you and cannot leave a Christian. But you can put him into a grief state.

Imagine you are a parent with a bad child. You would never give up your child! (At least most of us would not, though we might consider it in tough times.) Instead, you hang in there with them, persistently loving them and trying all that you can, even when they resist, deny, and disobey you.

In similar fashion, God will never leave you. Remember, in all you do he is with you, so you can make him sad with your worldly human-heartedness and sin. We can forfeit his blessings by acting badly. It is often too easy to say, as we do with family and friends who also love us, "Well, just this once," or "They will get over it and be okay." We do not realize how much we lose out on when we grieve God. We cannot do good alone, as Paul says in Romans 7:19–25. There he laments how he still does the evil things he does not want to do even when he wants to do good. This is because he is merely a "wretched man."

Contrast this with Romans 8, reviewing the life of the Spirit, and also consider Job 15, which states that worldly joy is but momentary. After the brief happiness or excitement of a committed sin, are you in truth not sad, feeling badly, or feeling guilty?

Think of sin examples from your life. Those adverse feelings you experience are conviction by the Spirit. You knew it was wrong to do what you either did or failed to do. You must see that the sin will never fulfill you, no matter how many times you do it or how much you escalate the behavior. Such happiness or excitement is all too transient, all too brief. It even becomes boring for you, unless you go into escalation tactics, which delay but never eliminate the ultimate emptiness of the sin!

Alternatively, Christians have a lasting joy that emanates from the Holy Spirit. He gives us peace as well as joy that are different from anything in this world. These gifts are lasting and cannot be taken permanently away by anything, not even by our sins. While we can reduce these blessings temporarily by our actions, we can easily get them back by confessing these sins and repenting of them to God.

This lets us feel confident and more in control in any and all circumstances and temptations, as we realize that he is always in charge of our lives. Our joy comes because we know God is in control. He has our ultimate benefit as his plan in and through all that is happening to us, both the good and the bad. This joy can never be taken away from us (unless we choose to give this up). So, rejoice in him, even if not in your circumstances! Remember his promise: "Your power will save me. The Lord will work out his plans for my life—for your loving-kindness, Lord, continues forever" (Psalm 138:7b–8a).

Next, we shall examine in more detail some of these blessings that God bestows on his children.

IV. Peace

"And the peace of God, which transcends all understanding, will
guard your hearts and your minds in Christ Jesus."
(Philippians 4:7 NIV)

Why me? Why them? Why is this tragedy, this pain, this evil, still allowed to go on? These are prevalent questions today. Yet they are
queries that remain unanswerable to our human minds. No answer
we could understand would help heal our hearts. And even if we did
possess God's divine knowledge of why each event occurs, we would
still have our pain.

We instead need faith and a strong trust that God is working all
for our good. I like the example of Shadrach, Meshach, and Abednego
in Daniel 3:16–28. Threatened with execution when they refused
an unreasonable demand to worship king Nebuchadnezzar, they
responded, "Our God can save us. But even if he does not, we still
won't worship your gods." In this case, in response to their faith and
trust, their God saved them in dramatic fashion by rescuing them from
a white-hot furnace.

In a similar way, we must realize that even if God does not respond
in whatever timing and circumstances our human minds feel that he

should, we must still trust him and pray for his peace and comforting presence so we may get above, and ultimately get through, the trial. It is helpful, besides asking for deliverance, to pray for the gift of his perfect peace rather than that of understanding. Consider this verse:

"But now you belong to Christ Jesus, and though you once were far away from God, now you have been brought very near to him because of what Jesus Christ has done for you with his blood. For Christ himself is our way of peace." (Ephesians 2:13–14a)

***

Peace in today's world can be many things. Certainly, this is a prominent topic politically with so many conflicts ongoing in our crazy age. Worldly peace means no longer fighting with one another. But the peace of God is much more than this. It is a mental, physical, and spiritual calmness that emanates from an understanding. It is when you know that, by trusting God and having him always with you, you are without a doubt able to endure, to rise above, and to outlast your trials. With this perfect peace, no suffering should ever change our trust in him!

To first achieve and then maintain this peace, we need to understand and know him as our friend and heavenly Father, and as our lord and savior. We also must try to avoid all negative thinking. In our great trials, negative thoughts keep us down, making us bitter, depressed, and apathetic. In a word, they can leave us feeling squashed. We may simply feel like giving up. Nevertheless, if we will do our best to think positively at all times, even in crises, by looking for the good and seeing

Rise and Soar

some blessing in whatever comes our way, we will rise above these trees, these bad times, which, in actuality, are shaping us into exactly whom God wants us to be.

Just as steel and diamonds are forged and strengthened through continued pressure, and gold and silver are purified and refined by fire burning away their dross and impurities, these trials are ultimately positives for us. It is extremely beneficial if you can avoid negativity. Ask God to help you remain a positive thinker in your trials. You cannot control all things in your life all the time, but you are in control of your attitude and your outlook.

Additionally, while it may seem contradictory, it is also helpful to remain conscious of how to help others as they go through similar difficulties! Thus, our trials will help not only ourselves but others as well.

Saint Ambrose once appropriately penned, "In Christ, we have everything. If you need help, he is strength. If you are afraid of death, he is life. If you desire paradise, his is the way. If you flee from darkness, he is light. Happy is the man who hopes in him."

***

Peace can be difficult to achieve in our hearts and minds, especially if we are always thirsting and striving after the latest and greatest things: that newest technology, a better vehicle, a better stock portfolio, a raise, that next promotion, and so on. We must understand that there is no way any of these will ever completely satisfy us. Nothing will ever fill the empty hole inside of us. It will be ever empty, unless it finds its true satisfaction in the Lord God. Recall that Saint Augustine said, "Uneasy is the heart until it rests in thee." This means we need to relinquish our continual striving to have control over every situation and trust instead our God's love and guidance, his shepherding! He is always with us, no matter where we are or what mess we are in. Perfect peace comes to us only if we can give our worries and concerns up to him!

Trying to be stronger or to control it all paradoxically will lead us into more confusion and chaos. We are not the center of the universe; rather, we are mutually dependent and interconnected, with God our Father at the center. As Romans 11:36 states, everything is made by him and is maintained by him, and its purpose is to serve and contribute to his glory.

> "I will lie down in peace and sleep, for though I am alone, O Lord, you will keep me safe." (Psalm 4:8)

> "You will keep in perfect peace those whose minds are steadfast, because they trust in you." (Isaiah 26:3 NIV)

***

Here is a thought: what would you give to have the world by the tail or to be on top of the world? Could anyone ever truly obtain such satisfaction here in this crazy place? We may think of the billionaires. Surely, they must have the world in their grasp, right? Yet, think of the worries they have, including those that are the same as we less well-heeled persons: illness, family issues, old age, frustration, bitterness, and so on. I strongly suspect they often have such stressors to exponentially increased degrees beyond the average person, given the added stress of managing all their wealth and possessions too!

But consider this: if you have Christ and his promise of salvation, then at the conclusion of this life, don't you truly have it all? You have the world by its tail. You control it, through Christ, rather than allowing it to control you. Its fickle winds will still buffet you in its wild seasons, but it can never overwhelm you nor alter your final destiny!

If you are a Christian, you understand that this life is as bad as things are ever going to get for you, especially if you become severely ill or disabled or are dealing with other difficult issues. The best for you is yet to come! But if you are not in Christ, then your life now, as imperfect and hard as it often is, is as good as you are ever going to get. It will unfortunately become worse for you as you age, with all the compounding physical ailments and afflictions of time, as well as at the judgment, which will be much, much worse and will last for the eternal ever after!

You must see that real peace comes only to our human hearts when we let Christ, the one true Prince of Peace, into them and submit to him fully. Stop fighting for your own will. Our worldly minds want to act against his will. You need to make a conscious decision to say yes, allowing him to forgive your sins and give you his amazing peace and grant you his eternal life! Consider these scriptures:

"Christ's death on the cross has made peace with God for all by his blood." (Colossians 1:20b)

"So now, since we have been made right in God's sight by faith in his promises, we can have real peace with him because of what Jesus Christ our Lord has done for us… We can rejoice, too, when we run into problems and trials, for we know that they are good for us—they help us learn to be patient. And patience develops strength of character in us and helps us trust God more each time we use it until finally our hope and faith are strong and steady. Then, when that happens, we are able to hold our heads high no matter what happens and know that all is well, for we know how dearly God loves us, and we feel this warm love everywhere within us because God has given us the Holy Spirit to fill our hearts with his love." (Romans 5:1, 3–5)

"Those who love your laws have great peace of heart and mind and do not stumble." (Psalm 119:165)

"Those who trust in the Lord are steady as Mount Zion, unmoved by any circumstance." (Psalm 125:1)

"I will lead them and comfort them, helping them to mourn and to confess their sins. Peace, peace to them, both near and far, for I will heal them all. But those who still reject me are like the restless sea, which is never still, but always churns up mire and dirt. There is no peace, says my God, for them!" (Isaiah 57:18b–21)

"And the Lord gave them peace, just as he had promised, and no one could stand against them; the Lord helped them destroy all their enemies. Every good thing the Lord had promised them came true." (Joshua 21:44–45)

***

So, let's imagine this pastoral scene: You are in a hammock on a warm autumn day. All you can hear are gentle birds and soft breezes rustling the falling leaves. There is warm sunshine on your face, lighting up the brightly colored trees on the hills beyond. Puffy clouds billow and drift across a deep blue heaven above. Now, close your eyes. Take a deep breath and hold it for three seconds. Then, let it all out. Can't you feel that relaxed sense of peace? How we savor, yet rarely experience, such brief interludes of peace, even though these are transient, worldly types of peace. Now, multiply that human perception of peace by one million times or so, plus infinity. Such is the very peace we will one day have when he takes us up into his high heaven to forever coexist in that perfect place with our God, our Creator Father!

> "I am leaving you with a gift—peace of mind and heart! And the peace I give isn't fragile like the peace the world gives. So don't be troubled or afraid." (John 14:27)

V. Joy

"You will rejoice; and no one can rob you of that joy."

(John 16:22)

The terms joy and happiness are defined by people in many ways, perhaps as a state of contentment or as the feeling that all, or almost all, is going well in our immediate lives. But are they the same thing, just mere synonyms?

I feel a more appropriate definition of joy is a state of mind or a state of being. Happiness is merely a feeling. True joy is what we acquire when we establish and maintain a good relationship with God. Joy can be imagined as looking up to God and realizing and thanking him for one's blessings. In a prior season, I tried thanking him for five new blessings each day. Try this, and you will see how truly blessed you are! From this joy will evolve a true happiness, which can be imagined as looking out toward others and being visible to others in your joy, as well.

This joy is so unlike the world's happiness, such as on Christmas morning or your birthday. Genuine happiness results from joy. And both then shine brightly through this world's darkness. No, we are not going to be happy about our sufferings and sadness, but we should rejoice that Christ stays with us in and through all our sorrows! This realization makes all the difference!

I recall an excellent example from Pastor Adrian Rogers. He described joy as a thermostat and happiness as a thermometer. You can set a thermostat, much as you can set your own internal degree of joy. It will not vary despite the outside conditions or temperatures. Happiness, on the other hand, will vary as a thermometer does, changing with the different weather systems and storms that come through. I believe this is an excellent way to compare joy and happiness. You control the joy factor. You can set it at an appropriately joyful level, which persists, if you know Christ, no matter what tempests, temperature extremes, or other situations are going on around you.

We will only achieve this joy, which is a blessing from God, if we first seek, then find, and then continue to hunger after him. He then will, as he promises, add all these blessings to us! We must come to realize and then definitively know that seeking only the world's pleasures, its goods, riches, foods—its stuff—cannot and will not ever meet our inner spiritual needs. Only Jesus can. Therefore, we must seek him if we are to achieve true and lasting joy and happiness. As he says in the Beatitudes of Matthew 5:6, "Those who hunger and thirst for righteousness are blessed, for they will be filled" (HCSB). Other translations alternatively use the Word *satisfied*. This means that if we seek Christ above all, first and foremost, we will find him. And then we will have everything!

Yet, we must seek him with the correct attitude. We should hunger for him as if we are starving for him. We should thirst for him as if parched from days in a burning desert. What prevents us from doing such? Well, if we are already full of worldly desires or excessive worries and concerns, we will have a distracted, unfocused mind and spirit.

Then we will be less likely to hunger and thirst for Christ. Eating too many snacks minimizes one's desire for food at dinner!

In other words, each of us has as much of God as he or she wants. Those with small hungers get small amounts, while those with larger hungers get larger amounts of him! As Christ says in Matthew 6:32–33, "But seek ye first the kingdom of God, and his righteousness; and all these things shall be added unto you" (KJV). Or, per the Living Bible, "But your heavenly Father already knows perfectly well that you need them, and he will give them to you if you give him first place in your life and live as he wants you to."

So, we must seek him first, above all else, and then he promises we will be joyous and have many more blessings. Contrast this with seeking worldly happiness by itself. Doing this makes God second place as if to say, "I will seek God after I achieve this or earn that, or after I become such or get that promotion or buy this thing or get married," and so on.

Do you see how we can become trapped in a never-ending cycle of worldly desires and cares? Do you see how we can put aside God, the one and only source of true joy in our world? Focusing primarily and one-sidedly upon any desire starts an insatiable hunger, like good food does. Our desire may satisfy our hunger for a bit. But once satisfied, we soon get hungry again and return repetitively to our desire, always needing more. Why not try Jesus instead? Why not focus on Christ and see for yourself what occurs? Once you realize what you find, and what you get in Jesus, you will not be able to stay away! Try to desire and to seek him above all else. Strive to know him better and better.

As you get to know him, he will fill you and bless you, as the Bible states. He will, in addition, seal you for eternal happiness with him when either you pass from this life or when he returns, whichever is first.

People may ask us, "Why are you so happy?" or "What's your secret?" Christ, through the Spirit, gives us joy. No person can ever steal it away, nor can any severe and dire trials. Our joy will still shine out of the darkness, revealing our great Jesus to others. No, we do not have to be happy for our sufferings or our sadness. Christ was not. But we should rejoice and stay generally joyous overall as we recall that he stays with and supports us in and through each of these sorrows and, too, because we know how the story will so gloriously end!

Do not ever give this joy up, no matter if family, finances, work, or other issues may seem unalterably bad. If this joy has already left you, you must realize that it is gone and work toward restoring it, asking Christ to help in this endeavor. Ask yourself, do your trials really compare in any way at all to the joy of knowing Christ? Consider the much more severe trials of so many other less-fortunate souls in our world, or even more so, the trials of Jesus himself on the rugged cross that he bore for us! Always remember: "No mere man has ever seen, heard, or even imagined what wonderful things God has ready for those who love the Lord" (1 Corinthians 2:9).

One thought I have regarding this verse is: why doesn't God simply reveal these things to us now so that we all can know just how amazing they truly are? Consider this: what if we knew exactly what joys really awaited us in heaven? Imagine if God gave the entire world a five-minute peek at heaven! My young daughter stated that she felt all people would then believe in him, although I disagree. There are still many selfish, evil people who care nothing about God or about having a relationship with him.

Rather, I believe that if God did so, many of us in relationships with him would, to our detriments, look to check out a bit early, especially when in bad situations such as severe chronic pain or illness, grief or depression. We also probably would be much more careless and reckless with our lives and our activities! Therefore, we are left to believe and to trust him regarding his promises.

> "You love him even though you have never seen him; though not seeing him, you trust him; and even now you are happy with the inexpressible joy that comes from heaven itself. And your further reward for trusting him will be the salvation of your souls." (1 Peter 1:8–9)

> "He grants good sense to the godly—his saints. He is their shield, protecting them and guarding their pathway. He shows how to distinguish right from wrong, how to find the right decision every time. For wisdom and truth will enter the very center of your being, filling your life with joy." (Proverbs 2:7–10)

> "Whatever happens, dear friends, be glad in the Lord." (Philippians 3:1a)

***

To find true joy, we must realize God has put each of us here to know him and to make him known, in essence, to glorify him! Our true calling is to be in a personal relationship with Christ and thus to develop his character as best we can. Do not miss your true calling. If you do, you will never become the beautiful butterfly you were meant to be. You will stay a caterpillar. Serving him in your true calling, that is, glorifying him each moment, becomes new and unique. It will never return. So, we must remain alert to actively engage and thus to bring each moment to its fullest potential, that of helping in God's kingdom work.

Every single moment spent, from actively evangelizing to family time, and even in your sleeping, is therefore done with meaning and put forth with purpose. Resist simply trying to get through that course, that workday, that meeting, that year. Do not just try to endure events and the passing of time. Rather, strive to look at each moment's possibilities through God's viewpoint and from the viewpoint of being his faithful follower. Try to be like Christ.

> "Put on heartfelt compassion, kindness, humility, gentleness, and patience, accepting one another and forgiving one another if anyone has a complaint against another. Just as the Lord has forgiven you, so you must also forgive. Above all, put on love." (Colossians 3:12–14 HCSB)

God, at this exact point in your life, is asking you to strive to do the work you are currently engaged in for his glory. He has placed you in that job, with that family, and in that social circle for definitive reasons. Let this thought improve your attitude. You will put forth your very best effort and achieve optimal results. Your interactions with others are extremely important also, as it is not solely the finished product that counts. Let them, through all things, always see Christ in you!

Therefore, true joy should be a constant in every Christian's life, while happiness will be intermittent and transient per circumstances and events. While happiness is a great feeling, it only occurs when things are well with us, which for most of us is not too often. True Christian joy, however, does not ever leave you, unless you choose to lose it by sinning. It otherwise stays with you always, even in times of troubles and sadness!

***

Rise and Soar

Now, we should realize that, to gain true joy, we must first repent and return to God, turning back to him and accepting Christ's payment for all sins. This gives us a joyful peace as we firmly come to know that there is no sin whatsoever left between us and God (Romans 5:1–2). The Father accepts Jesus's blood offering on our behalf, washing away all our guilt. This ultimately lets us have real peace, because of the true and certain hope that he will do exactly as he says. We already know how it is going to end. And it will be great!

***

"I don't seem as happy as I should be sometimes, not as joyful!" A pastor friend spoke these words to me. I replied that I think we need to extrapolate and to look outward. Real joy consists of several components. These are, first, peace: the knowledge that we are always in God's own hand, no matter what happens. Second, fulfillment: we firmly know we have been placed by God here on this earth at this exact place and time, and we are doing exactly what he made us to do. And third, his rescue: we are delivered from this world's craziness. Peace, fulfillment, and rescue comprise an umbrella of true joy for us. And our forgiveness of sins by Christ's blood helps us to remain persistently joyful.

Yet, this joy is not as some may expect. It is not happy as a child is happy on Christmas morning via some sky-high, albeit brief, happiness spike fueled by worldly events and stuff that can never fully satisfy and that breaks or is lost. For example, after the impressively dramatic (yet transient) happy spike each Christmas morning, by early afternoon, my daughter, when younger, routinely demonstrated an equally dramatic crash to the downside. It would come on after gifts were opened, dinner was done, and her slice of pumpkin pie eaten. It is impossible for human beings alone to maintain happiness of that sort at such a high degree for any length of time.

True joy is lasting. It evolves from the certain knowledge that we been forgiven of all sins, sealed by Christ, and guaranteed a forever paradise with him! Read about how King David danced, sang, and proclaimed his joy as the ark returned to Jerusalem in 2 Samuel 6:12–22. How much greater should our persistent joy be when we realize what our Christ has done for us!

Yet, how can we definitively access, read, review, and be reassured by the promises God has made to us? The answer lies solely in our accessing the Bible, which is God's Holy Word, his instruction manual for us. It allows us to be joyful and happy here in this world. It tells us truthfully of this great joy and then begins constructing such in our own hearts and souls. It describes God's granted hope through all trials, as well as his help and guidance in storms and his healing through and after our trials. His Bible explains, as best our human minds can comprehend, why things are as they are. It describes the peace, fulfillment, and rescue mentioned above, including his ultimate promise of eternal happiness with God in heaven. Therefore, God's instruction manual for being happy in this crazy world must be consistently consulted! You need to spend time in his Word every day!

***

So, how is your life going? Do you already have this persisting joy? If not, you need to reach out and choose it by prayerfully asking God for it and by picking up and reading your Bible regularly, in order to gain this joyfully happy life for yourself through God, he who can do all things. Choose him as your authoritative and unchanging rock. Heed this word from our Creator. Place its wisdom far above all the noise of this world.

Rise and Soar

The Bible explains things to us and gives us the promise of a much better time to come if we actively choose Christ and follow the Bible's advice to make him our friend and savior. The Bible is God's Word, our own personal guidebook for living a joyful life!

In conclusion, no matter what situation we are in, no one can ever take this joy from us. Do not let it fade! If you have lost it, ask for our Lord's help to get it back! We are not to be happy for our sorrows, as Christ also was not, but, as we shall see later, sorrow is unfortunately part of every life in this world, whether one is Christian or not.

Finally, it is worth repeating the following statement Jesus made just before his death: "Your hearts will rejoice, and no one will rob you of your joy" (John 16:22b HCSB). We must strive to always keep this in our minds, no matter how desperate, dark, or dire our earthly circumstances may be! Also consider:

> "But for you who fear my name, the Sun of Righteousness will rise with healing in his wings. And you will go free, leaping with joy like calves let out to pasture." (Malachi 4:2)

> "This is the day the Lord has made. We will rejoice and be glad in it." (Psalm 118:24)

VI. Fulfillment

"My success—at which so many stand amazed—is because you are my mighty protector. All day long I'll praise and honor you, O God, for all that you have done for me." (Psalm 71:7–8)

What is fulfillment? I believe it is a contentment, an inner peace we receive when we know, without doubt, what we are doing is exactly what Christ wants us to do with our lives for his kingdom. How would you like to feel that at this point in your life, finally, every moment is being done with a real purpose?

Like the first Christmas Magi, whomever those wise men were, we are modern searchers. We search for the true God as our life's goal, whether we admit it or not. If we are sincere and earnest, steadfast and not distracted in our search, he will guide us to himself! We must, however, avoid being lesser Magi, easily distractible, worldly thinkers who obsess over trivial issues and fear losses as King Herod did, such as the loss of power, family, a job, money, a relationship, or something else. We presume our worldly security hinges on these unimportant issues. We may feel we are in control, but in truth, we are helpless sinners who control nothing!

We need to change our thinking, our decisions, and our subsequent actions in order to rise above those of this world. We do this so that we may meet our one true Lord. He alone will give us life's answers, he who is our real treasure while we are here in this world. If we are steadfast and sincere in our search for him, Christ always guides us to himself! And without him, we will be truly lost. Consider this story:

Once in a deep winter wood, darkness fell sooner than I had anticipated. A storm blew in. The sun was gone. And I had inadvertently left my compass at home. Everything looked the same, so it was impossible to tell which direction was which. Even the tree moss looked about equal circumferentially on most trees, so true north could not be estimated that way. I had no pin or needle to make my own compass, and shadow directions with stick and stone were useless in such dim light. I saw only hardwoods, not any of the tall pines that typically point their tops toward the east and are often bushier on their south sides.

Suddenly, I heard a nearby howl. Then several more joined in. There was a known pack of very large coydogs in the area, which I helped thin out regularly, as they would kill many a beef cow on the large ranches nearby. Two of my neighbors had been charged by these canines, and I was charged once, even though that fearless brush-wolf knew that I was a human. I saw him at a hundred yards, and he reminded me of Alaskan timber wolves I have camped amongst and called down out of the mountains. I will never forget his face. He put his huge head and ears down and charged straight at me. I then had had a gun with me and finished that ninety-three-pound threat. But this night I had no weapon. I grabbed a stick and a few large stones and picked the most likely direction home.

As I walked, the pack stayed right with me, always lurking just out of sight in the dense undergrowth I was fighting through. When I stopped, they stopped. When I resumed walking, they did also. Though they were just ten to fifteen yards to my right, it was so thick that I never once saw any of them. In a few small clearings, I considered stopping to make a stand or to try to scare them off, but in the near-pitch darkness, I decided it was better to keep pushing on.

This continued for the better part of an hour until I saw a cloud-break overhead. There were a few stars, but, more importantly, a waning crescent moon peeked through the opening! Now, in our hemisphere, tracing an imaginary line from this moon's top to bottom tips is a definitive North-South line, so I instantly realized I was moving in the correct southerly direction toward the end of the woods and home, rather than deeper into my lostness. I confidently picked up the pace and reached the open fields just as all remaining light vanished. I neither saw nor heard more of my trailing stalkers thereafter.

In the same way, once we learn to recognize and see just who God and his Son, Jesus Christ, truly are and what they can do for us, they become similar guiding beacon lights. Throughout our lifetimes, they lead us to the safe and the appropriate places where we long to be. They make our trials easier to endure because they are with us throughout our storms and sojourns.

***

We must keep in mind that we are the continuing works of Christ that he began two thousand years ago. We act as his priests in this modern world, carrying on the works of the apostles and all those who have succeeded them right up into our very time. As we do this, the message of Christ and his kingdom, along with the salvation he brings, spreads ever farther. It is visible through our evangelizing and our good works! Through us, his human conduits, Christ often reaches out and touches others, bringing his love and his peace, joy, and fulfillment, as well as his hope and rescue and, ultimately, his salvation. He indeed is with us still!

***

> "My nourishment comes from doing the will of God who sent me, and from finishing his work." (John 4:34)

This is what Jesus said to his disciples while they were speaking about worldly food. He then said, "Vast fields of human souls are ripening all around us and are ready now for reaping." In subsequent verses he declared how the reapers, those who help to harvest souls, will be paid good wages. And he also foretold "what joys await both the sower and the reaper" together.

From our limited viewpoint, it is often hard to see and to understand the fact that Christ has huge plans for every one of us for as long as he keeps on giving us our successive breaths and heartbeats. My view is that if we are still here in this world, no matter how small, insignificant, helpless, or sickly we may feel, there is a mission he wants us to accomplish. Once this is completed, he is going to take us up to be with him forever.

Do you ever think, "Does my life really matter at all?" or "What is my purpose here?" Jesus tells his followers to act as both salt and as light in fulfilling these purposes. He did this in the Beatitudes of his Sermon on the Mount:

> "You are the world's seasoning, to make it tolerable. If you lose your flavor, what will happen to the world? And you yourselves will be thrown out and trampled underfoot as worthless. You are the world's light—a city on a hill, glowing

in the night for all to see. Don't hide your light! Let it shine for all; let your good deeds glow for all to see, so that they will praise your heavenly Father." (Matthew 5:13–16)

Let us look at these commands. Regarding salt, the metaphoric comparison here is that, just as table salt seasons food, we are also asked to season and change for the better all whom we encounter. Nevertheless, we must remember that Jesus asks us to sprinkle our saltiness, not to overload it. We must learn this distinction. Just as too much salt can easily ruin any meal, so too can it destroy any relationship or discussion!

What about light? This example means that we are to be a representation of Jesus's light to all whom we meet. Light makes things more visibly attractive. It also exposes dirt and eliminates things such as vermin and mold. Just like Christ, the true Son, light improves things, making the world more attractive by enhancing and beautifying it.

Imagine overlooking a predawn mountain landscape as the sun rises. The land below changes from a dimly lit, hazy outline into a brightly illuminated and clear vision with pink and yellow alpenglow beauty on its snowy peaks. Similarly, we are to instigate change rather than simply exist or coexist in a quiet, private Christian life. You cannot keep his light to yourself. His news is too good. Others truly need to hear it, no matter how hard they rage against you. That will happen, however, as described in Jeremiah 15:20: "They will fight against you like a besieging army against a high city wall." Yet, God assures us that "they will not conquer you, for I am with you to protect and deliver you."

Recall how light exposes and disperses what is in the darkness. Have you ever turned over a log or rock in a dark forest and watched the snakes, spiders, centipedes, and other critters scramble away? That is exactly what God's Word does when applied to all evils!

We Christians are called to be his agents and to thereby act as both salt and as light. Salt kept only on the shelf, isolated within its shaker, can never season anything! Light kept dimmed or turned off altogether helps no one! Our world needs us to stand up, speak up, and step out, now! If we truly know him, then wherever God has placed us, we are in the spot from which we are best able to fulfill what he desires us to be. We must do exactly this: we must forget and forego trying to be popular in this world. We must instead become the changers. You will glorify God with these actions when, because of you, someone will want to know Christ, to honor him, and thereafter, to be saved by him! He has you in your current place for a reason. You are his arms, his hands, his feet, and his voice. You are his agent of change!

In so doing, you are modeling Christ's love, forgiveness, saving grace, and power to all whom you meet so that they will want to meet Christ also. And he will change them as well and propel them into their true purpose for their own fulfillment, all further glorifying our God!

Now, does this sound boring? Perhaps it may, if you have not yet lived it, but it absolutely is not because, in reality, your adoption of this plan, this outlook, and this mindset for your life puts you directly into the leading action role of an exciting, non-routine, day-by-day adventure as you stand up, speak out, and step up for him! Consider:

> "The backslider gets bored with himself; the godly man's life is exciting." (Proverbs 14:14)

> "And I am sure that God who began the good work within you will keep right on helping you grow in his grace until

his task within you is finally finished on that day when Jesus Christ returns." (Philippians 1:6)

Therefore, ask God to fill you with his Holy Spirit! Yield yourself, your desires, your dreams, and your goals to his purposes. Ask him, "Lord, what do you want me to do?" Do not quench or extinguish his Spirit; rather, ask to be filled with him, and believe that it will be so. But remember, he will never enter or fill nonbelieving dirty hearts, so always confess and repent. Bring your sins before God and ask his forgiveness. He is always gracious to forgive! Next, simply believe and seek the Lord in his Word and in prayer, remaining always hopeful and positive in your thinking. Then watch out! Hold on tight! Your own specifically designed, individualized adventure is about to begin!

Let's conclude this section with some encouraging promises from our heavenly Father.

"In everything you do, put God first, and he will direct you and crown your efforts with success." (Proverbs 3:6)

"They are like trees along a riverbank bearing luscious fruit each season without fail. Their leaves shall never wither, and all they do shall prosper.... For the Lord watches over all the plans and paths of godly men, but the paths of the godless lead to doom." (Psalm 1:3, 6)

"For I know the plans I have for you"—this is the Lord's declaration—"plans for your welfare, not for disaster, to give you a future and a hope. You will call to Me and come and pray to Me, and I will listen to you. You will seek Me and find Me when you search for Me with all your heart." (Jeremiah 29:11–13 HCSB)

VII. Rescue

Peace, joy, and fulfillment. This trio of gifts that God grants us leads to a dual rescue. The first is a rescue from the folly and insanities of this world, while we are yet here. The second rescue is when his grace delivers us for all eternity into a final redemption, that of eternal life in a never-ending, amazing, and close communion with him!

I can sincerely say my life with Christ has been a refreshingly happy and exciting adventure compared to how I used to try to get my happiness. If you have never tried Christ's way, you absolutely need to go ahead and try the experience for yourself! Consider his promises, the direct words of our God:

> "The Commander of the armies of heaven is here among us. He . . . has come to rescue us." (Psalm 46:7)

> "For this great God is our God forever and ever. He will be our guide until we die." (Psalm 48:14)

> "God has rescued me from all my trouble, and triumphed over my enemies." (Psalm 54:7)

"Though the tide of battle runs strongly against me, for so many are fighting me, yet he will rescue me. God himself— God from everlasting ages past—will answer them!" (Psalm 55:18–19)

"I will say to the LORD, 'My refuge and my fortress, my God, in whom I trust.' He Himself will deliver you from the hunter's net, from the destructive plague. He will cover you with His feathers; you will take refuge under His wings. His faithfulness will be a protective shield. You will not fear the terror of the night, the arrow that flies by day, the plague that stalks in darkness, or the pestilence that ravages at noon. Though a thousand fall at your side and ten thousand at your right hand, the pestilence will not reach you.... Because you have made the LORD—my refuge, the Most High—your dwelling place, no harm will come to you; no plague will come near your tent. For He will give His angels orders concerning you, to protect you in all your ways. They will support you with their hands so that you will not strike your foot against a stone. You will tread on the lion and the cobra; you will trample the young lion and the serpent." (Psalm 91:2–13 HCSB)

"In my distress I prayed to the Lord, and he answered me and rescued me. He is for me! How can I be afraid? What can mere man do to me?" (Psalm 118:5–6)

***

The snowy season was ending, although bitter winds still swept the coastal mountains. They whipped up thousands of whitecaps on the brilliant dark-blue waters of Shelikof Strait visible to the north. On

Alaska's Kodiak Island, I noticed a pile of rocks and other debris high upon the mountainside, being pushed outward from the mountain's face. A brown bear was coming out of its winter den. I climbed a steep, slick, and mossy—at times almost vertical—cliff up to its cave's height, getting within twenty yards. Once, my large backpack nearly pulled me over the side of this extremely steep cliff, which would have been a very rough fall. Hiding in the nearby brush, I watched a sow come out, truly one of God's miracles of nature. She lingered a bit, looking at the new spring world around her for the first time in five months. But then, given the storm that was blowing in, she decided to return to the warmth and protection of her cave.

I successfully scaled the cliff face back to ground level and attempted to find my camp, which was several miles away. However, the vicious storm that had blown in off the sea pelted me with blinding snow. Its wind gusts were so strong I had to walk with my trunk bent over so that my upper body was parallel to the ground to keep from being blown over. There was no way to see anything. So, with no visibility, my options were either to try to wait this out or to go on blindly looking for my tent shelter, which could be disastrous if I blundered into a bear, dropped off a cliff, or hurt myself with some other misstep.

A third and better option was to employ my knowledge of an appropriate alternative in order to get out of this potentially dangerous situation. This knowledge I speak of was my knowing which way the storm and wind had come from, in this case off the ocean. I therefore could discern my true bearings and know which direction I needed to go to reach safety, based upon the direction it was blowing in from. Thus, knowing that the north coast was in one definite direction, and that my tent was at a ninety-degree angle to this, I walked at that angle, keeping the constant wind at my right side, until I eventually found the shelter of camp. It was relatively easy, despite blinding conditions. Nevertheless, without this prior knowledge, I would have been in much more dire circumstances.

In the same way, appropriate knowledge of our Lord God and his Son, Jesus, knowledge obtained by knowing God's Word contained in the Holy Bible, provides a solid knowledge of our most appropriate bearing and direction. God's Word allows us to safely weather and maneuver through any and all storms in life, no matter how severe or blinding they may seem. Its veritable lifelines provide a steady, ever-present, and always-reliable rescue for us!

Christ performs his saving rescue mission for us in this life. He helps us through the fires, and at times he keeps us from them. He will help us through our hardships and protect and spare us from specific trials, although not all. Nevertheless, always remember that Christ can and does rescue his followers from all that truly endangers them! "The steps of good men are directed by the Lord. He delights in each step they take. If they fall, it isn't fatal, for the Lord holds them with his hand" (Psalm 37:23–24).

In order to be rescued, you must step out and seek God and his kingdom. Do not merely sit back and wait. Consider God's message to Judah's King Jehoshaphat on the eve of a major battle in which the Hebrews were greatly outnumbered by soldiers from Moab, Mount Seir, and Ammon. The Lord says,

> "Don't be afraid! Don't be paralyzed by this mighty army! For the battle is not yours, but God's! Tomorrow, go down and attack them! . . . But you will not need to fight! Take your places; stand quietly and see the incredible rescue operation God will perform for you . . . Don't be afraid or discouraged! Go out there tomorrow, for the Lord is with you!" (2 Chronicles 20:15–17)

Also consider these verses:

> "You will be filled with his mighty, glorious strength so that you can keep going no matter what happens—always full of the joy of the Lord, and always thankful to the Father who has made us fit to share all the wonderful things that belong to those who live in the Kingdom of light. For he has rescued us out of the darkness and gloom of Satan's kingdom and brought us into the Kingdom of his dear Son, who bought our freedom with his blood and forgave us all our sins." (Colossians 1:11–14)

> "I want you to trust me in your times of trouble, so I can rescue you and you can give me glory." (Psalm 50:15)

> "My health fails; my spirits droop, yet God remains! He is the strength of my heart; he is mine forever!" (Psalm 73:26)

Ultimately, the choice is yours. Are you going to pursue and to worship mankind's worldly creations and wisdom, such as that of the Tree of Knowledge of Good and Evil in the garden of Eden? Will you eat disobediently from the tree that condemned Adam and all of humanity? Or will you choose the cross, the tree of salvation? I tell you sincerely that only the second tree, the cross of Christ, can give you real purpose in this life, as well as his hope and his peace, his true joy and fulfillment, and, ultimately, his rescue.

Let us conclude by looking at more of his rescue promises.

> "Come, let us return to the LORD. For He has torn us, and He will heal us; He has wounded us, and He will bind up our wounds. He will revive us after two days, and on the third day

He will raise us up so we can live in his presence. Let us strive to know the LORD. His appearance is as sure as the dawn. He will come to us like the rain, like the spring showers that water the land." (Hosea 6:1–3 HCSB)

"Yet I will rejoice in the Lord; I will be happy in the God of my salvation. The Lord God is my strength; he will give me the speed of a deer and bring me safely over the mountains." (Habakkuk 3:18–19)

"As for me, I look to the Lord for his help; I wait for God to save me; he will hear me. Do not rejoice against me, O my enemy, for though I fall, I will rise again! When I sit in darkness, the Lord himself will be my Light." (Micah 7:7–8)

"The Lord is good. When trouble comes, he is the place to go!" (Nahum 1:7a)

VIII. Talents and Time Management

"We glide along the tides of time as swiftly as a racing river and vanish as quickly as a dream." (Psalm 90:5a)

"For man is but a breath; his days are like a passing shadow." (Psalm 144:4)

"Teach us to number our days and recognize how few they are; help us to spend them as we should." (Psalm 90:12)

Let us talk next about our talents and skills, those gifts we are given to use, those things we are good at and that come easily to us. Sometimes we like to do them, and other times we deny or defer these abilities. Nevertheless, they have been given to us by God our Father, and we need to realize that God can use anyone regardless of their means, popularity, job, location, past history, family, the year on the calendar, or their place in history. Look at the examples of Paul, who severely persecuted early Christians, and Jesus's eleven uneducated disciples. All were used by God to fulfill his plans and purposes!

In a similar manner, we must realize that we are saved by his grace and thus are meant to serve by his grace and be accompanied with his grace. He has given each of us a special gift or gifts, which we are absolutely meant to use for his kingdom purposes!

What is also important is that we see our own sinfulness and, realizing such, that we ask Christ for his grace and forgiveness! He then comes in and transforms our lives into existences that will glorify him!

Sharing and spreading God's love is easy. It does not require any special abilities—just your availability. I have always liked this saying derived from 1 Corinthians 1:27–29: God does not call the qualified; he qualifies the called!

But you may ask, in using our talents for God and, in particular, with evangelizing, won't we meet opposition, anger, criticism, rebuke, laughter, scorn, and mockery? Yes, indeed, we will. We must expect it. Christ also received these. Think of these as golden opportunities to share the gospel in a loving way. Never respond with an angry, upraised voice (or worse). Realize instead that your response to the lost can make the greatest case for Christianity to your opponent, much more than any clever, mortal-minded speech ever could! In loving our opponents, we should try to understand and to assist them as part of an attempt to help them get beyond their blindness. Consider this example:

At a Muslim mosque festival in Central Asia, I approached the tent of *Hasen*, an Islamic missionary group. Having never met a Muslim missionary, I was keenly interested in discussing their methods and tactics. One question I often ask my Muslim friends is, "If Islam is so great, then where are all of its missionaries? We hear of the many Christian missionaries all the time, and indeed, the very term 'missionary' connotes a peaceful Christian effort in most minds. So, why do we never hear of

Islamist missionaries? Why do we only hear about Islamic attempts to spread its faith by the sword?"

I asked this same query at the Islamist missionary tent, and what followed was an intense discussion with a man named Ersuoy who told me that he was "doing this good work because it was needed to earn paradise" for himself. Our lengthy conversation was initially cordial, as we discussed facts about Islam and Christianity. I talked about how Jesus is, in truth, not just a lesser prophet, which is how they see him in their faith, but rather is the Son of God. I also discussed how, being God himself, Jesus died for mankind's sins so that all can be saved, if we will only believe upon him.

I discussed, too, how his prophet Muhammad was uncertain whether even he would be granted salvation by Allah. I then asked the big question: if even their greatest prophet was unsure, how then could Muslims ever be confident or certain about paradise for themselves? Ersuoy agreed with me and said no one could ever follow the Koran perfectly. I asked if this bothered him and if he could ever be as good as they feel their Muhammad was. Next, I reviewed how Jesus had already done it all for his followers and reiterated how we only need to believe on him for salvation into our paradise.

Ersuoy also talked about his beliefs. Muslims are taught from an early age that the Old Testament is good, but the New Testament is corrupt. I challenged him here and discussed its first-generation post-Christ authorship and its writers' strong ethics of truthful reporting. I talked about its extensive textual evidence of more than twenty-five thousand New Testament copies that are all remarkably similar. But Ersuoy still maintained that language changes made the New Testament corrupt, while his Koran had been preserved only in Arabic. He also believed translations of the Koran into any other language were likely corrupt as well. And he stated that he felt Allah and Jehovah are the same god we all worship.

Later, I asked a question that finally elicited his great anger and caused him to stomp off, after he shouted into the growing crowd, pointing at me and calling me a jihadist. My inciting question was, "How can you reconcile the fact that you say you are a peaceful Muslim, yet your Koran in thirty-five places, per my count, commands and commends executing the infidel (that is, anyone who is non-Muslim)?" He first replied that he felt the militant and violent Muslims were not right. Later in the conversation, however, he contradicted himself and said, "Muslims using jihad were and are only acting in self-defense versus Christian crusaders and other armed groups."

Then I asked, "So, who truly is right? Is it you, the peaceful Muslim, or is it the militant, infidel-executing jihadist? How can you both be right? Isn't it also true that you yourself are a target for the radical Muslims due to the fact that you call yourself peaceful and also given the fact that you are here speaking to me, a Christian, since your book commands you not to associate with us? Again, which of you is right? You cannot have it both ways!"

Ersuoy denied that the Koran said such, revealing that he did not know his book fully. I assured him that it did. Surah 5:51 says, "Take not the Jews and Christians for your friends," and also, "He among you that turns to them for friendship is of them." Also, Surah 3:C:57 (3:64–120), says, "Muslims should be true to their own, and seek help and friendship only from their own."

I said, "Thus, the way that I read and interpret it, either you are not following your Koran well by associating with me here, or else other Muslims do not follow it correctly by avoiding me. So how do you deal with this disparity? Do you try to ignore it, and if so, does this ever keep you up at night? Does this ever prick at your conscience?"

At this point, the Hasen missionary became extremely angry and began yelling as the crowd built up more around us. "What are you even doing here? This is our place, our mosque festival, and you come and tell me these things! You should not even be here!" He ended by pointing at me and yelling even louder, "I am not jihadist. You the jihadist!" Then he stormed off. And though I waited there for half an hour more, he never returned.

***

Many stories abound of persecutors who, amazed at their lack of results with torture and their inability to get Christians to fight back or to retaliate, themselves convert, either at that time or even many years later. I recall many, many stories from Richard Wurmbrand's amazing personal life and from his excellent Voice of the Martyrs organization. It publishes a monthly periodical, which I encourage getting on the mailing list for, as well as a superb website of videos and other stories regarding persecution worldwide. They clearly demonstrate how the gospel is spreading and Christianity is growing ever stronger, despite and even because of the growing oppression against it.

So, we should welcome opposition as a perfect way to tell the good news and to show our faith and trust in the Lord! Ask his Spirit to help, as he has promised he will. He has told us that he will be with us and that we do not need to worry about what to say, but rather, he will give us the words that are appropriate each time they are required. Thus, we must strive to imitate Christ in our response to opposition! Consider Christ's own words: "I say: Love your enemies! Pray for those who persecute you! In that way you will be acting as true sons of your Father in heaven." (Matthew 5:44–45a)

***

While spreading the gospel and using your talents for God's kingdom, always remember that God's truths are self-evident. One need only to openly examine and consider them without being blinded and while asking for God's wisdom and guidance. The pressure is not on us, his messengers. We must simply tell the gospel's good news clearly and simply without complicated discourses and proofs. At the same time, we also must live it so that our hypocrisy does not close others off from the Lord.

Give the results to Christ, go and tell the gospel, and let Christ work on their hearts! Step out and take a chance, do it for others and, especially, for his kingdom, not for yourself. It will help you too, more than you can imagine. But you will never know unless you go. Deciding to be an active witness for the gospel changes your whole perspective on your boring and arduous daily grind.

In all we do, we are to do it in the name of our Lord Jesus Christ, as his representative. As we step out and help others, we also help ourselves by obtaining the peace, joy, fulfillment, and rescue that Christ offers. These are his blessings, which he promises to all his followers. Consider this quote from F.H. Gillingham: "Only one life, 'twill soon be past. Only what's done for Christ will last." This means our present world's concerns and stressors will soon be left behind. We should, thus, examine our habits, especially regarding our leisure time, and decide how to best spend our remaining time here. This is your mission.

Now, contrary to typical connotations and perhaps our initial thoughts, a mission is not some far-off place we go to every year or so to do kingdom work. Instead, a mission is an attitude and a behavior in which, through all our daily circumstances, relationships, and activities, we keep ever in the forefront of our minds what we are asked to do for Christ's kingdom! We do mission right where we are. We are planted in our own mission fields: our homes, workplaces, or schools.

Those who deny God, especially those who do it loudest, in truth, have great insecurity and retain unmet desires deep within their hearts. They search for something to satisfy their inner selves: their souls, hearts, and minds. Their sinful, self-oriented behaviors are their attempts to fill this void, this inner emptiness! God makes each human with a special need, an empty hole, that only he can adequately fill. He is therefore mandatory for human completeness!

Those who have searched for him have, to this present time in their lives, either responded with faith and trust in Christ or, alternatively, rejected him with denial, anger, and bitterness. They get angry with the content and at-peace Christian. Many atheists, after initial angry and critical verbal attacks toward me, have later told me quietly, "I wish something could restore my faith," or "I wish I had that kind of faith." Their confessions came after one long visit or, more typically, several discussions. Often, they started out quite hostile and accusatory against the good news and Christianity. Yet, at the conclusion, they addressed their wish in a much different, quieter, at times almost pleading tone and manner.

Therefore, it is important that we try to stay in the game with such persons, keeping up personal contact and praying for them, because we know that no atheist, no denier, no anti-Christian, is ever, while still here in this world, beyond God's grace and forgiveness. God has a good and special plan for each of them, as I tell them. The very fact that he keeps their breaths coming one after another in succession and allows their hearts to keep beating is testament to that! It is only by his mercy, grace, and favor that we are all still breathing, all still living. This is because he still has plans for us in this world. If he no longer did, then our breaths and our hearts would stop at that very time.

In evangelizing and telling others the good news, Jesus wants us to testify to what we have experienced. Our personal experience with

Christ is a powerful persuasion for faith in him. Each Christian is an expert witness for his Christianity! Remember, when the time comes, he promised to give us the exact words we need to be the best witnesses for him! We simply need to rely on him to supply these words of wisdom. And he always does! Try it, and you will see for yourself! Look to these encouraging words:

> "Preach the Word of God urgently at all times, whenever you get the chance, in season and out, when it is convenient and when it is not. Correct and rebuke your people when they need it, encourage them to do right, and all the time be feeding them patiently with God's Word. For there is going to come a time when people won't listen to the truth but will go around looking for teachers who will tell them just what they want to hear. They won't listen to what the Bible says but will blithely follow their own misguided ideas. Stand steady, and don't be afraid of suffering for the Lord. Bring others to Christ. Leave nothing undone that you ought to do." (2 Timothy 4:2–5)

Does this text's prediction not appear to be ringing true in our current age? We need to show the lost there is something better than money, a job, prestige, family, their straight or gay relationship, their worldly goals and achievements, their merits and honors. We must go to these lost people and humbly tell as well as show them by example how much better Christ's love, peace, joy, fulfillment, and rescue are, compared to the goods of this world.

This is best begun through an established relationship with them, if possible, one which builds an initial trust and friendship. Then, when Christ is introduced and when you demonstrate Christ to them, the lost are more open to understand rather than to turn a blind eye and a deaf ear. Keep your focus on God's Word. Let it shine through the world's darkness. Stay in the game with them. Pray for them. And let your life be a loving testimony to the prodigal, the doubter, the skeptic, the defiant, the persecutor, and the sinner.

***

Let us talk for a minute about something I call evangelistic pressure. Most Christians feel a pressure to spread the gospel's good news, because, as Christ said, "the harvest is great and the workers are few" and the "time is short until all work ends." Thus, we feel pressured. We know we must initiate these discussions. Yet, we should feel less pressure when we realize he is here to assist us. We can start the conversation and let the Holy Spirit take it from there, all the while hanging in there with the nonbeliever and the seeker. This is like having a superstar on the ballfield or court with you, one who, while you assist, carries your team to victory. The Holy Spirit is that special, trusted one who is expected to win every time! As we are told in the verses below, do not worry about what to say. The Holy Spirit will speak through you. Our aim must be to initiate and then to let God himself do his kingdom work.

> "Therefore, don't be concerned about how to answer the charges against you, for I will give you the right words and such logic that none of your opponents will be able to reply!" (Luke 21:14–15)

> "But when the Holy Spirit has come upon you, you will receive power to testify about me with great effect . . . to the ends of the earth, about my death and resurrection." (Acts 1:8)

"Life is worth nothing unless I use it for doing the work as-signed me by the Lord Jesus—the work of telling others the Good News about God's mighty kindness and love." (Acts 20:24)

Knowing Christ's saving message is like having an amazing secret that can help everyone, such as having a cure for cancer or Alzheimer's disease, or even for physical death itself! It is such a good thing that we cannot keep it to ourselves. It is so great that we must tell it!

Paul also discusses his abilities to become a spiritual chameleon by always trying to find common ground with each person in order to better develop a relationship with them. This makes it easier for them to hear about and eventually come to Christ. Paul said:

"I have freely and happily become a servant of any and all so that I can win them to Christ. Yes, whatever a person is like, I try to find common ground with him so that he will let me tell him about Christ and let Christ save him." (1 Corinthians 9:19b, 22b)

As you build a relationship with someone and conversation progress-es and you are both feeling more comfortable, I believe these are key evangelistic points to make:

1. Discuss that Jesus is not a myth, given the verified historicity of Christ's birth, death, and rising. He was a real person, a true historical figure, with a documented death as well as a documented rising, testi-fied to by more than five hundred eyewitnesses (many testifying at the cost of their lives). Jesus's empty tomb is still unexplained by man. We have archaeological, scientific, historical, and eyewitness testimony, all of which sufficiently document the facts about Jesus of Nazareth.

Christianity is the only world faith system with this rock-solid foundation. No other faith has this!

2. Discuss Christ's love for them and his gifts of peace, joy, fulfillment, and rescue. Discuss them broadly and illustrate them by your personal testimony. This lets what Christ has done for you shine out brilliantly. The evidence of your character is extremely important.

3. I also like to discuss that all other religions are systems in which human beings are seeking a divine source. All of them consist of checklists, works to be done, and a hope of a heaven or some other higher state. I contrast them with Christianity in which God and Christ have already done it all. Often, people say, "I am not religious." I like to reply, "I am not religious either, as my belief is that religion is man's attempt to reach for a higher power or god-like being or to become as such himself, whereas Christianity is God reaching out to man!" There is indeed a major difference!

4. I have also approached many people by stating, "I can see you are very intelligent and that you have to 'know' something first, rather than just being told a doctrine to believe. So why not check out this Christianity thing for yourself first, adequately and fully, and then make an educated, calculated, and logical decision, just as you do for any other major life choice like buying a house or car or getting married? Look at the historical, archaeological, scientific, and eyewitness (both religious and secular) proofs for Christ's life, death, and resurrection, as so many other brilliant human minds have done the past two hundred years of the modern era. Then, and only then, decide for yourself. Use your intelligent, rational, legal, and scientific approach. Examine all the evidence. Do not blindly snub it, ignore it, or minimize it! You would not do so with any other major life decision. And this is the most important decision you will ever make! So, do not trivialize or delay it! Begin your investigative and seeking process now! If the gospel is true,

make it yours. Or, if you perceive it still to be false in your now educated opinion, you may then say you reached your conclusion after a fully evaluative study."

I also tell them, "I say this because I, through Christ, am lovingly concerned and desire that you, through his Spirit, might have your eyes truly opened. Please understand that Christ loves you and longs for you. He wants you to see him through clear eyes, now, as the only real path to God, the only way to eternal life with him. Therefore, put aside all shame and don't be proud, ignorant, too busy to bother, or stubbornly close-minded. The most important thing is not how long it took you to get to Christ, and thus he to you, but rather, that you take this step now, before it is too late."

I further tell them, "I know well where you are, as I personally mis-understood the truth of his grace and salvation by faith alone for more than two decades, despite practicing as a diligent and strict Roman Catholic. All through school, I was told that we could never know for sure if we would go to heaven but that we instead must try our best to be good. I was told that the Bible was not literal but instead just broad symbols and examples. For instance, I was taught that Adam and Eve represented a group or tribe of people rather than two specific indi-viduals. Rituals and zealous works were needed to get in good with God, like boxes to check to stay in God's favor so that, hopefully one day, he would allow me into heaven. I was always trying to do better yet always failing, as I relied on my self-effort, my resolve, cute ratio-nalizations, and lack of realization of my sinfulness. I recall reading the Bible and thinking, "Boy, I am really good. Only one or two points on those sin lists refer to me. Wow! Thank you, Lord, that I don't have to worry about those other sins like so many other people do. Yes, maybe some anger and maybe a little bit of pride, but those bad ones like greed, lying, lust, and judging others are not in me!" My self-perception mimicked the classic story of the Pharisee and the publican in Luke 18:9–14. Even then, while foolishly believing and trusting in my apparent goodness, whenever I thought of or was asked about my chances of going to heaven, I replied, "Well, I hope so, as I am a good person. But until we die, none of us can know for sure where we will go. Hopefully, God will be merciful to me, but it's all up to him."

Now, after my regeneration (a returning to fellowship with God, my heavenly Father), I am sealed for him by his Spirit. I, too, am progressing in sanctification, which is once again the process of humbly growing in holiness and getting closer to God and Christ daily. I with now-opened eyes fully realize my completely sick human heart, my utter inability to ever be truly good on my own or to do things that could save me by causing God to decide to let me into his kingdom when either I die or when Christ returns. I now see that only with him is my glorification guaranteed, so long as I never purposely and intentionally renounce him or choose to stop my relationship with Christ as my Lord and my Savior.

When Protestant Christians (Protestants do not follow the Roman Catholic model I was taught through sixteen years of Catholic school, including high school and university) would present their seemingly strange ideas to me, I considered them overconfident and prideful. I thought their beliefs provided a blank check excuse to do whatever one desired, yet then be able to simply ask for forgiveness later, an all-too-convenient escape route for sinning.

I think of Saul of Tarsus. For perhaps three years or so, he mistakenly hated and persecuted Christians. His mistake is common to many such converts from false religions. You may ask, as Saul must have done, "Were those years wasted?"

My view is absolutely not! Those years were not uselessly spent. Through Christ, they have forged me into what he needs me to be for his kingdom. Those years were in God's will and timing. They were his way of shaping me for his glory to help further his kingdom work in this dark world. Thereafter, with his Spirit leading, he began to use me as his instrument to help bring other lost sons and daughters to him. Still, I must humbly reiterate that this is not at all of myself. I am not great or special. It is God who uses me, as he does all who simply commit themselves. This is indeed so! Ask him to help you see clearly what he would have you do.

> "Ask also for the special abilities the Holy Spirit gives, and especially the gift of prophecy, being able to preach the messages of God. . . . one who prophesies, preaching the messages of God, is helping others grow in the Lord, encouraging and comforting them. . . . one who prophesies, preaching messages from God, helps the entire church grow in holiness and happiness. . . . If I speak plainly what God has revealed to me, and tell you the things I know, and what is going to happen, and the great truths of God's Word—that is what you need; that is what will help you." (1 Corinthians 14:1b, 3, 4b, 6)

> "They can see that you are a letter from Christ, written by us. It is not a letter written with pen and ink, but by the Spirit of the living God; not one carved on stone, but in human hearts." (2 Corinthians 3:3)

We are God's works of art, the masterpieces of his own hands, and he wants to use you as his tool to create more beautiful things. You are his sculpture knife and his paintbrush to apply his color, his paint, to this world. Nevertheless, to do this, you must learn, understand, and develop your individual spiritual gifts.

We all have at least one thing we can do very well. Learn to walk in this good gift that your God has given you. Find your best one, your primary gift, and spend most of your time and effort there. Secondary gifts are great bonuses, but we must learn the place of each one in our lives. Using your primary gift will give you joy and fulfillment as you mirror God and Christ to others. It will lead you on an amazing life adventure!

God has a plan specifically for you! How do you find it? Look at your life. What makes your heart most happy? Ask your spouse, your family, or your friends for advice. Better yet, ask God to reveal his plan to you. And if you do not yet know him, ask him to reveal his very self to you as well. Tell him that if he does, you will use your gift for him!

Being a Christ-follower does not mean that you accept him and then live a boring life without fun from then on, simply following a list of rules! Once you find your gift, you will learn how and where he needs you to apply it. This makes for an exciting ride indeed! Look here to God's Word for encouragement: "Be strong and courageous and get to work. Don't be frightened by the size of the task, for the Lord my God is with you; he will not forsake you. He will see to it that everything is finished correctly" (1 Chronicles 28:20).

Consider also Matthew 25, the parable of the talents. Our talents and gifts are illustrated by the money a man gave to his three servants before leaving on a trip. The first two servants invested their talents wisely. They doubled their money! But the third servant hid his money in the ground because he was afraid of losing it. He did not use his gift. When the master returned, he praised and rewarded the first two servants who used their resources wisely and bore much fruit. But he punished the man who hid his talent in the ground and refused to use it. In the same way, it is not appropriate for us to deny, defer, or not use our gifts from God. They are meant to glorify him. They are for his purposes.

Look to the example of Paul in the New Testament. He gave his very life for the vocation Jesus called him to. He dedicated his everything to it. He cast off his lifelong Jewish religious and political affiliations and his social status as a Pharisee. Christ called him directly to be an apostle, and he accepted the call. He then physically brought the good news of God's grace and mercy to many, many persons. And he wrote a large portion of the New Testament. Through it, his mission continues to this very day, two millennia later!

Recall Jesus's final command to his followers, which is called the Great Commission: "Go, therefore, and make disciples of all nations, baptizing them in the name of the Father and of the Son and of the Holy Spirit, teaching them to observe everything I have commanded you. And remember, I am with you always, to the end of the age" (Matthew 28:19–20 HCSB).

Jesus told the apostles to go, baptize, and teach. And this is our mission today. We must accept God's call and do likewise. We must boldly yet humbly proclaim his good news, explaining what Jesus did for us, and we must remember there is nothing else in this world so important as bringing the knowledge of Christ, of what he has done for us all, to people who do not yet know him.

Look also at the example of Gideon. He is described as a weak and frightened lad, yet he became a mighty warrior when he accepted God's call to battle the Midianite hordes (Judges 6–8). And how about Peter, John, and the other disciples: they were mere net fisherman! Jesus used these uneducated and simple men to change the world by proclaiming his kingdom on earth, a kingdom that grows stronger and stronger by the day, despite the persecutions that rage against it.

Looking at these people in Scripture, you may think, "Yes, those are great Bible characters, but I am not one of those men or women." You must realize that Christ has an exciting plan for your life in the very same way he did for them. He has made you as a unique creature, one who can only do the special job that he needs you to do!

***

So, are you on board yet? Change your thinking, and therefore change your life. Know that each step you take, each person you speak to, and each event that occurs are all a part of his master plan for your specific role in his kingdom and for his glory. Thinking about it this way changes your attitude and the way you live your life.

Okay, so what exactly is our role, besides believing in Christ as our Savior? Or, if we are not at that point yet in our journey to Christ, how do we achieve it? Well, we must come to know him. Then we will realize all else is transient. Only he and his Word are unshakeable here in this crazy world.

What should matter most to Christians in this dark and imperfect world is, above all, mirroring Christ and incorporating him within us so others can meet him too. To do this is to enact the above-noted Great Commission Jesus gave to his disciples, instructing them to bring the good news to all nations, races, and tongues. We are to bring Jesus to them so that they will come to him and obtain the benefits Christ confers on all his flock: his peace, joy, fulfillment, and rescue!

> "Make the most of your chances to tell others the Good News. Be wise in all your contacts with them. Let your conversation be gracious as well as sensible, for then you will have the right answer for everyone." (Colossians 4:5–6)

So, how do the lost, those nonbelievers, get to know him? They do so as we encourage them to stay daily in his Scriptures, his Word, thereby getting to know Christ better and better day by day. I like to tell seeking people what Jesus said in John 8:31-32: that his follow-ers must stay in his Word. "If you continue in My word, you really are My disciples. You will know the truth, and the truth will set you free" (HCSB). As always, his advice is indeed best!

You may reply, "Really? His Word? Is it reliable?" Okay, great question, one that we will discuss in much greater detail later in this text. For now, let's see what Scripture says:

"Heaven and earth will disappear, but my words remain for-ever." (Matthew 24:35)

"God's words will always prove true and right, no matter who questions them." (Romans 3:4b)

"Your love and kindness are forever; your truth is as enduring as the heavens." (Psalm 89:2)

"God's truth stands firm like a great rock, and nothing can shake it." (2 Timothy 2:19a)

His Word stands forever, eternally unchanged, like a house built on a rock (Luke 6:47--49). The wind and rain washed away the house built on sand. But the one built on a solid rock, that is, upon Jesus, stands unscathed against all assaults, because he is per Revelation 1:5, "Jesus Christ who faithfully reveals all truth to us."

***

So, in summary, how do we discern the direction God would have us go? In order to learn it, we need to give God our true and undivided at-tention. We get rid of distractions in order to speak with him and learn what he wants us to do. Fasting can help. It is not a way to convince or influence him to work faster or to grant a different outcome simply because "I am so good in denying myself." Rather, it gets rid of the distraction of food, thereby allowing you to focus more on God alone and to thus be more open to his voice.

When I fast, I am on a dramatically better conversational link with my heavenly Father. It is as if there is a clearer channel or wavelength from God in heaven down to me, and from me back up to him.

You humble yourself when you worship before him, whether you pray, fast, or do any other type of worship activity, including even an inner conversation or brief contemplation upon him and his Word. Humility allows you to better learn his plans for you and perhaps to understand more clearly why things are happening as they are as you gradually become more open to hearing and thus discerning God's will. Then, as you begin to better and better understand his will, you find yourself to be at peace. Do not go through your whole life being too busy to listen to all that he wants you to do. Do not miss out on all the blessings he has planned for you only to realize in later life they have passed you by!

To have time to listen, you should set aside at regular intervals some special time for just you and him! If you do so earnestly, he will indeed speak to you! Then listen and follow his path, staying in close communication with him:

> "If you want to know what God wants you to do, ask him, and he will gladly tell you, for he is always ready to give a bountiful supply of wisdom to all who ask him; he will not resent it. But when you ask him, be sure that you really expect him to tell you, for a doubtful mind will be as unsettled as a wave of the sea that is driven and tossed by the wind; and every decision you then make will be uncertain, as you turn

first this way and then that. If you don't ask with faith, don't expect the Lord to give you any solid answer." (James 1:5–8)

***

What about time management? Satan can use God's blessings—our possessions, jobs, homes, families, and other things in our lives to trap and distract us. We get too comfortable and less willing to step out, as worldly things preoccupy most of our time. As a result, we devote less time to our king and his mission! Instead, we must use wisely the little time we have left for God's service!

Think of it this way: in a year there are thirty-two million seconds. If we live to eighty, that is two billion five hundred sixty million seconds. Once each second is used, whether for good or merely wasted, it cannot be brought back. It is completely gone forever. Christ on the cross did not waste even his final, torturous moments. He saved a thief, comforted his mother, arranged for her care thereafter, and even forgave his killers, in addition to speaking to his heavenly Father! We, too, must similarly accomplish our important purposes with our precious remaining moments!

Imagine also, as my daughter once profoundly stated, that you have a visible timer or stopwatch ticking backward until, at the final 0.00, your life ends. How wisely would you use your time then? In truth, we must all admit that this stopwatch exists for every one of us, although we cannot see its timer display. No one can know for certain how much of their game time remains.

So, do not wait. Why would you delay? You may become physically or mentally disabled or severely ill, which might limit you from doing God's work. Do not put off seeking God until you have more money or your children are grown or after you retire. You must decide to start now! Ask what he wants you to do and step out. It will be a guaranteed, exciting, and fun adventure! Remember that he is with you every step of the way, with growth and blessings for you vastly exceeding your imaginings. Consider:

> "How do you know what is going to happen tomorrow? For the length of your lives is as uncertain as the morning fog— now you see it; soon it is gone. What you ought to say is, 'If the Lord wants us to, we shall live and do this or that.'" (James 4:14–15)

> "Be careful, or your hearts will be weighed down with . . . the anxieties of life, and that day will close on you suddenly like a trap." (Luke 21:34 NIV)

> "How can my dust in the grave speak out and tell the world about your faithfulness?" (Psalm 30:9b)

> "All our greatness is like a flower that droops and falls; but the Word of the Lord will last forever." (1 Peter 1:24–25)

***

Next, let us talk about the physical blessings we have been given: our possessions, our money, and such things. My thought on money is that it is like manure-based fertilizer. If you hoard it in a pile and it sits only in one spot, it begins to stink and grows moldy. But if you spread it around, it does great good in stimulating growth, crops, and fruit.

God wants us to give and be generous just as he is generous! He has given you your job, your work skills, and your ability to earn money.

It is ultimately his money in truth and not yours, no matter how hard you feel that you worked for it. He has given you your very breath, strength, and energy, to be able to work. So, it indeed is his money, and we should give an adequate percentage of it back to him through our spreading it around!

The long-accepted Biblical reference regarding donating to charity, be it your church, impoverished adults and children or other charitable foundations, a local food kitchen, leprous or persecuted persons overseas, anti-trafficking or anti-abortion agencies and such, is that we are asked to give 10 percent of our income per year. I am not going to go into tithing in detail here. The most important thing is that you give with a generous, honest, and heartfelt sense of charity. Without this, it is not worth giving anything at all. If you are bitter about donating, it is best to keep the money, in my opinion. If you are a follower of Christ, your desire is to help others. You will go above and beyond the 10 percent, often donating 20 or 30 percent or more. A helpful attitude is not to be extremely picky about an exact 10 percent but, rather, to do the very best that you can do. Give the most that you can from your financial means as well as of your talents and time. Giving may not be purely monetary. One's time, goods, and expended efforts in volunteering, driving, and other service all count. This is the appropriate heart attitude that you need to develop.

Understandably, this is not easy. Yet you no longer have the typical selfish human heart within you. It has been transformed into your new Christian heart, the very heart of Christ. Ask him for his help. He understands. He will help you make this change, and he also will pay you back many times over, multiplying his blessings to you! Take a chance. Step out and try this. And then watch the results! These are helpful verses demonstrating God's own views on this subject:

"The purpose of tithing is to teach you always to put God first in your lives." (Deuteronomy 14:23b)

"It is possible to give away and become richer! It is also possible to hold on too tightly and lose everything. Yes, the liberal man shall be rich! By watering others, he waters himself." (Proverbs 11:24–25)

"Trust in your money and down you go! Trust in God and flourish as a tree!" (v. 28)

"When you help the poor you are lending to the Lord—and he pays wonderful interest on your loan!" (Proverbs 19:17)

"Happy is the generous man, the one who feeds the poor." (Proverbs 22:9)

IX. Prayer

"When you pray, I will listen. You will find me when you seek me,
if you look for me in earnest." (Jeremiah 29:12b–13)

Roaaaarrrrrrrrrrr!!!! We awoke with a start. The noise had come from immediately outside the tent my wife, my daughter, and I were sleeping in. We instantly knew it was a lion, and he was angrily upset. The night before, he had walked around the tent, verbalizing in his rumbling bellow, yet without aggression. However, on this second night, he was enraged. We found out the next morning that four males had come in this night, trying to take over the pride of the simba who shared our camp area. They now chased each other about our camp for a good hour and a half. Then, for perhaps twenty minutes, the big male sat just meters away from the back of our tent, snarling and roaring defiantly and generally causing a great degree of fear for we humans tucked inside! The adrenaline spike was amazing. Besides prayer, we had no physical weapons. (We were in the protected Serengeti reserve, and weapons were not allowed.) I was praying, and I told my family, "Do not worry, as Jesus will protect us."

We lay there as still and quiet as possible, recalling how the camp overseer had forewarned that if a lion is angry, one should not make any noise. Lions had come into tents before to noises, tearing right through the wall in thinking there was another challenger lion to defend against. I did have a plastic ice pick in my hand, but the odds of putting that in any place that would do harm to a lion were nil.

Lying there physically defenseless in that tent quickly made me realize how frail we humans are. If the lion were to come in, he hopefully would be more interested in fighting than eating. Yet an angry lion in your tent is certainly no fun. "If he comes in," I told my wife and daughter, "cover your heads with the blankets and lie still."

My daughter needed to cough several times during the encounter, and she did her best, as I had instructed her, to cough into her pillow. After the hour and a half, the brawl moved far enough away that we could barely hear it any longer. Yet, with the adrenaline rush, it took me as long to finally go back to sleep—and lightly so at best!

The large tracks around the tent the next morning were amazing. One man said he looked out and saw four male lions chasing the resident male through the darkness. So, did prayer help us? Perhaps so, but it certainly did not hurt us. It allowed us to remain calm throughout the event by speaking with our protector.

One lesson here is that we should always pray regularly to our Lord and not wait until we find ourselves in a difficult event or situation. If we are used to conversing with him through an open, regular, daily prayer channel, then our prayers will flow easily over that well-established open wavelength. But if we neglect prayer, our attempts to pray in hard times will be like fumbling to look up his cell number! It is harder to call up trust in his strength and protection if we have not yet developed our faith in such by a regular prayer habit.

***

Rise and Soar

Why do we need to pray? Doesn't God already know everything? Yes, he does. But prayer's purpose is not to tell him but, rather, to glorify him and to invite him into conversation. To pray is to commune with him.

I often hear the valid question that if God already knows all our wants and already gives us all that we need and controls our paths, why then do we need to pray? The answer is that prayer done regularly, rather than merely occasionally whenever we are fearful or have something going wrong, keeps us in daily conversation and relationship with God. It also shows him we realize how much we need his help. We are always dependent upon him, even for our very heartbeats and pending breaths.

As supporting evidence, consider the example of Jesus Christ. He was God in our world, perfectly holy, sinless, flawless, unable to be harmed without his permission, and with divine knowledge and insight. Yet, as demonstrated repeatedly in Scripture, Jesus was in constant, prayerful conversation with God, his Father. My thought here is, if I am so imperfect a sinner, then how much more so should I be praying? Yet, I often feel convicted of having a less-than-optimal prayer life. And my conviction hits home all the greater when I read about Jesus's prayer habits.

Prayer puts us on the same channel with God! We should always strive to keep this channel open with him throughout our daily lives. We should think of him as a best friend or as one who is always available and involved during both our good as well as our bad times.

> "Pray all the time. Ask God for anything in line with the Holy Spirit's wishes. Plead with him, reminding him of your needs." (Ephesians 6:18)

"I will bless the Lord who counsels me; he gives me wisdom in the night. He tells me what to do. I am always thinking of the Lord; and because he is so near, I never need to stumble or fall." (Psalm 16:7–8)

"I love the Lord because he hears my prayers and answers them. Because he bends down and listens, I will pray as long as I breathe!" (Psalm 116:1–2)

"When I pray, you answer me and encourage me by giving me the strength I need." (Psalm 138:3)

***

In actuality, the entire Trinity plays a part in prayer. God the Father is the prayer receiver or hearer and also the judge. Christ's role is as our advocate to God. You can consider him your defense attorney. He mediates and pleads our case for us, reminding the Father that "this one is mine" and claiming us for himself. The Holy Spirit's job is to help us prepare our case and pray the correct things!

We should always enter prayer in humility, being fully aware of our complete dependence upon God. We each have needs, even if we are not sure how to express them. The Spirit also helps us claim the blessings God gives. "Whatever you desire," Christ says, "when you pray, believe that you will receive them, and you will." He also states, "I will give you whatever you need!"

Our prayers should not be a checklist or an unthinking, unconscious, rote repetition. Neither should they be Santa's Christmas wish list. Rather, they should be in God's will, and they will be if we truly get to know the Spirit. He gives us encouragement, with a promise of God's mercy to all who truly recognize they are sinners, repent, and return to

God. At his encouragement, we gain peace enough to pray. The eternal security of the believer and also the realization that Christ will indeed meet our needs descends upon and stays with us.

There are also sinful things that block the powerful results of prayer. These include idolatry, which is putting any other thing above God, be it money, career, family, kids, success, leisure and entertainment, or sexual activities. Another prayer blocker is unforgiveness. You cannot hold bitterness inside of you. Still another is not being regularly in his Word. If you are not in the Word, you will not know his will nor live in his desires and plans for your life. A further prayer blocker is having no compassion or sensitivity to others. It is not loving others as God does. A heart of prayer is compassionate and sensitive, and it does not lack care for the poor, the imprisoned, your spouse and children, your coworkers, and the persecuted in this world.

***

Regarding what categories can constitute a prayer, I learned as a young man about the commonly used acronym ACTS. I often like to think through the four ACTS categories in my prayer routine. The categories consist of:

A for Acknowledgment. This means we acknowledge that God is truly our Lord, our great Father and Creator, and we give him the glory that he is due.

C stands for Confession. We admit our wrongdoings to God. God is like we are with our children. He already knows what we did wrong. But until we come clean, the relationship with him is affected until we confess our misdeeds. Then, all becomes positive once again.

T is for Thanksgiving. We thank him for all those many blessings he has bestowed upon us: our very life, our relationships, possessions, health, and other goods.

Last, the S stands for Supplication. Supplication means we humbly present our petitions, requests, and desires before him, although this does not mean unemotionally or unemphatically. Think of some of the spirited prayers of David as well as those of other prophets! I believe there is certainly a place for emphatic prayer. Yet that does not mean we can demand that God do something at that immediate moment. I often pray emphatically with ill patients, including many who are nearing the end of their lives in this world. Humbly realizing the great privilege of being able to do so, I ask the Lord emphatically to heal them of their affliction, to help them, and especially to let them feel his loving presence upon them. I ask him also to continue holding them and their families in the palm of his healing and loving hand. Yet, I will always qualify this by stating that we request this, certainly, with respect to God's will and in his timing and, ultimately, for his glory.

***

In terms of how to pray, let's next discuss the where, the physical location, which is also very important. I recommend finding a quiet place where you can be alone with God without distractions. Jesus often went off by himself to quiet places to be completely alone in order to best pray to his Father. You also need to eliminate all distractions, including TV or music, your phone and computer, kids, pets, or even noise from outside. I sometimes use earplugs or will get out and lay in a grassy field or sit up against an old oak.

Then you must prepare your mind to communicate with your Lord. Get down on your knees. Or, even better, lie prostrate upon the ground, properly humbling yourself.

Further, have a list of specifics, not generalities, to be prayed for. And pray verbally right out loud. Praying aloud keeps your thoughts from straying from your primary prayer focus. And keep on praying regularly, even if you get no answer for what seems a long time. Keep it up. Such delays are often further trials for you to get through.

As you pray, you will see how getting on the same wavelength as God links you more and more into a progressively positive relationship with him. It also clears your mind of the chaff, namely those bothersome things that can cloud your attention and take over your consciousness. Prayer lets one rise above distractors and detractors to optimally commune with God.

It is also helpful to pray together with others for common needs and plans as well as for personal goals. Praying with others can be a very powerful advantage. Remember Christ's words, "I assure you: If two of you on earth agree with any matter that you pray for, it will be done for you by my Father in Heaven. For where two or three are gathered together in my name, I am there among them" (Matthew 18:19–20 HCSB).

Let's conclude by looking at the Bible's input on prayer.

"Don't worry about anything; instead, pray about everything; tell God your needs, and don't forget to thank him for his answers." (Philippians 4:6)

"Don't be weary in prayer; keep at it; watch for God's answers, and remember to be thankful when they come." (Colossians 4:2)

"Pray first that the Lord's message will spread rapidly and triumph wherever it goes, winning converts everywhere as it did when it came to you." (2 Thessalonians 3:1)

"Pray much for others; plead for God's mercy upon them; give thanks for all he is going to do for them." (1 Timothy 2:1)

"The earnest prayer of a righteous man has great power and wonderful results." (James 5:16b)

"And we are sure of this, that he will listen to us whenever we ask him for anything in line with his will." (1 John 5:14)

X. Reading the Bible

How do we know the Bible is trustworthy and not corrupted? And how should we best read it?

"Isn't the Bible chock-full of contradictions?" This is a question I am commonly asked. I recently used God's Word to try to explain a difficult situation in the life of a man and his wife. The man, a self-proclaimed "very-centered Buddhist," retorted loudly, "Ha! The Bible is the biggest collection of mythology that has ever been collected in the history of the world!" I told him he needed to sit back for a discussion. I could not let his statement pass without giving an accurate view. When I asked if he had ever read the Bible, he admitted that he had never looked deeply into it, having read only some small parts. I said his statement was absolutely not true, as is clear to anyone who has studied the historical and archaeological basis of these texts with an open mind.

More and more of the Bible's questionable issues and suspected controversies are proven to be true and accurate as time passes. Problem texts are being explained or verified by new discoveries in archaeology. For instance, the Jerusalem sheep gate by the pool mentioned in the Old Testament was long felt to be a myth. Nothing consistent with it had ever been found within the city's walls, Yet, this area was uncovered recently in ongoing excavations. Another example is the Hittites. It was believed for many centuries that this tribe was a myth. Mentioned frequently as one of the pagan tribes of the Old Testament, there was no proof the Hittites existed. Yet, proof of their existence was recently discovered.

Consider Dr. Robert Dick Wilson. He spent forty-five years studying and investigating the Old Testament and then wrote his life's work, *A Scientific Investigation of the Old Testament*.[1] Dr. Wilson challenged any and all Old Testament critics to cast doubt on its truthfulness. He said he could fully disprove any skeptic or objection against it!

In a verifiable statement of fact, not one single confirmed case of any suspected biblical mistruth has ever been verified, to my research and knowledge. An error has never been found, despite innumerable critical textual examinations that have attempted to do so over these past centuries.

Do people know absolutely everything? For example, when a scientist finds a confusing quandary or anomaly in nature, does he just give up on science because he cannot explain it? No! He gives it the benefit of the doubt and delves further in his search for the truth. Similarly, the Bible should be thought of as innocent until proven guilty, especially because, once again, no fault or error has ever been proven. The evidence is there and is valid if people will only look open-mindedly and objectively at the data—and, of course, if they will choose to believe it.

In truth, we do not turn from God because of lack of evidence. We do so because of our pride and our belief in our intellectual superiority. God is not going to force us to believe. His love works not forcibly but persuasively. We need to openly and honestly look at the hard evidence that he provides!

Now, if you have examined the evidence appropriately and yet still disagree, I will certainly respect that opinion. Nevertheless, I highly doubt this will occur in any human mind that is open to looking at the

Bible and weighing all the evidence supporting it. It, unfortunately, is all too common in our culture for one to make loud, seemingly knowledgeable declarations without having correct data and expertise on one's subject. So, I urge you not to come to an opinion regarding the Holy Bible until you have examined its history and other evidences for its accuracy. It is too important an issue to avoid or ignore. And in our age of data at our fingertips, one can research this easily, right from one's own home or apartment, without any trips to the archives, a museum, or an Old Testament scholar.

***

When we consider the books of the New Testament, a common accusation is that the Gospels were written much later than the actual time of Christ. Nevertheless, it is common sense that the Gospels had to have been written before the year AD 70, as none mention Rome's destruction of the Jerusalem temple. If these accounts had been written much later, as critics say, they most certainly would have mentioned this as part of Christ's prophecy in which he foretold the temple's destruction. This would be solidifying proof recognized by the people of that time, proof that Jesus's predictions were amazingly correct! Therefore, this never would have been left out of Scripture if the Gospels were written after that event. It would have solidified Jesus's authority in the minds of people of that day as prophecy fulfilled less than forty years after Jesus made it!

Also running counter to the argument that the New Testament accounts were written centuries later is the fact that the author of the Book of Acts, Luke, must have penned his history prior to Paul's documented death in AD 62. If written later, Acts surely would have mentioned Paul's martyrdom, as it does the martyrdom of other early Christians. Because we know Luke wrote his gospel first and penned

Acts second, Luke's gospel then had to have been written even earlier. Further, Luke includes parts of Mark's gospel. Therefore, Mark clearly predates both of Luke's books. Mark was probably written in the late 50s, less than twenty years after Jesus's death!

Additionally, we know that some of Paul's letters, which include the early church's specific creed and other beliefs, predate the Gospels. Paul's conversion was about two years after Christ's death in AD 33. So, his letters were written within five to twenty years after Christ's crucifixion and rising! These facts have been proven as definitively true, so there is absolutely no logical way to reason that the New Testament was written centuries after these events! Also, as noted above, John 5:2–5 mentions the Bethesda Pool (by which Jesus healed the paralytic who had lain there thirty eight years) "by the Sheep Gate with five colonnades" (which can mean rows of columns, platforms, or porches). This pool was doubted to exist. Yet, it was finally identified after being originally found in an 1888 excavation. Its identification demonstrates still more proof of the Bible's accuracy, joining the above-noted Hittite discovery in Turkey as well as the Siloam Pool (John 9:1–11, where Christ healed the blind man), which was also used by skeptics as evidence against the Bible until being excavated in 2004! In his book *Archaeology and the Religion of Israel*, master archeologist William Albright states: "There can be no doubt that archaeology has confirmed the substantial historicity of the Old Testament tradition" (Albright, 1953, 176).[2]

Let's look at several more examples. When Isaiah wrote, the earth was generally believed to be flat rather than being a sphere. Yet, look at Isaiah 40:22, written about 700 BC, which states, "He sits enthroned above the circle of the earth." Also, Job, the oldest biblical book, in 36:27–28 describes the water cycle. Even in the middle ages, rain's source was still a mystery. Yet, Job described it amazingly well more than three thousand five hundred years prior! How can one explain that knowledge that human beings did not possess until two or three thousand years later is clearly found in very early biblical texts? The only valid explanation is that the Bible must be divine in its origin. Only God would have had such knowledge! Or, take Psalm 22. This psalm accurately describes a crucifixion hundreds of years before such method ever existed. Christ quotes this very psalm in Matthew 27:46 while upon the cross, "Eli, Eli, lama sabachthani," or "My God, my God, why have you forsaken me?"

There are many, many other proofs that verify the Bible, and we will look at them in more detail later. The conclusion here is that, yes, the Gospels and the rest of the New and Old Testaments were definitively written by firsthand witnesses of the events of those very days. These are not mere stories contrived centuries or more later by deceitful men and women!

***

Okay, what about the differences between the Gospels? Critics continue to state the variation argument, implying that too much has been added to the Bible and that the Gospels are not enough alike. They question how the four the versions of Jesus's life here can be so different.

As separate individuals, the four gospel writers would naturally have variability in what events they decided to report or not. As John 21:25 states, "And there are also many other things that Jesus did, which, if they were written one by one, I suppose not even the world itself could contain the books that would be written." Here we are officially told that, as one would naturally expect, not every single deed and Word of Jesus was nor could have been recorded in written form.

In addition, consider this: Imagine you had four eyewitnesses to a vacation that you took, let's say four members of your family. Once at home, if you asked each to write their account of the trip, would they ever be the same? They would not. And I would add that, if indeed such were just the same, this would raise suspicion much more highly for false reports. I recall, as an example, the cheaters in school who were caught by turning in the exact same answers. If the Gospels were all exact carbon copies of each other, with the exact same events reported, each in the exact same way, that would suggest that somebody was intentionally doctoring them to force an opinion or make an extremely specific point.

The variations between the Gospels are something that valid legal witnesses will then always manifest naturally. Seasoned prosecutors and judges are rightly suspicious if the stories told by multiple witnesses are ever exactly the same! Therefore, the differences between these four books, written by four separate individuals with thus four expectedly distinct viewpoints, provides strong evidence of their veracity and further proof of their truthfulness!

***

How about the text of the Bible? Is the New Testament corrupt as Ersuoy, the Muslim missionary, suggested? More than five thousand six hundred copies were transcribed into Greek from the original Hebrew manuscripts. And the earliest copies were written within one hundred years of the original, making it by far the most extensively copied literature ever in the history of written language. In addition, there were at least twenty thousand copies later transcribed into Latin as well as into several other languages. Contrast the Bible with other ancient sources: Plato has only seven copies of his oldest manuscript. And these were all written one thousand two hundred years later. Homer's *Iliad* has six hundred forty-three copies. All were written five hundred or more years after Homer's original. There are so few of these texts that were written so long after their originals, and yet these secular documents are never questioned!

Furthermore, despite such prolific copying, there are very few omissions, additions, or other changes in the text of the New Testament—although one, the story of the adulteress and her attempted stoning, is a later addition. The reason why this was added is uncertain. It may have been passed down in oral tradition first then added to the written text later, or it may have been felt necessary to be placed in at that later time, if perhaps there was a perceived need to address more so the attitude toward adultery in that day (perhaps the culture was too lax or even too strict). The events of the story could have happened during the ministry of Jesus. The scene is so tense and dramatic that it would have been well-remembered by the disciples even if it had not initially been written down.

In summary, while the story of the adulteress was not present in the earliest manuscripts, it was still added in the fifth century, which is early on. Maybe it was added to teach a lesson or to give more guidance. But it could as well have been something that did occur during Jesus's ministry. I personally think the event did occur as described since Jesus is reported to be in the story.

Jewish copyists were held to an extremely strict standard of honesty and integrity. They were not men who would intentionally lie. They knew they could not get away with lying before their peers or their God. So, they were on guard against spreading falsehood and were very careful to write and copy only the exact truth as it existed in written form. Therefore, we can logically extrapolate that they would have done likewise with any later additions of existing oral tradition. They wrote and copied these documents with a very strict and stringent standard of accuracy in order to be certain to pass on only the truth to the best of their abilities, as we will review in more detail later in this book.

So, when we review the textual evidence, only a few words differ between the initial autographs and their later copies, and none of these slight differences alter the Bible's meanings or messages. Take, for example, the five thousand six hundred Greek New Testament manuscripts all produced within one hundred years of the original text. How did they ever manage to achieve this accuracy through multiple translations over an entire century? If left to mere men, such is highly unlikely, and indeed, it would be more unlikely than likely. The fact that these were so well preserved over time shows how the Bible is not merely the work of specific men but that it has a divinely supernatural basis underlying it. As a comparison, consider Shakespeare's writings. Some of his plays, although written a few hundred years ago, have missing parts. Even today, some retain huge gaps to the degree that modern scholars have had to add significant amounts of text in order to complete whole sections.

***

Isaiah 53, in addition to Psalm 22 noted above, also describes a crucifixion. Doubters had always declared that Isaiah must have been written after Jesus died, given its extremely accurate and detailed description of crucifixion. And for centuries the oldest copy of Isaiah was from AD 900, nearly nine centuries after Christ died.

But then in 1947, a young Bedouin boy throwing rocks into caves heard a strange noise in a cave high upon a cliff. He heard an urn break when struck by a rock. He climbed up and, upon reaching the cave, found urns containing what we now refer to as the Dead Sea Scrolls.

The scrolls contain forty thousand different manuscripts written over one thousand years. Many of them predate anything we previously possessed. And one of these was Isaiah.

The scrolls contained a complete copy of Isaiah that dated to 700 BC and was nearly identical to the copy from AD 900! Only seventeen letters are in question between the two texts. So, after a thousand years of copying, the differences were minimal, and none affected the text's meaning!

Because of the Dead Sea Scrolls, historians and theologians can compare ancient texts to later copies. We also now have an extremely accurate version of the entire Old Testament, excluding only Esther, one that dates to hundreds of years before Jesus's birth.

This is solid evidence that people did not make up the Old Testament histories and prophecies—including the predictions that Christ fulfilled. The evidence shows that God does indeed preserve his Word throughout the centuries and millennia, not allowing major changes and revisions to be done by men!

This is confirmatory evidence for my firm belief that God wrote and preserved his book, his Bible, beginning with the oral tradition and then continuing as people wrote eyewitness accounts on paper. God first established its written form and then oversaw and guided its copywriters, making certain that all copies were valid. I see no other way to fully explain this. It would be impossible without divine input.

***

Further strong proof for the authenticity of Scripture is its prophecies which have been fulfilled. Every single prophecy in the Bible thus far has come true, excepting of course the ones in Revelation, Daniel, and Ezekiel regarding the end times which are still to come.

So, if the rest of this book is true, why would you ever feel that the conclusion is not going to happen? The rest of it has already occurred exactly according to its predictions! For example, the prophecies of destruction on Moab, Tyre, and Sidon came true. These peoples were, as promised, wiped completely off the face of the earth so that no trace of these civilizations remains today, just as God had predicted would occur. So, awaken and be aware—Christ is indeed coming soon!

**

Therefore, the Bible is God's own Word. So, your next question is: "What do I choose to do with it?" We are asked to believe it. Believe without doubt that the Bible is truly the word and the will of the one true God, our Father Creator in heaven, he who loves us and has given it to us for our benefit as a guidebook or map, if you will. It makes our life here the best that it can be and grants us access to eternal life with him when we are ultimately rescued from this world!

While many people deny the Bible, I feel that, in truth, one can never really deny nor disprove it. Once again, many great minds have tried, but these have either failed or given up or ultimately realized the truth and become Christians themselves. They converted through the process of examining these texts in detail, including both their historical bases and their impressive preservation over time.

So, what is the bottom line? Accept it! It is his book, consisting of his living Word, given by God to us so that we may know him and his will!

**

In addition to believing the Bible, we also have several duties to it. First, we must study it. As a takeaway from this studying, we must learn how to apply and obey it. Additionally, if we spend time in it, I am absolutely convinced we will learn to love it, meaning that we will continually yearn for more.

Certainly, our schedules are busy. Nevertheless, longing for more time to spend in the Word and being blessed and refreshed by it when you do is a significant lesson. It keeps you constantly coming back to the Lord's fountain of wisdom and love for more and evermore. Once this habit develops, it is extremely difficult to break!

Finally, once we have learned the Bible, what God asks us to do is to preach it. We need to tell others this good news. It is too good to keep to ourselves!

***

In summary, the Bible itself is its own best proof. If you diligently study it with an open mind while asking God to show you its truth, you will see its divine nature, its validity, and its truthfulness. It has changed many, many skeptical and doubtful human minds! Amazingly, the more time one spends in it, the less doubt one has, and the greater the confidence that it indeed is what it claims to be. We become convinced that we are holding the living Word of our holy God in our own human hands, given to us for our benefit!

If you are still not certain, I would challenge you with this: Read the Bible every day for one month. Read at least one chapter daily or better yet, read for thirty minutes a day if you can, beginning with the Gospels. As you do, ask for God's help in understanding it. Then wait and watch to see how this will change you!

This Bible challenge, to spend thirty minutes each day in his Word for one month, will change you. I believe you will want to continue to do this after the month is over. You will hunger for it, treasure it, and absolutely delight in your time spent within it! Let his Holy Spirit fill and feed you through the Bible!

***

Okay then, what is the best way to read the Bible? I feel it best to pray first, asking to be shown what is meant in the words, asking to receive God's enlightenment. Next, read it slowly, word for word, thinking about each one. Rapid reading is never as beneficial. Then, meditate on it. Look again at each word and think more deeply about its meaning.

It helps to put yourself into the scene. For example, put yourself in the place of Jesus and his followers or of those who were against him. Don't only be David, the hero battling Goliath; be the other Israelites, the Philistines, including Goliath himself, as well as Saul. In the prodigal son story, see yourself not only as the lost prodigal, but also as his angry elder brother, as a servant, or as the father himself. Try doing this with every single person discussed in the passage. Ponder how they may have felt in their attitudes or emotions. Put yourself in their sandals. Contemplate, "If this was to happen to me today, what would my feelings be? What would be my thoughts and concerns?" You will see how your feelings and opinions change when you place yourself into these different roles.

I also have found that writing down questions, thoughts, and ideas while reading is very helpful, whether in the margins or in a separate journal.

***

Next, we must incorporate the Scripture into our lives. It is not enough to read it and then let it pass out of our minds. Incorporating it into us makes us more and more like Christ as time goes on.

Further, we then must pass it on. We must tell others how important God's Word is to us, how it has changed us, and how it is alive and speaks to us. It reassures us and explains life's mysteries, such as why there is evil, suffering, and disease in our world.

A common theological acronym I like, which is helpful in remembering how to approach any biblical text, is OICA.

O stands for observation. How does it read? What exactly does it say on the surface?

I stands for interpretation. What is the actual meaning of the text? This requires us to think more deeply about what we read.

C stands for correlation or context. Where else in God's Word does this idea or topic appear? None of God's themes are ever stated in isolation. Rather, these recur throughout his scriptures. Therefore, when interpreting, always check context. This is very important. If you take a single line of Scripture by itself, you can erroneously presume this to mean something completely different than what is intended. For instance, you can derive a completely erroneous and opposite message if you take the phrase, "There is no God," and exclude the succeeding words "but Yahweh." If you look only at part of a verse or theme without also looking at its context, you can misread of God's message. Only a fool would do this, obviously, but it can easily happen if this extremely important step is forgotten.

Another way to check context is to see what other Christian theologians and scholars have thought the text has meant over these past hundred years or so. Bible commentaries are written and published every year and are available to help us. These are excellent devices to assist us as we study Scripture. As Peter said, "there is no private message in scripture." The message should be clear to all who are saved even if you cannot understand it 100 percent by yourself. On standard questions, you should be able to realize the essence of a scholar's interpretation, not counting mysteries of major degree, such as the Trinity or predestination. If you or any other person comes up with a brand-new, novel message from the Bible, you are wrong! I like what I heard James MacDonald once say here: "If it's new, it's not true, and if it's true, it's not new!"

Last, A stands for application. How does this passage relate to me, to us, and to life generally? How should or does it affect me?

***

Finally, the Bible has conclusively and without doubt stood up to the greatest intellects and investigators of the ancient as well as the modern world. Yet, it has remained completely infallible and has never been proven wrong! Therefore, when you hold the Bible in your hands, you need to realize that this is God's living, breathing Word. It is his decree about how we are to live. It is also the way in which he speaks to us today, in order to teach us how to be as happy as we possibly can here and to rescue us into his eternal, perfect happiness in the afterlife as well. It is the absolute truth from the One who created the world, from the One who created you. It tells us how we can optimally function in this broken place. Without it as your guide, your instruction manual, you are lost in a very dark place, a black wood, perhaps even a deep canyon. Yet with it, you have a "lamp for your feet and a light on your path" (Psalm 119:105). So, keep it close. Read it daily. Incorporate it, live it, and tell it. Value it as the great treasure it truly is! If you let his Word be your guide, he will positively affect your life throughout the rest of your days!

So, how is your life's happiness doing? How is life's joy going? You can have it, easily, by making a conscious decision to choose it and make it yours on a personal, individual basis. The Bible is the authoritative word from our Creator, and it gives great wisdom and explains many things to us, at least as much as our human minds can comprehend and understand. So, choose it, pick it up, read it, and incorporate it. Make his Word your life's guidebook! Let us look at some scriptures discussing this:

"Man must not live on bread alone but on every word that comes from the mouth of God." (Matthew 4:4 HCSB)

"All Scripture is inspired by God and is profitable for teaching, for rebuking, for correcting, for training in righteousness, so that the man of God may be complete, equipped for every good work." (2 Timothy 3:16–17 HCSB)

I also like the Living Bible's translation of these same two verses:

"The whole Bible was given to us by inspiration from God and is useful to teach us what is true and to make us realize what is wrong in our lives; it straightens us out and helps us do what is right. It is God's way of making us well prepared at every point, fully equipped to do good to everyone." (2 Timothy 3:16–17)

"But if anyone keeps looking steadily into God's law for free men, he will not only remember it but he will do what it says, and God will greatly bless him in everything he does." (James 1:25)

"You will do well to pay close attention to everything they have written, for, like lights shining into dark corners, their words help us to understand many things that otherwise would be dark and difficult. But when you consider the wonderful truth of the prophets' words, then the light will dawn in your souls and Christ the Morning Star will shine in your hearts. For no prophecy recorded in Scripture was ever thought up by the prophet himself. It was the Holy Spirit within these godly men who gave them true messages from God." (2 Peter 1:19b–21)

These verses state in no uncertain terms that the Bible came from the Lord's inspiration to holy men of God who wrote it as they were moved by the Holy Spirit to do so. Thus, if the Bible is God's own Word rather than just something written by men alone, as I believe we have been able to prove here, we must make a choice. Do we embrace it and do our best to learn from and to follow it? Or do we deny it and foolishly refuse it? The choice is yours, but your heavenly Father is waiting, hoping that you will choose him! In so doing, he will amazingly bless you, as promised in what follows:

"Never forget your promises to me your servant, for they are my only hope. They give me strength in all my troubles; how they refresh and revive me! From my earliest youth I have tried to obey you; your Word has been my comfort." (Psalm 119:49, 52)

In conclusion, let me ask you: what else in your life can never be shaken, never changes, and can, solely by itself, be always, always constantly relied on? It's not your spouse, your parents, your kids, your minister, your job, your possessions, your investment portfolio, your car, your health, your abilities, or your talents. It is solely God and his mighty and unchanging Word!

XI. Faith, Works, and Doubt

"You will be judged on whether or not you are doing what Christ wants you to. So watch what you do and what you think; for there will be no mercy to those who have shown no mercy. But if you have been merciful, then God's mercy toward you will win out over his judgment against you. Dear brothers, what's the use of saying that you have faith and are Christians if you aren't proving it by helping others? Will that kind of faith save anyone? If you have a friend who is in need of food and clothing, and you say to him, 'Well, good-bye and God bless you; stay warm and eat hearty,' and then don't give him clothes or food, what good does that do? So you see, it isn't enough just to have faith. You must also do good to prove that you have it. Faith that doesn't show itself by good works is no faith at all—it is dead and useless."

(James 2:12–17)

What is faith? It is a firm and uncompromising belief in God and his Word. It is fully believing his promises for you and letting this strong belief direct your life.

Faith is not a blind, unthinking entity, nor is it a perpetual high. It is separate from feelings! We cannot get it by our own willing or our own choosing. It is a gift from God, often coming and then being strengthened through prayer, Scripture reading, and by experiencing his providence and protection in our lives.

Now, can faith ever waver or doubt? Absolutely. In fact, if someone tells you they never, ever have doubt, you should be concerned. The human heart doubts quite regularly in almost all cases.

This brings up a major question that many people have: how can I be a Christian if I have doubts? My response is that you certainly can be a Christian yet still struggle with doubts. Faith, especially early on, typically always includes some questions and doubts. Using an example from the Catholic Church, its criteria for the anointing of a saint includes that the saint-candidate had a defined crisis period of doubt at some point during their lifetime. While perhaps not an optimal example, this shows that doubt is going to occur in us all, if expected even in those rare people labeled by the Roman Catholic Church as good candidates for sainthood!

It is fine and even normal to have intellectual doubts, but do not stop there! Go deeper to find out what is driving you away from God. Find and assess what is causing your doubting. Why do we choose not to believe? As stated previously, the reasons I have come up with for this, per my thinking, include pride (feeling too smart) or being afraid of giving up or losing things, or perhaps fear of judgment for prior sins. Others say they simply have no time. Some of us may even like the pain we experience in a life without God.

Nevertheless, if we choose faith in him and begin to do his will, God then confirms to us that Jesus is indeed the Messiah! Then, as more time passes, our faith becomes stronger. Our doubts become weaker and less frequent and certainly less bothersome. This happens because you have examined and defined the faith that you have. You explored and found God, who has helped to build your faith into a much stronger instrument. A major benefit of our years is that the longer we live, the more instances we have in which we see God helping us throughout our lives. These experiences all help forge our beliefs and build our faith into a firmer foundation.

I encourage any seeker to read the Gospel of John and then to ask himself, "Can I trust Jesus?" All your questions and concerns will never be fully addressed, especially not before you begin a relationship with him. But all in all, the question remains: can we trust him? The answer is yes, we absolutely can!

Once we decide to trust and to believe, we must start to read the Word daily and to spend time in other faith-building materials, such as Christian music or books. We should also get with others who have our same faith (a church or a small group), and then let Jesus direct our steps from there. Rest assured that if you start this endeavor, he will do this for you! Consider Psalm 34:8, "Taste and see that the LORD is good" (HCSB).

***

Okay, do Christians have variable degrees of faith as well as different degrees of doubt? Certainly they do, as we are all separate individuals. Consider an example of two Israelites entering the promised land of Canaan to fight the *Anakim* (the giants). If one man was bold and courageous, yet the other was frightened and unsure, were not both still protected and saved by God's almighty hand? Or consider two Hebrew families on the eve of the first Passover. Both were told to spread lamb's blood upon their doors to keep God's angel of death from killing their firstborn. Both were told the blood application would allow God to pass over, or spare, each one's house (Exodus 12). If one family strongly and fearlessly believed that the blood would save their firstborn, while the other was less sure and still afraid, yet both still did what they were told with the blood, then which one was spared? Yes, both were!

Similarly, we all have varying faith levels, but faith in Christ as our Savior is the bottom line. It is belief enough to follow him and his commands and to have faith in his saving blood! Do you have it? Or, do you feel too smart, maybe too grounded in this modern era's technology, science, or some other worldly small-g god that keeps you from realizing that accepting what Christ has done for you is the most important decision you will ever make? If this describes you, how much longer will you continue to deny and refuse his great gift?

Our mind is so gifted by its Creator that we can question his very existence, his goodness, and his plans. Yet our mind's basic, essential need is to worship the one Creator alone. God stays close to us, holding us in the palm of his hand throughout our lives. He speaks to each of us in variable ways, trying to get our minds, our hearts, and our souls upon the correct track. Unfortunately, many never get there, due to their pride, ignorance, defiance, or obsessions with other gods of this world.

So, what must we do? We must do as Christ says: we must believe, and then we shall see its validity. This is like riding a bicycle. You cannot merely watch it or read about it. Rather, you have to get on board and learn to do it. Then it becomes second nature. Faith is an action, a life direction, and thus a verb, not a noun, not a thought, nor a feeling. Consider:

> "'Has there ever been a time when you cried out to me that I haven't rescued you? Yet you continue to abandon me and to worship other gods. So go away; I won't save you anymore. Go and cry to the new gods you have chosen! Let them save you in your hour of distress!' But they pleaded with him again

and said, 'We have sinned. Punish us in any way you think best, only save us once more from our enemies.' Then they destroyed their foreign gods and worshiped only the Lord; and he was grieved by their misery." (Judges 10:12b–16)

***

I like John MacArthur's description of good works in his book *Twelve Ordinary Men*: Zeal must always be harnessed and tempered with love. But if it is surrendered to the control of the Holy Spirit and blended with patience and long-suffering, such zeal is a marvelous instrument in the hands of God." He also writes, "The Kingdom needs men who have courage, in ambition, drive, passion, boldness, and a zeal for the truth. John certainly had all of those things. But to reach his full potential, he needed to balance those things with love." Also, he pens: "Zeal for the truth must be balanced by love for people. Truth without love has no decency; it's just brutality. On the other hand, love without truth has no character; it's just hypocrisy." [3]

As God's disciples, we need to know Christ as well as his truth, his Word. And we must express as well as live it in love. We are never simply to tolerate it or deny it. Rather, we are to proclaim his love in a direct and firm, yet humble and loving, manner. As we do this, we will become more and more like Christ and mature toward his perfect example.

What about faith in the actual gospel, specifically, as it is stated so well in John 3:16? John states, "believe in him," that is, on Christ, which means you cannot just believe intellectually, but you must make him your very own foundational support, a veritable part of yourself!

Then, the challenge is that once you claim and get this gospel as your own, you are told to get it out to others, that is, to take an active role in making sure they also incorporate it rather than just thinking about it or even denying it.

***

A great controversy throughout many churches over the years has been whether faith alone and of itself is all that is needed for salvation, versus faith plus good works where both are considered mandatory.

My view is stated in our New Testament: if you have faith in Christ, you are absolutely going to do good works—you simply cannot help it. You will spread his good news, taking it to the poor, the needy, the emotionally distraught, and all the imprisoned lost souls you encounter.

Some churches, however, also doctrinally demand good works. They state that, along with faith, good works are necessary for salvation. Such churches include, for example, the Church of Christ and the Roman Catholic Church. This is not what our Lord tells us in his Word. In its pages, he tells us unquestionably that faith in him is enough for salvation: "For you are saved by grace through faith, and this is not from yourselves; it is God's gift—not from works, so that no one can boast" (Ephesians 2:8–9 HCSB).

Of course, I must reemphasize that good works will indeed flow from one with a true faith. Faith that does not bear the fruit of good works is not genuine faith. It is not in step with Christ's command. I like the thought that once we accept Christ's gift and exchange our rags for his righteousness, we naturally begin to do righteous acts in his name!

However, there is no specific list of things we must do in order to gain our salvation with Jesus. He merely asks us to accept his gospel and also, despite our human weaknesses, to strive to become as much like him as we can, reaching out to others and becoming part of the great progression of his kingdom throughout the remainder of our lives. A well-known Christian statement nicely summarizes this. It says that our salvation is by grace alone, through faith alone, in Christ alone.

***

In summary, no human mind will ever be able to answer all the intellectual questions and objections about God and his saving plan. Yet, this should not matter to one who has faith!

This is because the farther we walk on our faith journey, the more we come to see that it really is the true path. We see that Jesus and Christianity aren't true because they work; rather, they work because they are true. We should ask Christ, as did the man with the demon-possessed son in Mark 9:24, "I do believe! Help my unbelief!"

Doubt, once again, has its benefits, as it spurs more questions and investigations. It acts as a purifying fire for our faith, making it stronger and more battle tested. Thus, we cannot and do not need to resolve every single issue with God in order to have true faith. Rather, we can still make the choice to believe and then ask God for help with our unbelief and doubt issues!

Also, consider this: should not my God and our God be beyond our total knowledge and at least partly obscured from our full understanding? Do you truly want your God to be someone whom you can fully rationalize in your limited human pea-brain? If we mortals could fully explain and understand him, how could he be God?

Yes, big questions, such as the reason for evil and suffering, certainly can make some wonder about God's existence. But these are outweighed by much greater evidences for the facts that he does exist and that he loves us. He redeems our sufferings by drawing ultimate good from them. He is always turning negatives into positives. So, although we do not fully understand questions such as why suffering or evil exist, we can trust that God is present, is still just, and is still acting appropriately. He will give us a full understanding someday!

These big questions and multiple other commonly raised objections are addressed in more detail in Part II below. But let's address one question for now.

The human intellect alone cannot credibly account for the big bang that started life's emergence, the fine-tuning of the universe, the existence of our moral laws, the Bible's supernatural confirmation, nor the resurrection of Jesus. The only hypothesis that explains these reasonably well is that there is a divine Creator whose own Son is Jesus Christ!

Thus, we do have evidence enough to step out and express faith in God. Objections do and will always exist. But we do not demand such level of conclusive proof in any other area of life! Yet again, because of our issues of pride or our fear of giving up things, we have many excuses that can keep us from God, as Satan and this, his world, desire us to do!

We thus need to step out in our faith, unafraid, and say as per Mark 9:24, "I believe! Help my unbelief!" He who wants to know God has God revealed to him. Each of us has either a will to believe or a will not to do so.

Therefore, we must decide exactly this: Do we want to know God personally and experience peace, joy, fulfillment, and rescue with him? Do we desire a release from guilt while living the fulfilled life we were meant to live? Do we want to pursue his purposes for our lives, tap into his power for daily living, and commune with him in our lives now and eternity next?

Come as you are, right now, and he will clean you. He will change you into his new creation. We truly have nothing to lose and everything to gain!

XII. Dealing with This World

When was the last time you were disappointed? Your day did not go as planned, or you didn't get that promotion or raise, or what you wanted for Christmas or your birthday. What, the washer broke again! Another flat tire. You're sick with another cold. You get no respect from your spouse or family. It's raining on your big, planned, fun-activity day. How can this house be dusty and trashed again after you just cleaned it yesterday? Your job is not as great as you'd like it to be. Your finances aren't right. Family or friend relationships aren't where they should be. The list unfortunately goes on and on and on.

A major and extremely successful tactic of the enemy, the evil one of this world, is to keep us busy with worldly things, thereby distracting our minds and bodies from the things of God. If this was difficult to overcome in ages past, imagine how exponentially much more difficult it is now, given today's world of technology. Ours is the constant banter of communications exuding literally moment by moment from our cell phones and computers. Ours is video games or the media in print and song. Ours is working so hard to be able to pursue and then maintain a certain lifestyle and income.

Such things keep us from quality time spent with our families, driving divisional daggers into our relational foundations. We desire those sleek sports cars and boats, the glamorous airbrushed magazine and TV models, that mansion on the hill, and so on. And we reduce our satisfaction with or even forget about the amazing blessings God has already placed into our lives. Even good works can be distractions if they are done for the wrong reasons.

We need to look at our lives and make sure that we regularly set aside time to unplug and to scale back. We need to keep our ultimate focus on God through his Word and by prayerful communication with him.

***

So how should we deal with these fields of worldly land mines, these waters full of protruding rocks? We must realize what great good is still to come for us. And we should remind ourselves that there absolutely is, ultimately, a known and ultra-positive endpoint coming for us, despite all the craziness, confusion, and disappointment we currently wallow in. We must know without doubt that we have a God of merciful rescue, one of hope and of love. He is ever with us in our daily disappointments, which pale when we compare them to his great plans for us.

Seeing life this way minimizes these troubles and disappointments. We see them in their true light, with respect to our eternity. Will most of our troubles really matter in ten years? How about in fifty or one hundred years? Remember 1 Corinthians 2:9: "No mere man has ever seen, heard, or even imagined what wonderful things God has ready for those who love the Lord." Also consider Colossians 3:1–2: "Since, then, you have been raised with Christ, set your hearts on things above, where Christ is, seated at the right hand of God. Set your minds on things above, not on earthly things" (NIV).

So, we already know exactly how everything is going to turn out for us. We also know the ending to the story of this entire world. Yet certainly, just as in any novel, movie, or other storyline, there will be bumps along the way. There will be disappointments, those things and happenings that seek to drain us of our hope, our energies, our endurance, and our faith, and therefore try to limit or even destroy our peace, our joys, our sense of fulfillment, and possibly even our rescue, if we are not careful!

When such obstacles arise and dwell gloomily within our paths and in our very souls, we need hold fast to our top possession, our constantly steady rock, our anchor of light, our own Jesus Christ. We must remember all that he has done and continues to do for us right up until the very moment that he either returns or calls us home, whichever is first.

We must always remember that we have an eternal God and Father who remains always faithful and true, never wavering toward us. He is our light and our life in this dark world where disappointments abound, springing up at us like lurking beasts, attempting to ruin both our spirits and our spirituality and thus limiting our relationship with our lord as well as with those around us.

Always keep in the front of your mind our ultimate, eternal rescue into paradise with him. All problems, all disappointments, and all concerns of this life will simply fade forever! Amen, come Lord Jesus!

Our prayer is that you, O Lord, would continue to comfort us here in this world, helping us to keep our hearts, minds, and eyes fixed upon you primarily, no matter our circumstances. We thank you for the eternal rescue you have promised to all who believe on you, a rescue that will occur in the relatively near future! As reassurance, consider:

"Fear not, for I am with you. Do not be dismayed. I am your God. I will strengthen you; I will help you; I will uphold you with my victorious right hand." (Isaiah 41:10)

"And now just as you trusted Christ to save you, trust him, too, for each day's problems; live in vital union with him. Let your roots grow down into him and draw up nourishment from him. See that you go on growing in the Lord, and become strong and vigorous in the truth you were taught. Let your lives overflow with joy and thanksgiving for all he has done." (Colossians 2:6–7)

"Don't be impatient. Wait for the Lord, and he will come and save you! Be brave, stouthearted, and courageous. Yes, wait and he will help you." (Psalm 27:14)

"The Christian who is pure and without fault, from God the Father's point of view, is the one who takes care of orphans and widows, and who remains true to the Lord—not soiled and dirtied by his contacts with the world." (James 1:27)

"But now the Lord who created you, O Israel, says: Don't be afraid, for I have ransomed you; I have called you by name; you are mine. When you go through deep waters and great trouble, I will be with you. When you go through rivers of difficulty, you will not drown! When you walk through the fire of oppression, you will not be burned up—the flames will not consume you. For I am the Lord your God, your Savior, the Holy One of Israel." (Isaiah 43:1–3a)

In this world, you will have troubles. Nevertheless, as Jesus (in John 16:33) says, "Be courageous! I have conquered the world" (HCSB). We must strive to remain confident and joyful. Get up and step out either against or into every challenge! Do not be afraid or ever believe your best days have already passed. Step up into God's plan, and he will do amazing things through you! Consider this relevant passage:

> "You have turned on my light! The Lord my God has made my darkness turn to light. Now in your strength I can scale any wall, attack any troop. . . . He fills me with strength and protects me wherever I go. He gives me the surefootedness of a mountain goat upon the crags. He leads me safely along the top of the cliffs. He prepares me for battle and gives me strength to draw an iron bow!" (Psalm 18:28–29, 32–34)

As we have discussed, Christ calls us to be both salt and light to others in this world. We as salt are to prevent the decay of society as best we can, just as table salt preserves. We add flavor to the world, in addition to making others thirst for God by our speech and our actions. As light, which exposes and attracts things (even bugs like mosquitoes) to itself, we are to show others the truth and bring them to Christ, the true light of our dark world!

We should pray and ask God to fill us and to use us and to tell us what he would have us do, as we empty ourselves before him and fully submit to him. If we risk nothing and do not step out, we will never accomplish the amazing and exciting adventure ride that he has planned for us, that which truly will be the time of our lives!

We must ask God to use us to bring hope, joy, peace, problem-solving, nourishment, encouragement, deepening of faith, and the reduction of pain and loneliness and suffering to others by touching their lives in the name of Christ. Let us show these broken and lost ones how infinitely valuable they truly are in God's sight. We need to let them know about the major plans he has in store for them!

***

Let us now look at several of the different pitfalls that commonly confront us in this world. Let's start with money. You know the old saying, "You cannot take it with you," meaning that when you die, any earthly goods and riches, no matter how many or how few, will stay here in this world.

However, do you know that you can take your riches to heaven with you if, while here in this place, you employ them for Christ's kingdom advancement by using them for others for the benefit of their souls? We are told in Matthew 5 to store up our treasures not here but in heaven. The question is: what will be left in your cold, dead hands when you die your earthly death? Paradoxically, it will only be what you gave away in his name that remains with you! You can bring these riches up to heaven. They will solidify your victor's crown. Consider these verses:

> "Beware that in your plenty you don't forget the Lord your God and begin to disobey him. . . . Always remember that it is the Lord your God who gives you power to become rich." (Deuteronomy 8:11, 18)

> "Throw away your money! Toss it out like worthless rubbish, for it will have no value in that day of wrath. It will neither satisfy nor feed you, for your love of money is the reason for your sin." (Ezekiel 7:19)

***

Rise and Soar

Let's next look at theft. This can include lying on work expenses or time cards, tax cheating, or even removing small things from work like office supplies. Revelation says God's wrath is indeed coming to all who do these things. We must, therefore, fully avoid these at even the smallest degree, allowing ourselves no other gods before him, our one true God.

Nevertheless, since we all, even the staunchest of Christians, will commit such sins at times due to the hardness of every human heart, we must continually repent, truly trying to change our sin patterns, our thoughts, and our actions. And we must return to him daily.

***

Okay, what about sexual immorality? Unfortunately, this is a very common major pitfall, a cliff that many fall off in our world today. It is defined as anything sexual besides that which occurs between one man and one woman together in a marriage relationship. It includes the use of pornography, as well as pre- or extra-marital intercourse, same-gender relationships, adultery, masturbation, and other sexual sins.

Yet, its pull can be so strong. How do we combat it? The only way to achieve a complete and lasting victory is by using God's Word to develop an aversion to the sin. Then you will not allow it to draw you into its trap. You must then do your best to avoid it. However, it is paramount to understand that you alone, as a human being, cannot ever steer completely clear of this (nor any other addiction-sin type) long-term without his help! Sure, you may pull yourself away from it for a week, a month or two, maybe even a few years. But without Christ and his Word to protect you, it is a pattern that you will most likely fall back into in time, given the right circumstances. We therefore need to read and incorporate God's Word into our hearts to ever have any chance of truly achieving a lasting change.

As an important aside, we must not view sexuality as impure or dirty. Appropriate sexuality in the pure and good form that God intended, that is, in a marriage between a man and a woman, is a true gift from our heavenly Father.

***

Okay, how about anger? Anger, we must remember, always stems from either hurt, pride, insecurity, or fear. It is an emotion we all encounter daily in others as well as in ourselves. Knowing that there is a reason behind anger helps us to deal appropriately with it. And how should we best do so? Well, getting back to that all-important principle, what does God's Word say about it? Look at James 1:19–20: "Dear brothers, don't ever forget that it is best to listen much, speak little, and not become angry; for anger doesn't make us good, as God demands that we must be."

You can see an emerging pattern here: whatever the situation, remember that God's Word holds the answers. Consider Matthew 4, where Jesus is being tempted in the desert. He uses God's Word to rebuff all three of Satan's offers. He withstands these temptations and makes the evil one flee.

***

What about regret? If you are stuck in past mistakes, sorrows, grief, or sins, you are living each day in unnecessary torment, focusing so much on the past that you are throwing away your todays as well as your tomorrows. Ask him to help you let go and begin living for him all the rest of your days. Cast all your cares on Christ.

"Let him have all your worries and cares, for he is always thinking about you and watching everything that concerns you." (1 Peter 5:7)

"Don't worry about anything; instead, pray about everything; tell God your needs, and don't forget to thank him for his answers. If you do this, you will experience God's peace, which is far more wonderful than the human mind can understand. His peace will keep your thoughts and your hearts quiet and at rest as you trust in Christ Jesus." (Philippians 4:6–7)

***

What about judging others? We are constantly making judgments day in and day out. Of course, we must make many daily judgments to survive in this world. However, with respect to judging other people, we must try to judge deeds and actions only, not the hearts or the motivations behind them. Matthew 7:1 says, "Judge not, and you will not be judged." Okay, but again, in our lives we must make many judgments, for example, regarding our children, family entertainment choices, or friends. So, we naturally make assessments and then form opinions, which then allow us to make choices based upon these judgments.

However, it is dangerous and nearly impossible to correctly judge another person's heart. We cannot know the motive behind their action. We do not know their past, nor can we ever stand in their shoes. Only God can know their hearts. While men see the outside, God sees inside and knows the heart. So, leave the verdict to God rather than judging for yourself. We can and should judge actions. But we cannot judge the heart or the motivation behind these acts.

Calling others out for their misdeeds is to be done for their benefit by pointing out their errors and trying to change them positively.

It also protects innocent victims from further abuse while leaving the actual judgement to our Lord.

Regarding our judging of apparent nonbelievers, let us look at this:

> "So be careful not to jump to conclusions before the Lord returns as to whether someone is a good servant or not. When the Lord comes, he will turn on the light so that everyone can see exactly what each one of us is really like, deep down in our hearts." (1 Corinthians 4:5)

This refers to Christians judging non-Christians. However, what is our responsibility if we know a self-professed Christian who continues to sin, whether it be drunkenness, substance abuse, sexually immorality, sins against his family, or greed, or cheating? 1 Corinthians 5:11—13 states that it is our job to deal with Christians who sin. If unrepentantly persistent, we are to cut them off before they spread and infect us all like a cancer:

> "You are not to keep company with anyone who claims to be a brother Christian but indulges in sexual sins, or is greedy, or is a swindler, or worships idols, or is a drunkard, or abusive. Don't even eat lunch with such a person. It isn't our job to judge outsiders. But it certainly is our job to judge and deal strongly with those who are members of the church and who are sinning in these ways. God alone is the Judge of those on the outside. But you yourselves must deal with this man and put him out of your church."

This is ultimately meant for the sinner's benefit:

"Take no part in the worthless pleasures of evil and darkness, but instead, rebuke and expose them. . . . But when you expose them, the light shines in upon their sin and shows it up, and when they see how wrong they really are, some of them may even become children of light! That is why God says in the Scriptures, 'Awake, O sleeper, and rise up from the dead; and Christ shall give you light.'" (Ephesians 5:11, 13–14)

***

What about bitterness and negative thinking, which occur so often in dealing with the problems of this world? Will you have problems? Absolutely. Do you know what you need to best help with these problems? There is but one answer: Jesus Christ in your life!

He wants us to refuse negative thinking in dealing with this world's issues. Remember how he reassures us that "I have overcome the world." If we focus negatively upon all our issues, we may turn angry and bitter. If, however, we think positively in our trials, we can rise above those dark woods. We help ourselves and become a saving beacon, a guiding lighthouse or signal fire, if you will, for others who are stumbling and wandering down below in disabling darkness.

Ask God for insight into your trials. There is a reason why everything occurs. Ask for the ability to think positively in storms, in dark times. Realize they are temporary and that they pale in comparison to your eternal reward.

When out camping, have you ever wandered from camp's safety out into the darkness to collect wood, to fish, or to view the stars, but then get turned around? In trying to get back to camp, you stumble around lost for a bit? Yet, then how do you feel when you finally see your campfire shining out through the dark trees, guiding you home?

One cold and rainy night I went out into the deep woods and purposely got lost wearing only cotton clothes, which offered little protection, and carrying just a flint and steel. After getting lost, I made a fire to dry out and warm up. I stayed there until nearly 3 a.m., then thought about going home to a warm and dry bed. But there was no moon, and I had no other reliable way to tell direction. One route home looked good. But being unsure, I built up an extensive fire in case my attempted direction home was wrong and I thus wound up getting even more lost. I then could look for that firelight through the trees in the hills where I was spending the night. The light would at least guide me back to protective warmth until the morning light allowed me to find my way out of those woods. I would be safe until the dark night was over and I could clearly see my way home. Christ is like that fire. He acts as our home base at all times, even when we are badly lost:

"For then you will prosper and succeed in whatever you do. Haven't I commanded you: be strong and courageous? Do not be afraid or discouraged, for the LORD your God is with you wherever you go." (Joshua 1:8–9 HCSB)

***

Next, let us examine what is called hardening your heart. Unfortunately, this is something that happens relatively easily in our world. One of the Bible's frequent exhortations is, "If today you hear his voice, harden not your hearts." This means that we are not to fight against him. We rather are to ask, invite, and, yes, actively seek out his calling, his Holy Spirit!

He is perpetually reaching out to us. Each day that you choose to avoid his voice and ignore his call, while staying in rebellion and sin against God, you lose a few more of the stepping-stones on your pathway back to him. Another plank is lost off your bridge into heaven, and you progressively care less and less. You will eventually barely hear the Spirit's voice at all as you further grow to care not at all about him. There is a point when you cannot hear or respond any longer. The voice becomes silent, not because he pulls it away or turns it off but because you have learned all too well to ignore it. You shut it out of your soul to keep it out of your life!

Consider the example of hot oven pans being handled without pot holders or of acid being handled without gloves. The first few times you do such, these are extremely painful experiences. However, as you continue to do them more and more often, the skin of your hands scars, and the sensation of pain from the heat or the acid burns becomes no longer perceptible.

These examples apply to our heart. Once this state is reached, how hard it is to ever reverse gears and return to God! You become blind to your true state, which requires God. You are blinded even to the fact that his very assistance is needed for that next heartbeat and that next breath. You can no longer see what you need to fill your life optimally and fully. And thus, you will never obtain true peace, joy, fulfillment, nor rescue. You instead become more and more entrenched in sin. You are its blinded captive, its slave!

The Book of Revelation mentions several blinders, or things that make us not truly see our sin. The first it calls the works of their hands— idolatry. This means those small-g gods that we worship, our idols, become demonic if they are worshiped instead of our one true Lord. A second blinder mentioned is murder, which, beyond the obvious definition, includes hatred of others or a bitterness of spirit against people. A third blinder to our awareness of sin mentioned here is sorceries, things we use to dull our senses. These include addictions and agents, both licit and illicit substances such as alcohol, prescription or illegal drugs, and even excessive food, video games, TV, and the like. Many people try to dull their pains and their senses until they are no longer able to realize their pains are the very things that God is employing in his attempts to bring them back to him!

I often tell my patients there is no pill that is going to fully take away their depression or anxiety. But I do know what will. Rather than trying to cover these issues up with medications, if they do not know the Lord, I will strongly recommend they begin the process of seeking him, as he is the only one who can heal their hearts and give them peace of mind. I do my best to resist prescribing medications until I am certain that people know the Lord (or at least have heard his good news) because I tell them I believe God is trying to speak to them. He wants to get their attention through what is happening to them, and I do not feel it to be the correct thing to do to try to cover these problems up with medications.

Again, God uses problems and trials to bring us back to him or to mold us into what he desires us to be. This is the root reason for our sufferings. Any substances that are contrarily used to keep us numb to our lostness and our godless state actually keep us blindly groping about in the dark. They only aid us in delaying or avoiding a confrontation with whatever it is that God is wanting to tell us.

***

"For the wise and fool both die, and in the days to come both will be long forgotten. . . . it is all so irrational; all is foolishness, chasing the wind. . . . So I decided that there was nothing better for a man to do than to enjoy his food and drink and his job. Then I realized that even this pleasure is from the hand of God. For who can eat or enjoy apart from him? For

God gives those who please him wisdom, knowledge, and joy."
(Ecclesiastes 2:16–17, 24–26a)

"I have learned to be content in whatever circumstances I am.
I know both how to have a little, and I know how to have a
lot. In any and all circumstances I have learned the secret of
being content—whether well fed or hungry, whether in abun-
dance or in need. I am able to do all things through Him who
strengthens me." (Philippians 4:11b–13 HCSB)

Do you want God, and therefore, do you want Christ, to be present with you always as you go through this crazy life? You can be certain that he always remains with you by checking a few items:

First, do you give excessive attention and time to other things besides him? As with anyone you love, the more time you spend with them and the more you invest in that relationship, the better it becomes. Do you spend enough time with God, speaking with and worshiping and praying to him? Strive to make him real in your life. He will not disappoint you!

An excellent indicator of our hearts and our true passions is how we use our time, our minds, and our bodies. For example, consider the relationship between a boyfriend and girlfriend or with a spouse. If a couple spends no time together, their relationship suffers. It cannot grow or remain healthy. This same principle applies in our relationship with our heavenly Father. Again, our Father God says that he will not share his glory with anyone or anything else!

So, do you love or spend more time with or serve or fear something else more than God? If so, then that thing or person is an idol as much as pagan statues were in the ancient world. If you worship an idol, God, who loves you too much to yet bless you fully or to be with you in an optimal way as your loving Father, will punish you. He cannot positively reinforce your idolatry with blessings, just as an earthly father would hold back on some blessings for his badly misbehaving child. That father would still provide all necessary food, shelter, warmth, and clothing. Yet, he may well not pick up that extra toy gift surprise for his child or buy that ice cream cone on the way home or read an extra story at bedtime. He would be much more likely to consider doing those things for a child who was being good. Consider: "The one who will not use the rod hates his Son, but the one who loves him disciplines him diligently" (Proverbs 13:24 HCSB).

Yes, even if you are his misbehaving child, he still blesses you with continued breaths and heartbeats—hopefully! He provides for you. But he is persistently calling you to give up that distracting sin and run back to him to receive the fullest blessings that he can give!

Second, in your life now, do you outwardly disobey God? Do you do things that you know are wrong? Like any disobedient child, this automatically puts you at odds with God, your heavenly Father. Once again, such actions limit his blessings. For example, consider a child who is discovered to have stolen money from a parent's purse or wallet. Like God our Father, the parent already knows what their child did and will still provide and care for the child. But they will not give additional blessings as freely. What best heals the situation is, of course, for the child to admit his error, say he is sorry, and try his best not to do it again. Does this not then heal the injured relationship, allowing a positive progression onward from there? In the same way, we need to admit our sin to God our Father, ask forgiveness and repent of it, and prepare to receive his bountiful blessings, which he wishes to heap upon us!

Third, do you resist him as he tries to direct you into the doorways and paths that he has specifically designed you for and that he wants you to follow? Do you do what he asks you to do when he puts something on your heart? Is there a person to help or to witness to, a job, a family, a mission, or a church work that he is calling you to? 2 Timothy 1:3 says, "My only purpose in life is to please him." Consider what would happen if we all tried this perspective! Do so and wait and see the amazing and plentiful blessings your loving Father will shower upon you!

In such light, consider this prayer: Dear Lord, I do want you to be fully with me so I can receive your greatest gifts and blessings and grow to know you better with each passing day. Please help me to be obedient to you and to give you my full attention. Help me give you all the love and worship you truly deserve. Help me to rely more on you than on myself and my own personal abilities and tools. Please help me to realize that these are all gifts from you. Grant me a real and complete relationship with you, God, and show me what you need me to do. Then, with your help, I will do it. Thank you, Lord Jesus, for loving and for saving me! May I keep my eyes ever fixed upon you through the rest of my worldly life until I see you face-to-face!

***

Over my fifty-plus years in this crazy world of ours, I have learned a few lessons. In trying to best deal with this world, the following are what I refer to as my Ten Rules for a Very Good Day. Feel free to add your own!

Number 1: Watch the sunrise, thanking God for another day and asking for his Spirit to fill and use you as he would in the new day.

Number 2: Realize and count your blessings.

Number 3: Smile and laugh often.

Number 4: Enjoy your family, your friends, and your pets.

Number 5: Seek and talk with God regularly through daily Scripture reading and prayer.

Number 6: Get outside to enjoy God's amazing natural works and their beauty. Unplug from technology as often as you can.

Number 7: Live boldly for him. Try your best to model Christ's example, and tell others of his love and his salvation offer.

Number 8: Don't worry! He's got you in the palm of his hand!

Number 9: Praise and thank him at day's end.

Number 10: Sleep well under the safety of his wings.

PART II

XIII. The Big Questions

We have thus far covered many major points and issues; using these as existing foundations, now is the appropriate time to address and discuss what I call the Big Questions. These are the recurring questions that we all have, whether believer or nonbeliever, at least once in our lifetimes, and sometimes quite regularly. If you have not thought on some of these yet, chances are that you will, and you will certainly meet other people who will ask about these, thus it helps to think on these things ahead of time so that you have already formed your thoughts on such when the questions arise. Let's get started.

1. Why Does God Allow Evil, Suffering, Sorrow, and Pain?

I feel this is the most asked question by both unbelievers and Christians alike. It is also typically the nonbeliever's first and foremost reason that they will state for their doubts about God's existence. If we can help someone understand this, it can be extremely beneficial in easing their misconceptions and doubts about God.

So, how should we respond when persons ask, "How can God even exist when there is so much evil?" I like to approach it first by explaining that part of the answer is that we have free choice, or a free will, which God has given to us. One of the very best gifts he has given to us all is the ability to be aware of who and what we are, as the created children of God. It is indeed a great privilege to have such a free will, to be able to say yes or no to anything, even to God.

We reviewed how, since man's sinful mistake in the garden of Eden, the human heart, left alone, always leans toward evil. I know people who doubt this, who feel that man is inherently good. I ask them to look at examples from the animal kingdom. It is a dog-eat-dog world, tooth-fang-and-claw. I have seen brown and grizzly bears trying to eat bear cubs, some genetically proven to have been even their very own progeny! Even the cerebrally highest species, such as chimpanzees, treat each other extremely poorly and often with great malice.

Extrapolating to mankind, we, despite our more advanced brains, are not too far beyond them, unless we hold to God's higher standard. And, in the case of a human mind that becomes bent on evil and even preplanning it, can it not be argued that humans are much worse than those in the nonhuman societies?

Beyond the animal kingdoms, over my five-plus decades of dealing with the kingdom of man, I have seen five major motivations for every human action, that is to say, actions apart from those with Christian intent. These five motivating factors are either: power, pride, money or financial gain, something relative to sexuality, or a need for acceptance by others. I believe that if one cuts to the basic motivation behind any deed committed from a purely human purpose, at least one of these factors will be the underlying etiology or etiologies, the foundational motivation for such action.

Rise and Soar

Further, look at Revelation: at the end of the thousand-year reign of Christ on earth, despite ten centuries of the most perfect world since Eden, with much less suffering, sickness, and tears, countless numbers of evil men "more numerous than grains of sand" (according to the reference) will yet rise against God and his people.

Therefore, God, by our free will that he gifts to us, has created the potential for evil, but humans make evil reality by choosing evil things! God made evil possible but man made it reality. God then allowed it because he does not wish to force himself upon anyone. Think. Can you really force someone to love you? And if you do so, is this love?

So, we conclude that our world's evil exists by human choice, as is evidenced by these verses:

"They have thrown away the laws of God and despised the word of the Holy One of Israel." (Isaiah 5:24b)

"So it was that when they gave God up and would not even acknowledge him, God gave them up to doing everything their evil minds could think of. Their lives became full of every kind of wickedness and sin, of greed and hate, envy, murder, fighting, lying, bitterness, and gossip." (Romans 1:28–29)

"For we naturally love to do evil things that are just the opposite from the things that the Holy Spirit tells us to do; and the good things we want to do when the Spirit has his way with us are just the opposite of our natural desires. These two forces within us are constantly fighting each other to win control over us . . . But when you follow your own wrong inclinations, your lives will produce these evil results: impure thoughts, eagerness for lustful pleasure, idolatry, spiritism (that is, encouraging the activity of demons), hatred and fighting, jealousy and anger, constant effort to get the best for yourself, complaints and criticisms, the feeling that everyone else is wrong except those in your own little group—and there will be wrong doctrine, envy, murder, drunkenness, wild parties, and all that sort of thing . . . . But when the Holy Spirit controls our lives, he will produce this kind of fruit in us: love, joy, peace, patience, kindness, goodness, faithfulness, gentleness and self-control . . . Those who belong to Christ have nailed their natural evil desires to his cross and crucified them there." (Galatians 5:17, 19–24)

***

Logically, one cannot have free will without the categories of good things and bad things coexisting. If only one of these choices exists, then there is no ability to choose from one classification scheme or the other. Evil possibilities must exist as an available choice or else you would have no true choice. Our love for God and each other must always involve a choice that includes the alternative, which is hatred. When we choose evil rather than God, suffering will result. You thus cannot create a world with free will without the possible choice of sins and evil being within it.

When one rejects God, and thereby chooses to follow a different path for their life's journey, God then allows them to proceed upon their own way. He does not force his path upon people. However, because this is not God's way, this straying from his path usually has poor, at times even evil, consequences.

Also, we are only able to define evil because we can compare it to God's goodness. God is the measuring standard. If there were no God here and thus no good, and evil was all that we knew, would we even recognize evil as bad or as the opposite of good?

Therefore, it logically follows that we can only recognize and label something as evil if it diverges from God's standard. We use his supreme nature as our measuring stick!

God is never evil. Consider Psalm 111:7–8: "All he does is just and good, and all his laws are right, for they are formed from truth and goodness and stand firm forever." Also, as per James 1:17, "Whatever is good and perfect comes to us from God, the Creator of all light, and he shines forever without change or shadow."

So, a great counter question to why evil exists is to ask in response to doubters, "So, if there is no God, as you propose, how then do you explain there being so much good in this world?" Again, God must be the standard, that supreme good by which we classify and judge good and evil. A secondary question is, "So, if there is no God, then where do we get this measuring standard?"

***

Ponder how one can explain that over 90 percent of the world's people who have ever lived, most existing in much more dire and painful circumstances than we do, have believed in a divine Creator God? The world's pains and problems may seem to not justify the belief in a good God, yet he still has been almost universally believed upon throughout the ages. How can one ever explain this away?

As an example, I will never forget seeing the account of three young North African boys. They were orphaned by jihadists who had executed their Christian parents. In a photo, they hugged each other tightly with big smiles while standing in the doorless entry of their makeshift hovel of wood, sheet metal, and plastic scraps. And the hand-painted sign over the home read, "God Is Good."

***

Consider why, if everything was good all the time and there was no evil, would we even need God? Everyone would go happily along throughout life, with all things seemingly perfect, never needing to seek God for help or support. Therefore, God would receive no glory or recognition for all he has done and continues to do for us.

***

Additionally, it is not fair to look only at the world's evil and ignore its good. As above, there is much good in this world, and there exists an interplay between both good and bad that must be recognized. Open your eyes to see it! You cannot comment upon this world's evils without considering its goodness as well.

***

More so, while it can certainly be hard for our human minds to come to this conclusion, all suffering does result in some good. Romans 8:28 states that all things work together for good to those who love the Lord and walk in his ways. As hard as it is to see at times, he always has a plan and is always in control, working out everything for good, albeit of course in his timing, according to his will, and for his glory!

God works out all things for good to those who know and walk with him! Scripture tells us this, and we can look at examples of how things first seen as perceived evils are later viewed as good things. There are times when evil results in ultimate good, even though it may go unseen by us.

Consider the example of nuisance bears. These are bears that become unsafe for both people and themselves if they become habituated, meaning they get too close to or become too unafraid of people. Should that happen, nuisance bears are caught in traps and moved to safety. The bruin does not like the time it spends in the trap. Yet, once snared and moved for release into a better and safer natural sanctuary, he is in a better position. Or consider physicians like me. When we give an injection or perform a surgical procedure, we often cause some temporary pain and suffering. Yet our goal is always to produce a good, a healing. Similarly, God sends trials our way to produce a healing of our hearts and souls through a deepening of our relationship with him! Consider this relevant scripture: "How enviable the man whom God corrects! Oh, do not despise the chastening of the Lord when you sin. For though he wounds, he binds and heals again. He will deliver you again and again so that no evil can touch you" (Job 5:17–19).

As another, and I feel the optimal, example, let's look at the worst tragedy ever, that of Jesus's crucifixion on Calvary. It was a great injustice and a savage death wrought by evil. It nevertheless resulted in the single best event in human history, although the disciples could not see any good in it at first! Yet, once Christ rose, the benefit of salvation for us all because of this tragedy became very clear!

Therefore, God may tolerate bad things, such as starvation, cancer and other illnesses, poverty, crime, or natural disasters like floods and tornados for a time because he foresees that people will become better and will turn to him from their pain. Therefore, he may not immediately intervene miraculously in a beneficial way. We see no good in suffering. But as occurred at the cross, God has a plan we need to trust. We must allow him his time to bring forth his good and to bring us closer to him. So, God is not being evil, nor does he turn his eyes from evil, by allowing pain to exist for a time.

"You punished them in order to turn them toward your laws; but . . . they were proud and wouldn't listen and continued to sin. You were patient with them for many years. . . . But in your great mercy you did not destroy them completely or abandon them forever. What a gracious and merciful God you are!" (Nehemiah 9:29–31)

We learn from the bad things. They form and forge our souls into what God needs them be to accomplish the unique and special task he put us here to do. Consider how a diamond is formed. It begins as carbon deep in the earth and would never reach its brilliantly valuable end state without enduring overwhelming pressure and stress! Consider:

"So you should realize that, as a man punishes his son, the Lord punishes you to help you." (Deuteronomy 8:5)

"For God sometimes uses sorrow in our lives to help us turn away from sin and seek eternal life. We should never regret his sending it." (2 Corinthians 7:10a)

Jesus learned obedience from suffering as per Hebrews 5:8. We are not here for our comfort but, instead, for training in preparation for eternity. We learn, grow, and mature through hard times. If the world was without suffering, we would all be spoiled brats without any need for the love of God or for loving others.

***

Since we don't have complete knowledge of the universe's workings, we cannot definitively say why God allows evil. Yet, one does not have to say exactly why in order to be a Christian. Realize, instead, that God and evil can and do coexist until the end of this world, when we

Rise and Soar

are told all evil will be eliminated as it was in Eden, in God's initial, perfect creation before human beings messed it up so badly! Consider Proverbs 20:24, "Since the Lord is directing our steps, why try to understand everything that happens along the way?"

Being reassured by this ultimate ending, we know that God and Christ are the final answer to all evils. God is not the cause of evil, nor is our God one who simply neglects to do anything about it. Therefore, the existence of evil is a problem only for nonbelievers. It does not trouble Christians who know that Jesus is the final answer to evil. If you have done evil, he has paid for it with his blood, if you will only believe and repent and stop your evildoing. Or, if you are a victim of evil, fear not! There will be justice. He will either make the evildoer pay or will cover him with his blood at the judgment, depending upon that person's ultimate response to the question of belief in Jesus!

Through Christ, then, evil is addressed and taken care of by our Lord. He will either judge or justify all persons who have ever lived. He overcomes evil and is its only true answer. Evil is, therefore, only a problem for those who refuse him! "I will see that right prevails. My mercy and justice are coming soon; your salvation is on the way" (Isaiah 51:4–5).

Okay, you may ask, but how do God and Christ bear the immense burden of all our current suffering? The answer is they already did it. And they did so once and for all! Christ entered our world. He became a human being to bear it, and thus he knows our pains, having also suffered. How can you not love him for this, for what he has done for you?

Remember also how our ongoing sins and evils hurt him. Our sins are part of the burden he suffered on Calvary. So, how can we knowingly, repeatedly, and purposely sin now, knowing that each sin hurts him so much more?

We do it because we are sinners, despite our efforts. Nevertheless, in knowing him and growing in him, his thoughts become our thoughts, and his actions become our actions—and increasingly so over time. Therefore, we also become part of the answer to evil during our lifetimes here!

***

To allow us to make sense of evil and suffering, we need to stop seeing the world from our self-centered view. Instead, we must expand our minds to see it as it is God-centered. Remember that not just evil, but all our life experiences, both good and bad, will find true meaning and answers only in a God-centered world. We thus should glorify him forever! We should let the light of the Son enlighten and optimize all our views and understandings, like the physical sun's light allows us to stop stumbling about in the darkness of night!

We need to thank him not just for the good, for our sunrises, but also for our storms and our sunsets, such as illness, pain, hardships, or death. Just think: are the most beautiful sunrises and sunsets those without clouds or those with them, such as when a storm or a front is breaking? Going through or enduring these clouds (as representatives of our trials) will lead to a more beautiful time in our lives. The sunrise becomes so glorious after a night of bad storms!

If we want to be with God, we need to step out and go to his cross. There, all suffering can be laid, as this is where the focal point of suffering is located! Following Christ means that we, too, will suffer and obtain our own scars. They will bring us closer to him. Suffering reinforces people's faith instead of making them question God. Most who do object and question are not actually experiencing the pain. They are more often the well-fed, the comfortable, the well-to-do.

Those who suffer are more likely to be stronger believers. For example, simply look at the strong testimonies and bold evangelism of those Christians suffering extreme persecution in places like North Korea, the most persecutory country toward Christians in the world today. From them we conclude that severe suffering is as likely to strengthen one's faith as it is to cause disbelief or denial of God altogether.

***

Further, Christ calls us to minister to those who are suffering. We are asked to be part of the answer here in this dark world. We are asked to clothe, feed, warm, visit, encourage, and do other good works. When you ask God why he allows evil, he asks you the same question! And yes, he did do something about evil. He made you, so you can go out there and oppose it and thereby help to reduce it. Christians, therefore, need to live out their faith by helping others and by embodying Christ's love to them. Consider Matthew 5:44–45, "But I say: Love your enemies! Pray for those who persecute you! In that way you will be acting as true sons of your Father in heaven."

Christ is the answer! He entered our world and suffered for us, making our suffering meaningful and manageable in light of his sufferings. Of all the world's religions, only Christianity's God is a suffering god. And he endured incredibly severe agonies: Christ on his cross and the Father in sacrificing his only Son.

Certainly, this question of human suffering is very hard. But stamping his cross over it does let us see suffering in a different light. It lets us see our afflictions in the shadow of Jesus's suffering on his cross. And in so doing, we must remember that we do not possess God's foresight and reasoning. We can never fully understand why suffering is allowed in our world. We must trust and continue onward with God's will and

God's work until our time in this world, and thus our work for him here, is finished.

Becoming a Christian does not mean our lives are suddenly from then on going to be perfect. No, we are still here in this dark, imperfect world, albeit temporarily. We still fight and struggle, many times seemingly in vain. We grieve and we mourn. Yet it is different for us because we do none of this without hope. We have faith that Jesus will one day make everything right and perfect for every one of us who knows him! Consider his promises in these verses:

> "Those who mourn are fortunate! For they shall be comforted." (Matthew 5:4)

> "What happiness there is for you who are now hungry, for you are going to be satisfied! What happiness there is for you who weep, for the time will come when you shall laugh with joy!" (Luke 6:21)

> "Come to me and I will give you rest—all of you who work so hard beneath a heavy yoke. Wear my yoke—for it fits perfectly—and let me teach you; for I am gentle and humble, and you shall find rest for your souls; for I give you only light burdens." (Matthew 11:28–30)

Here in Matthew, Christ tells us we shall have burdens. If you are a parent, don't you allow your kids to endure hardship, a trial or some suffering, perhaps even for a prolonged duration, so they can achieve, become, or gain something better?

Perhaps those times when our heavenly Father allows us to endure hardship, he, as in the prodigal son tale, is taking us down a few pegs so we can not only hear his voice, his call to us, but also so we will listen!

Why would we seek or realize that we needed God if everything was perfect for each of us all the time?

***

In summary, we are all God's creations, but not all of us are his children. Hell is full of good people who lived good lives and may well have done many good things. They may have even believed in God. Yet, they remained independent. They never established a relationship with the Father or his Son! If we do not have a relationship with God and with Jesus, the question of evil and suffering is a difficult one to manage. Yet, alternatively, when we have a relationship with them, we receive their gift of peace of mind and reassurance. If you are not in a relationship with God, then seek him out now. Ask him to help you find him and receive such peace for yourself!

Our world is a fallen world. It is not at all the one God had originally set up. That perfect place is evident only in his goodness and holiness.

Someday, we will be back in his heaven, the New Jerusalem. Yet, while we are here now, he is still a just and a fair God, although his justice is not always timely as per our human view and not always fair, to our perception of such. Yes, all is for good, but only in his perfect timing and in his will, not ours. And all is for his glory, not for ours! He will allot justice but not necessarily as we feel it should be, in either its severity or its timing.

But take heart! He will always take care of us, making all that occurs be for his glory, and thus, by definition, ultimately for a good outcome, as hard as it can be for us to see it now. Yet, if we are in a close relationship with him, we are somewhat able to understand, as much as our little worldly minds will allow.

More importantly, that understanding gives us a true sense of peace through all trying circumstances. Lean on God. Give up your trials to his one, wise, all-knowing being, and let him take the reins. Ask him to show you what he wants you to do. Ask him to strengthen your belief and your trust and to help you realize that he is in total control. And when he then shows what he wants you to do, be sure to do it! Remember Christ's own words: "I have told you all this so that you will have peace of heart and mind. Here on earth you will have many trials and sorrows; but cheer up, for I have overcome the world" (John 16:33).

***

Another commonly raised and related question is, "Why do bad things happen to good people?" Let's look at this basic premise. We have already established that there are no good people or perfect people. We are all sinners. God sees all as bad, yet he sees us as bad in one of two ways: either as those who know him and thus are forgiven of their badness, or as those who do not know him and thus are not forgiven. C. S. Lewis once said, "When you understand the sinfulness of man, the question is not why we do suffer, but rather, why do we not suffer more?"

***

There is no other answer that can easily explain or help us to comprehend the existence of evil and suffering. The only real options are either that there is no loving God, or that there is one, yet one beyond our understanding who uses all evils for eventual good. Again, for verification, we need only look to the best answer to this question in all of history, the crucifixion and resurrection of Christ.

"You have sorrow now, but I will see you again and then you will rejoice; and no one can rob you of that joy." (John 16:22)

I above discussed two severe storms I experienced on Alaskan waters. Both threatened to sink the boat I was in. With one, our engine died during a big blow in Glacier Bay, and we were forced to navigate by sail only. All the while, gigantic waves broke over the eighteen-foot vessel, and it was tossed wildly back and forth. (This was the only time I have ever been seasick!)

Suddenly, the boom swung round unexpectedly and struck the more experienced sailor (the boat's owner) smartly in the head, and it seemed I had to handle the storm alone. I remember glassing different rocky outcroppings and beaches, trying to decide which ones were best to run aground upon if absolutely needed. Given the storm's great fury, it seemed beyond my control, no matter what I decided or tried to do. Fortunately, the sailor remained lucid enough to help get us through the gale safely.

In the other storm, it was dark, and we were caught in a sudden, fierce gale while in a small skiff trying to get back to our larger vessel. The waves pushed us nearly vertical at times, with the boat sometimes going fully perpendicular to the ocean's surface. I remember planning to remove my hip waders to use as flotation devices in order to try to swim out of the frigid seas to a shoreline should we capsize, which miraculously never happened.

Similarly, we each have our own storms that we manage, our own gales and tornados of life, which oft blow hard against us: jobs, family, illness, anxieties, responsibilities. We may be able to add and subtract some things while in our storms, yet other things get tossed in or pulled out beyond our control. We continually strive to gain footholds over these tempests, but we in realty cannot control or dictate much at all.

So how do we deal with these and avoid depression, worry, fatigue, or such? We must give these up to the Master of Storms. Let him take charge of your life's tempests, and then accept his peace, joy, fulfillment, and rescue!

Are you carrying your own heavy burden strapped crushingly across your back? God's view is that if you choose to do this, you are carrying it needlessly. Give it to him instead. Pray and keep on praying, firmly believing that he will lift it from you. Then all the while, by your improved relationship with him, he will help you bear it. You will no longer carry it alone!

***

Our questions about suffering, death, and evil should never be answered by stating that such are simply judgments or punishments hurled at us by an angry God. We should say, instead, that these problems are a result of choices, beginning with the disobedient choice of Adam and Eve and continuing in human beings ever since, whenever they persist in deliberately ignoring and disobeying God! Therefore, these problems in our world persist and multiply. And we see the result in the evil, the sadness, the trauma, and all those other consequences, which continue to grow worse by the day.

So, human beings make the choice to let sin enter and to stay in our world. Such was not a component of God's originally created world. God stepped in, however, in his being always loving and merciful, as he did not like to see us flounder and agonize in this morass of sin. Therefore, he intervened by sending his Son to redeem and to save us from ourselves and our bad choices, to pull us from the quagmire from which we are unable to extricate ourselves.

> "When Adam sinned, sin entered the entire human race. His sin spread death throughout all the world, so everything began to grow old and die, for all sinned. . . . What a contrast between Adam and Christ who was yet to come! And what a difference between man's sin and God's forgiveness! For this one man, Adam, brought death to many through his sin. But this one man, Jesus Christ, brought forgiveness to many through God's mercy. Adam's one sin brought the penalty of death to many, while Christ freely takes away many sins and gives glorious life instead. The sin of this one man, Adam, caused death to be king over all, but all who will take God's gift of forgiveness and acquittal are kings of life because of this one man, Jesus Christ. Yes, Adam's sin brought punishment to all, but Christ's righteousness makes men right with God, so that they can live. Adam caused many to be sinners because he disobeyed God, and Christ caused many to be made acceptable to God because he obeyed." (Romans 5:12, 14–19)

We must stop our bad choices, as these sins separate us from God and the blessings he wishes to give us! We tend to minimize sin by thinking, "I'm not as bad as so-and-so," and "It's not my fault," or "I can't help it." So, we deny any and all personal responsibility for our choices. We must instead, as Peter told the new church in Acts, take responsibility and make a conscious decision to turn from sin, repent, and return to God. We must pray for Jesus's help in this endeavor to help us overcome our temptations. Then we will avoid the sinful consequences we suffer as the result of giving in to such desires. Yes, these forces are very alluring and quite strong. But our Lord and Savior is stronger. Make him your strength, your tower, your rock, your anchor, and your lighthouse to remain fixed upon and to shield and protect you from sin's devastation for your life here and for your eternal soul!

Again, we cannot do this by ourselves. Our human hearts are not able to. Instead, ask for Christ's strength, and remain focused on him. It is solely with him alone that we can victoriously conquer!

Even when you feel you can endure no longer, when you are being torn down and cut deeply, being twisted and bent in your trial, allow yourself to be pushed down to your knees to communicate better with God. Realize that he is shaping you and making you into his perfect instrument for his specific purpose, which you are here to perform in this world.

Our commitment to Christ may exact a price beyond the expense of giving up or denying ourselves certain things. Following Jesus can bring suffering. But any suffering for the kingdom and for Christ only strengthens your heart, as you give up more of your own selfish being in order to gain more of him and to gain more for him as well! Suffering for him strengthens our relationship with Christ unlike any other experience.

While we are in the middle of our trials, we should not look at our situation but, rather, should strive to look up to Jesus. This lets us maintain a positive attitude in any and all circumstances, as Paul writes about. We then will always trust, having maximal confidence as we realize that God is indeed ever with us, forming and shaping us, as carbon under pressure transforms into diamonds and as young oaks in strong winds become stout hardwoods over time and through their trials.

Our own sufferings and trials are similarly productive and are used by God to either show us how far along we are in our spiritual growth and in our relationship with him or, alternatively, to reveal where we need to change and grow so we can better serve in his purposes for us!

But you may ask why. Why did someone need to get sick and die? Why did that accident disable me? Why did that person hurt me? Well, think in this way: why did Christ need to die? Let us examine such reasons: he died, first, to save all who believe on him and, second, to glorify God. This is the same with Christians. We are in him and he in us. In a similar way, each one of our problems, our heartaches and tragedies, illnesses, sorrows, and evils will ultimately glorify God, although it is so hard to see it when in the throes of the dark storm. But take heart—no storm lasts forever! They blow through. Then the light floods back in, illuminating all in a much more striking and brilliant manner, like the sunlight on a sleek and wet landscape after a summer or an autumnal rainstorm.

Think of the diamond example above. The diamond begins as a speck of carbonic matter on top of the ground. It then gets buried and subjected to extreme pressures, darkness, heat, and cold. Without all of these, no gemstone would ever result from that speck of dirt.

Or consider a seed that will only bear fruit and multiply if buried in the dark underground and subjected to extreme heat and cold and wetness, causing it to break apart. This is a key step in its germination and leads to its later bearing of good fruit!

Yet, what if the speck or the seed decided instead to say, "No, I refuse the pressure, the dark, the cold, the heat!" If they could choose to stay comfortable above the ground, neither would ever become anything but themselves. They would never change or grow for the better, not ever bearing fruit or doing anything for anyone else.

Similarly, dying to our old selves is exactly what Christ calls us to do. It is therefore what we must step out and do while having the faith that he will help us. We must allow our new selves to bear the fruit that derives from his specific plan for us. This is what God calls us to do, to embrace the life Christ asks us to choose as we follow him. What appear to us to be unloving or unclear trials from God may, instead, be major blessings. Consider Jesus's cross!

You cannot separate yourself from God's love, no matter what. He made you. He sustains you. And he keeps you. He even allows you to take your next breath and triggers your next heartbeat. Ease your worries. Remember what Jesus says in Matthew 6:27, "Can you add a moment to your life by worrying?"

Remember that we are all immortal in this world, until his work for us here is done, as per British evangelist George Whitefield. We must until such time stay in him, safe within his light, doing what his Word instructs. You must also stay in his will and do what he is instructing you to do. Please understand that this is always going to be your safest place!

Also, know that he is molding and building you by your life's trials and hardships, by your heartbreaks and joys. He wants your faith to increase, rather than to fail, because of these events!

Remember always that adverse events are the experiences that God uses positively to grow and build you up. Change your mindset from yourself to his. For his higher purposes, rarely understood by us in the here and now, some pain and sorrow are needed. They lead us to search for and find our God. Without them, if all were ever-well, we would never seek him and would never find him. Thus, we would never be saved, as we would not understand nor appreciate the great gift of his grace to us!

People always ask, "If God really loves us, why so much pain?" If you are in a bad place, you can only get out of it by going to God, by running into his loving arms. If your mind and heart still feel he should not allow suffering, aren't you trying to define your own god? Aren't you making a god with a love that completely buffers and always protects and prevents you from any and all pain and heartache? We must realize that God did not send Jesus here to take away our pain but, rather, to fill our sorrows with his own presence!

Through our hardships, he draws us closer, humbling and molding us, shaping us into what he desires for us to become in his perfect plan. He will bring us all the way through this life and to himself for eternity and salvation. Consider:

> "Though our bodies are dying, our inner strength in the Lord is growing every day. These troubles and sufferings of ours are, after all, quite small and won't last very long. Yet this short time of distress will result in God's richest blessing upon us forever and ever! So we do not look at what we can see right now, the troubles all around us, but we look forward to the joys in heaven which we have not yet seen. The troubles will soon be over, but the joys to come will last forever." (2 Corinthians 4:16–18)

So, can you see how sorrow and pain are actually loving interventions into our lives by God? Where would we otherwise be without him? We would all be lost in blinded, futile lives lasting mere decades, each unfulfilled, restless, miserable, and, worst of all, unsaved!

God's love is always with us. It never leaves us, not even in our trials. It protects and provides for us, yet it does not fully shield us or grant us perfect lives of comfort. Instead, while usually not in what we feel would be an appropriate timeframe, God acts in his timing within his will and for his glory, which is always for our greater long-term good, no matter how rough current events may seem. God's love molds us as he guides our steps and controls all details of our lives, including encounters, events, school and job choices, choice of spouse and all the rest. He does all of this for our ultimate goods. He shapes us more and more into his perfect creations.

Thus, you need to turn to God and consciously make the decision to choose his love. Speak to him in prayer and ask his help in this. You must believe in your heart that God loves you. A mental assent to what Scripture says about his love without believing and possessing a certainty in knowing it is not enough! It is not enough to merely memorize and spout verses such as John 3:16. No, we must accept these. We must believe them and always trust his perfect, all-knowing will and designs for us, his children. If we do not, we are described as follows:

> "Because you have forgotten me and turned your backs on me, therefore you must bear the consequence of all your sin. . . . You will suffer the full penalty, and you will know that I alone am God." (Ezekiel 23:35, 49)

> "'Oh, turn from your sins while there is yet time. Put them behind you and receive a new heart and a new spirit. For why will you die? . . . I do not enjoy seeing you die,' the Lord God says. 'Turn, turn and live!'" (Ezekiel 18:30–32)

***

Saint Thomas Aquinas wrote that God's true sovereignty is clear by the fact that he allows some evil through free human choices and that he uses even it for good. He writes, "This is the infinite goodness of God, that he should allow evil to exist and out of it produce good."

Therefore, God is still sovereign. He is still in charge, always. And although he permits evil choices, he still will always convert pain and suffering to good. Consider once more the example of Christ's cross, the most evil act ever. Christ was alone, sinless, and innocent. Yet he was still killed by evil-choosing men. Look to these reassuring promises from God's book:

"Yes, be patient. And take courage, for the coming of the Lord is near." (James 5:8)

"For since he himself has now been through suffering and temptation, he knows what it is like when we suffer and are tempted, and he is wonderfully able to help us." (Hebrews 2:18)

"God will tenderly comfort you when you undergo these same sufferings. He will give you the strength to endure." (2 Corinthians 1:7)

"Do not let this happy trust in the Lord die away, no matter what happens. Remember your reward! You need to keep on patiently doing God's will if you want him to do for you all that he has promised. His coming will not be delayed much longer." (Hebrews 10:35–37)

"Yes, and the Lord will always deliver me from all evil and will bring me into his heavenly Kingdom." (2 Timothy 4:18)

***

Further regarding the question about evil, some will ask why God does not stop it right now. We should respond that our God eventually will stop it all, as he promises in Revelation. He will eliminate it for all eternity. Unfortunately for us, his timing is again not ours, and the time for this intervention is not yet here no matter how much we might like it to be so.

***

Before we move on, I commonly hear two other questions associated with the question of suffering and evil, namely, how can any good God let innocent children as well as innocent docile animals suffer?

To answer these questions, we first need to remember why and how evil itself exists. The Old Testament writings are often brought up by critics who ask why God commanded the killing of innocent enemy children (and even all the domestic animals in some cases) when the Israelites wiped out certain Canaanite cities. Given that people are all born with original sin, no single one of us is innocent, not even children. God created us by breathing his life into us. So, he has the right to take our lives too. And he will eventually do so with every one of us. The only question is how and when. Thus, it is a definitive fact that we all will die at some point.

Additionally, looking at the battles that took place in the Old Testament, these almost exclusively were planned engagements. Aside from surprise attacks, it was widely known by people for days in advance that a battle was nigh. Israel's battles were not ambushes. Therefore, the pagan warriors would stay at the front to fight Israel, while noncombatant women and children could and indeed are believed to have often withdrawn to a safe zone before the fight, the exception being those living in the walled cities.

As for the adults in walled cities, not all were killed in every instance. For example, God saved Lot's family in Sodom and Gomorrah, Rahab's family in Jericho, and the entire Nineveh populace to whom Jonah preached. These people were saved because they came to know and follow the true God, having repented and turned to him. However, the unrepentant sinners in each of these cities were justly dealt with, per God's holy nature.

God never delights in the demise of evil people: "As I live, says the Lord God, I have no pleasure in the death of the wicked; I desire that the wicked turn from his evil ways and live" (Ezekiel 33:11). It is imperative that, given his righteous nature, God must deal with all corrupt and evil people who refuse to stop their sins, those who will not repent or turn to him. Throughout history, he is above all holy, just, and fair. At the same time, he is kind and merciful to those who repent. Therefore, he is not at all cruel, capricious, or arbitrary. Such traits are not in his character. He cannot act that way.

***

The second question was, how can a good God let animals suffer? Reading through the Old Testament, there are thousands upon thousands of animal sacrifices specifically mentioned. Yet, animal sacrifice was never part of God's original plan. He created all men and animals as herbivores (vegetarians), as is noted in Genesis.

But this changed after the fall of man. Man's sin caused this to happen. God did not! Human beings needed clothes after they sinned. The first animal sacrifices provided this. "The Lord God clothed Adam and his wife with garments made from skins of animals" (Genesis 3:21). And thereafter, perhaps to not waste the rest of its body, God allowed carnivorism as well.

What must be realized is that these were the result of man's sin. People thereafter needed to be covered with garments as well as by blood. Here, God first demonstrated that all sin comes at great cost. This first sacrificial death preceded the thousands upon thousands of

Jewish animal offerings meant to cover the nation's sins. It also foreshadows Christ's blood sacrifice to cover us all.

Whether we are reading the Old Testament or dealing with modern-day animal issues, what we need to realize is that, no matter what one thinks, if we base our belief upon Scripture, animals do not have moral rights. Humans are of course meant to care for animals and to be morally good to them, caring for, helping, and managing them as best we can. They have been given to us as gifts from God, and we are meant to care for and to use them wisely and appropriately, in some cases for food or clothing, and in others as our companions or for other products or benefits.

As a hunter, I have seen what happens to deer, coyote, and rabbit overpopulations, especially in years of excessively dry weather. It is well documented that when populations of any species grow exceedingly large, they become prone to disease. And disease comes to naturally reduce their numbers again, as God's natural world order cyclically brings such back into balance. Hunting performed in a controlled manner for the benefit of food, species management, clothes, or materials otherwise required, and which is done with full and appropriate respect for the dignity of the animal, is not animal cruelty. It is instead, by documented scientific truth, beneficial for their populations.

Consider the case of bears, including the polar as well as grizzlies, browns, and blackies. I have studied the research extensively on these amazing species and spent more than seventy days in the field with brown and grizzly bears in the wilds of Alaska, not including my many weeks spent with black and polar bears. It is a well-documented scientific fact that adult males kill cubs frequently, in some cases even their very own genetic offspring. They do this for either food or to put the female back into reproductive capacity sooner, for breed-ability once more. Statistics prove that taking a mature polar bear male from the population saves, on average, thirty polar cubs, that is, cubs that would otherwise be killed by him over the lifetime of that large male. This research is exactly why those Canadian provinces that want to boost the bear population allow a small number of male polar bears to be culled through hunting each year.

Further, one must realize that of the monies spent for the conservation of animals, fish, and birds, the vast majority of such (over 90 percent) comes from outdoorsmen and outdoorswomen, hunters and fisherman, through licenses and access and tag fees. These funds are used to help preserve habitat and to protect animals. And in verifiable truth they account for far more money than that which "well-meaning" anti-hunters and anti-fishermen contribute.

So, in addition to providing huge amounts of funds to preserve, manage, and conserve these species of wildlife, controlled hunting also limits animal suffering by reducing disease and starvation. While living in West Texas during severe drought years, I often saw deer that were mere walking skeletons, simply wasting away without enough food or water to sustain them, ripe with skin and systemic diseases, stumbling around like zombies, just enduring as they died extremely slow and agonizing deaths. No matter whether you consider yourself a hunter or a non-hunter, I strongly suspect that you would do the exact same thing I did if one of these poor, suffering creatures staggered blindly by you for the third time in the same afternoon, wasting away, losing her hair, covered with bugs, boils, and other skin lesions, clearly in her last days of life.

So, whether one is for or against hunting and fishing, one must realize and understand the existence of our natural cycles. These were divinely designed to function perfectly well. Yet, any extreme deviation from these, be it overhunting, overfishing, or, alternatively, species overpopulation via restriction of such activities, will upset the delicate balance that God put into place and motion, causing adverse population changes, disease, and starvation.

He has given us the job of caring for all living creatures. This also means managing them responsibly and appropriately to the best of our abilities.

***

Because the existence of evil is always such a commonly asked Big Question, let's summarize seven key answers that should be made to those who ask it.

EVIL EXISTS BECAUSE:

1. Human beings have been given free will by God and thus can choose good or bad.

2. The example and standard for goodness is God.

3. If all was good and perfect, we per our view would not need God, thus we would not seek him.

4. We must not only see this world's evil but its great goodness as well!

5. All suffering results in some eventual good.

6. God and his Son, Jesus Christ, are the answers to evil not the cause!

7. God and Christ call us to address evil and to minister to the suffering. We, therefore, are part of their answer to evil!

2. How Can I Trust the Bible?

"What? The Bible? The Bible is the biggest collection of mythology ever written in the entire history of the world!" This was the response

I got from a man when I asked if he read the Bible. He and his wife thereafter told me that he was a self-professed Buddhist because he was very centered.

I humbly replied that he could not simply drop this bomb without allowing me a response. In asking once more if he had ever read the Bible, he told me, "Yes, some of it." He told me how he felt it was full of contradictions, fairy tales, and falsehoods. However, when I asked him for one such contradiction or mistruth, he was unable to come up with any—not a single one. He did later call the many miracles of Jesus "simply impossible."

I then asked if he had ever researched the Bible at its foundations, namely examining its writers and the very significant correlation between its sixty-six books written by more than forty different authors over one thousand five hundred years. I said that in my view, if one dedicates oneself to open-mindedly trying to find out the truth, one will find it. I further discussed how no intelligent human mind of the past two hundred years that had undertaken such a quest had ever been able to refute or accurately disprove even one single fact within the Bible.

I said, too, that the Bible is God's living and breathing Word which can change anyone. And I challenged him to read a chapter a day from John's twenty-one chapters, then chapters from the other Gospels, for a total of thirty consecutive days. I asked him to then tell me, if he could, that he felt unchanged. I explained how reading about Jesus's life and mission would take only five to ten minutes daily. And, since he had never studied how the Bible was written and who wrote it, I said he needed to do so. I told him he needed to be certain rather than simply listening to others, before making such grossly erroneous statements.

So, was I harsh? Was I mean? No, I do not believe so. God's Word is exactly as it says it is. It is permanently unchanging. It is a guide for our survival upon this planet. It tells us how to make things go as well as possible for us, even during our bad times.

We must therefore strive to present God's Scripture exactly as such to those who are lost, who are misguided, or who misunderstand it. We must show them what it has done for us! We must also demonstrate its effectiveness regarding its gifts of peace, joy, fulfillment, and rescue, and make certain that others know that it can and will do the same for them, if they will give their hearts to Jesus and then, while asking for his help, devote themselves to a thorough study and reading of his Word!

Do not take my word for it, nor anyone else's word for or against it, but rather, check it out for yourself! You cannot afford to be wrong on this most important decision of your life. What do you have to lose? If you will simply get into his Word daily, while praying for his guidance in trying to know him better, then you will find him!

***

I meet many people of other faiths who state that the Bible is a good or influential book. Therefore, they read it or are told to read it by parents or mentors. Yet they tell me that they do not believe it is God's Word.

I see a problem with this. More than three thousand eight hundred times, the Bible states that it indeed is the Word of God, for example, when it says, "God said," and, "Thus sayeth the Lord."

So, for one to say that they think the Bible is good yet still refuse to believe that it is God's Word to us makes absolutely no sense. If you deny it is God's Word, but still think it is a "good book," consider what you are saying. Would you ever call any other book good if it contained more than three thousand eight hundred lies? How could you ever state such to be good or influential literature?

***

While we already examined this issue earlier in Chapter X, let us look more deeply at the trustworthy nature of the Bible as a book that is divinely ordained rather than compiled by men, as some infer. To do that, let's consider some of its unique characteristics. First, consider the Bible's transforming power. From its very beginning, its contents have given people hope, courage, purpose, wisdom, power, and guidance to show them the true way to salvation. It indeed can transform lives, minds, souls, and hearts. This has occurred innumerable times throughout history. There is no denying this. Just look at what the gospel did to the previously timid disciples after the risen Christ and his Holy Spirit transformed them! Similarly, this process has continued throughout the ages, right into our own present day!

Further, look at the Bible's unity of theme. We have sixty-six books written by more than forty different authors, each in his own different style, over a one-thousand-five-hundred-year duration. Yet, the text presents one continuous thread of events with a central message. The only way that this could happen, with so many varied human styles and personalities being represented in its contributors, would be if a divine mind had indeed inspired each. There is simply no other way to explain this.

Next, further evidence for Scripture's divine origin are the miracles presented within it. We will address the doubts some have with miracles in more detail below. But at this time, let us state how these suffice as strong evidence for the Bible's divine origin. Christianity, Judaism, and Islam all recognize miracles as signs that confirm a message from God. Further, the New Testament miracles are described in writing within a few years after their performance by Christ and his disciples. Eyewitnesses were therefore still alive, persons who could speak out against any embellishment or lies regarding such events. Contrast this with the hadith's described Muslim miracles, which were not added until one to two hundred years after Muhammad's death, with some added even four hundred years later!

These were made up and ascribed to Muhammad by Muslims who were attempting to give him further credit and better solidify their belief system. Yet by that later time, no eyewitnesses were still alive, so none could refute or confirm their validity! Also, the Koran itself contains no actual miracles, apart from the supposed miracle of the Koran itself: Muhammad, when once asked to do a miracle, refused and suggested one read a Koranic surah instead. Thus, while the hadith traditions do ascribe reported miracles to him, these were first written more than one hundred years after his death. More were then added as time passed. There are a reported three hundred thirty-eight definite miracles and more than six thousand possible miracles cited in the hadith.

Yet these are not at all like Jesus's miracles in the Bible's New Testament, which were written down within the first generation after Jesus. The importance of this living eyewitness support cannot be minimized or denied, as the importance of truth-in-reporting was so significant a virtue in Hebrew culture and society! Therefore, recording false events or even embellished accounts of lesser happenings would have led to a rapid failure of any propagated belief system as well as perceived severe judgement from God. The Hebrew writers would never have attempted it.

Further proof of the Bible's divine origin is its archaeological evidence. The Bible has never been disproven, not one single time ever. And this is despite a host of skeptics. Examples are, as we discussed above, the Hittites, a people for years thought to be fictional until the discovery of evidence confirming their existence. Even Pontius Pilate was doubted to have been a historical figure until a carved stone with his name and position as Judean prefect listed twice on it was discovered in Palestine in 1961. Additionally, a two-thousand-year-old ring bearing his name was found in the 1960s at Herodium, the palace and fortress near Bethlehem. Yet only very recently, with new technology, was the "Of Pilates" inscription on it able to be discerned.[4] As above, the Bethesda Pool, Sheep Gate, and Siloam pool were also thought to be erroneous biblical misstatements until they were excavated.

These types of things have all been used by skeptics to try to discredit God's Bible. Many sadly spent their entire lives upon such futile endeavors. Yet archaeology, which we must all admit is a valid and trustworthy science, has proven the Bible correct every time!

No, we do not presently have evidence for all of Scripture. Yet over time, people discover more and more evidence that confirms the truthfulness of the Bible. Even more important, we have never found anything that can definitively disprove the Holy Bible!

I highly recommend Sir William Ramsay's *St. Paul the Traveler and Roman Citizen*, an excellent archaeological treatise.[5] Prior to writing his highly enjoyable book, which is replete with impressive photographs, Ramsay was a public skeptic. He declared that he was going "to disprove the Bible and thus Christianity" through his archaeology. But after many years in this quest, he was forced to change his position, having in actuality done the opposite. Instead, he found undeniable evidence for the truth of the biblical text.

Regarding apparent Bible contradictions, newer discoveries continue to prove the Bible's accuracy. No single proposed disproof has ever been able to stand up over time, despite innumerable critical examinations. The Bible has stood up to every attack.

What type of person could ever make a valid and believable claim that human beings know everything? Really! Only the most arrogant person would make a such a statement.

If we admit we cannot know everything, do we throw away the things we cannot yet prove? When a scientist finds an unexplained anomaly in nature, does he give up on science? No, he gives it the benefit of the doubt and keeps looking for answers in a continual search for the truth. Similarly, the Bible should be thought of as innocent until proven guilty. But people do not do this. They rush without evidence to a guilty verdict!

The evidence is there, and it is valid. And, really, we do not turn from God because of lack of evidence. We do so because of our pride from what we perceive as our great degree of intelligence. God is not ever going to force us to believe. His love works persuasively, not coercively! We simply need to openly and honestly look at the evidence.

***

As reviewed in Chapter X above, it is worth repeating that there are more than five thousand six hundred Greek manuscripts of the New Testament in existence. All trace their source back to the original manuscripts, which were written within fifty to one hundred years from the events they describe. Such manuscript evidence makes the Bible by far the most extensively copied literature in the history of the world.

There are again very few omissions and changes in the manuscript tradition. Errors were monitored for fastidiously and obsessively. By contrast, we only have seven copies of Plato's oldest script, made about one thousand two hundred years after Plato's death. We only have six hundred forty-three copies of Homer's *Iliad*, and these were written about six hundred years after the original. Yet, interestingly, these highly celebrated, classic works are never questioned!

***

Old Testament prophecy provides further evidence of the Bible's divine nature. There are one hundred ninety-one Old Testament prophecies written between 400 and 200 BC. All of them were fulfilled in one man (if, in your skeptical view, Jesus was only a man). Even if we say he was only a man, he was a man who had no personal control over prophetic predictions. The odds of such happening merely by chance are beyond astronomical. Therefore, this supernaturally confirms the Bible as well. No other book has such evidence underlying its premises and foundations with complete fulfillment of its predictions to date, with those in Daniel, Ezekiel, and Revelation still to come to fruition!

***

Let us also review the literary tradition of the era in which the New Testament was written. First-century men writing an epic fable or legend would not have even remotely considered portraying their hero as the Gospels do, as a convicted felon crucified on a wooden cross. Such authors would not have women at the tomb be the first to see him alive again, given the societal male emphasis of that era. Nor would they have portrayed Jesus's loyal disciples as men full of doubt that he had risen, as they did at first. A person or group writing a legendary story to try to start a movement would certainly not ever present a saving hero in such manner, especially given the literary traditions in that culture and in that day and time.

As further convincing proofs, consider how Jesus's initially skeptical family later converted. Consider too Jesus's post-resurrection appearances to more than five hundred people, many of whom were later martyred cruelly without recanting. Consider also the thousands of Jews who in those early days cast off all tradition and inheritance that had been established for more than one thousand five hundred years, throwing all comforts and securities away for this brand-new religion. Consider too the survival of the sacraments of communion and baptism and even the persistence and exponential growth of Christianity itself!

***

Objections are sometimes raised about Jesus's resurrection. Some state that instead of Jesus rising, his disciples stole his body or that they went to the wrong tomb or that Jesus did not completely die and somehow snuck off to heal from his wounds. Some even say that God took him off the cross before dying. All of these are pathetically meager attempts to say that there was no resurrection.

They are futile efforts because the empty tomb is a known historical fact. Think of the psychology of Jesus's enemies, the Jews and Romans. If the tomb was not empty or had been confused with another and if there was a corpse of Jesus that they could lay hands upon, would they not have seized it, even opening his tomb themselves if need be, and paraded the body about the streets? Wouldn't this have easily snuffed out this spreading belief that he had returned from the dead? Of course they would have! Their problem was that there was no body to be found! The fact that they felt compelled to make up the story and offer bribes to the guards so that they would claim Jesus's body was stolen (Matthew 28:11–15) is solid evidence for the empty tomb. Were it not empty, why would they need to contrive a story and bribe others to pass on such a lie? Were the empty tomb untrue, no bribery money would be needed! The Jewish leaders, then, through their lies and their bribes corroborate the truth: the risen Christ left behind as testament his empty grave!

Other practical considerations that strongly argue against a stolen body theory are: how did the disciples get past a guard detail of

Roman professional soldiers and temple-guard security personnel? Further, even if such had happened, say if they had perhaps crept quietly past them or the guards really had all fallen asleep, how then did they ever quietly roll the great stone aside? This would obviously take a good number of people and would also likely be a rather loud and noisy effort. Are we really supposed to believe that Hebrew fishermen and some women pulled this off, besting professional soldiers? Consider the modern example of a group of average college students trying to not only sneak past but also to accomplish such a difficult mission against an elite Special Forces or Navy SEAL team. The odds of success are indeed extremely minimal. Therefore, to believe or to state such makes absolutely no sense.

The fact of the empty tomb must be dealt with. It cannot be swept under the rug. The Jews' made-up stories that they circulated about Jesus's followers stealing his body or about the tomb guards falling asleep, which they attempted initially as damage control, were quickly squelched by eyewitnesses and could thus never have stood long-term. These lies publicized by desperate men lasted only a brief time precisely because there were eyewitnesses present!

Further, if all of this resurrection stuff is a lie, a mere fable, then who got more than five hundred witnesses to agree for more than one or two days without recanting, fighting, or changing their stories? Who convinced them to go to their graves as martyrs for Jesus? This simply would not happen unless they were telling the truth about the resurrection.

Of note also, an interesting tradition is evidenced in John where it says the burial clothes were folded on the tomb's bench. If one was to steal a dead body, would you take the time to unwrap it and then not only leave behind but also neatly fold up its garments? Absolutely not! You would not take the time. You also would use the wrappings to help you carry the body as well as to keep it from touching you, given Jewish cleanliness rites and laws. What we have instead is an interesting Jewish tradition in which folding one's napkin means one is not done yet, one is coming back to his meal. The folded burial clothes were a sign from Christ that would be recognized by people of that day. Jesus was signifying that he was not finished and that he was coming back!

Evidentially, it is a historical fact that Jesus did rise from the dead. Any fact backed up by more than five hundred eyewitnesses cannot be overlooked or refuted! We all take the account of Pliny the Younger, a lone, seventeen-year-old Pompeiian lad who wrote about Mount Vesuvius's eruption, as solid fact, although it was written about twenty-five years later after he had become a Roman senator. Pliny's account is accepted as truth without questioning his details or motives!

In summary, the evidence for the resurrection is solid. It clearly follows that if Christ did rise, as the evidence has shown, he must therefore be God. And if so, then he cannot lie. So, all he says in his Word, in the Bible, must be true! This means that the Bible's prophecy about the end of all things is going to come true also. All people will be judged by whether they have accepted Jesus as Lord and Savior or not!

***

For further reading and research about biblical proofs and evidences, there are many excellent texts and investigations that I would strongly recommend so that you can personally solidify your understanding of Scripture as being valid and authentically from God. An excellent recent work is *Cold Case Christianity* by J. Warner Wallace.[6] Wallace was an initially atheistic police detective who researched the claims of the Bible, looking at it through strict evidentiality. His conclusion is that the Bible is an accurate and true document that readily meets all the criteria of modern forensic, legal, and evidential practices. He evaluates Scripture through the lens of modern policework and concludes that it passes all tests of truthfulness. I strongly encourage anyone to read this excellent text.

Referencing Wallace's wonderfully researched work for a bit here, because it answers so many questions that are often brought up by both skeptics and believers alike, let's look at several different areas. The first is from pages 99 to 108, which discuss added biblical material. These are things that appear in later copies but are not in the earliest manuscripts. The largest addition is the story of the adulteress who was about to be stoned until Jesus intervened. The story is in John 8:1–11. It is not found in the earliest manuscripts of John up through the 300s, the fourth century. The story of the adulteress first appears in the 400s in the Codex Bezae. It appears in Luke for the first time even later between the years AD 1000 and 1400. The questions are why was it added and is it true?

None of us can definitively know the answer. But using common sense, the story was most likely added to address questions about adultery, which were ongoing in the church at that time. I believe that the incident occurred and was passed down through the oral tradition. It was felt to be important enough to instruct the biblical reader on this subject, so it was later added to the written text as well.

That is my thought on it, but no one knows this for sure. Wallace, however, brings up an extremely important point that we must ask regarding any contested additions. He asks, if you look at each addition, does it change anything at all about the message of the Bible, about the gospel of Jesus Christ and his dying to save us? I feel that the story of the adulteress does not, but each must make his own decision.

Let's look at some other additions, all lesser in influence as well as in length: Luke 22:43–44, in reference to Christ's pre-crucifixion anguish, states that "an angel strengthened him." This is not in the earliest manuscripts of Luke. Also, John 5:4 describes an angel stirring the Bethesda Pool and promoting healing, and it is also not found in earlier manuscripts. Further, 1 John 5:7 has a line that states, "Father, Son, and Holy Ghost, these Three are One," which did not appear in copies until the 1500s. Acts 15:34 states "it pleased Silas" to stay in a certain area, and that is also not in the very early manuscripts.

With these last four references, some modern Bible translations either remove them altogether or add a footnote to each stating that they are later additions. But the question here is how we reconcile these. Just because they were added later, do they taint or pollute or corrupt the entire Bible, making it unreliable? No. I agree with Wallace in his conclusion that we have hundreds of early manuscripts before these additions, and these are extremely consistent, many to the very letter, with others having just rare misspellings and minimal grammatical errors. If we exclude these few small additions, we today see Scripture as it was in its original form.

We can therefore either ignore these few additions or take them as later additions and be aware that they are just that. Wallace very notably states that, as a detective, he would expect to see a few added articles and small changes in any text that was copied and recopied. It would be suspicious if they weren't there and suggest a faked, manipulated document! Wallace also states we must consider other ancient texts, such as secular Greek and Roman documents. These were also copied again and again over the centuries since they were written, and they collected the same sort of additions and spelling changes we observe in Bible manuscripts. Yet, no one holds so stringent a standard to them or doubts them as ardently as do so many regarding the Bible's text.[7]

***

Another extremely helpful section of Wallace's book examines hard evidence that suggests the Gospels were written by eyewitnesses rather than being made up or even exaggerated by later persons.[8] It also reviews how such testimony was passed on appropriately through the early pre-canon centuries. The New Testament was not passed on verbally as in the telephone call game in which each new person down the line says things a bit differently until the original message becomes an error-filled and distorted copy. That is what one Muslim told me he had been taught.

Well, could his claim be true? To answer such, in addition to my thoughts and research as we discussed earlier in Chapter X, let's dig deeper into the summary of the factual evidence put together so nicely by Wallace.

First, Wallace shows how the gospels were written early enough to be eyewitness accounts. They are not the writings of much later authors who could not have firsthand personal knowledge of what had occurred. But how do we know this for certain? Well, the New Testament does not describe the Roman destruction of the temple in AD 70. Christ predicted this in Matthew 24:1–3, so any later biographer, especially a writer attempting to magnify or exaggerate Jesus, would certainly have included it to corroborate his prophecy and support claims about his divinity.

The New Testament also does not describe the Roman siege of Jerusalem that went on for three years before AD 70. Therefore, it must have been written even earlier than this event, too, or it would have undoubtedly recorded it.

Also, Luke does not include Peter's death in AD 65 or Paul's death in 62 or the death of James in 62, despite writing about all three men in the Book of Acts. Paul is still quite alive at the end of Acts. I believe firmly that Luke in his detailed physician's writing style would have noted their martyrdoms, if such had occurred before his writings concluded. He does not merely censor or shy away from graphic material. He describes the death of Stephen quite graphically (Acts 7:54–60) as well as that of James the brother of John (Acts 12:1–2). Furthermore, Luke's Gospel is the first half of a two-part work. The Acts of the Apostles is its second half. Therefore, Luke's Gospel was written before Acts!

Additionally, Paul quotes Luke's gospel in his letter to Timothy, which was written in 63 or 64 (1 Timothy 5:17–18). He does the same in his letter to the Corinthians, which was written between 53 and 57 as well as in his letters to the Romans and Galatians written from 48 to 60. In these letters, he reinforces the Gospels' resurrection accounts and states that Christ is indeed God's Son. These are written from eyewitness accounts. People were still alive who could contest any claim. In Galatians, for example, Paul reports his seeing the risen Christ and learning his gospel, which occurred within five years of Jesus's crucifixion and resurrection!

Further, Luke's gospel quotes from the Gospels of Mark and Matthew, making them even earlier accounts, and Luke of course was not an eyewitness. He appears to have copied entire sections of these earlier Gospels over to his. Therefore, Mark and Matthew were already written and established before Luke, placing these texts even earlier into the gospel timeline!

Additionally, Mark's gospel is a shorter, less detailed account. Although Mark was not an eyewitness, church tradition and writings reveal that he heard these accounts from Peter, an intimate eyewitness, with whom he spent the most time, as well as from his travels with Paul and Barnabas. He then wrote them down as they were told to him. Wallace makes the important point that, as a first account, Mark may intentionally not have named some eyewitnesses to keep them safe from the Jews, who were at that time persecuting and killing Christians. For example, after Jesus raised Lazarus, the Jewish council began plotting to kill not only Jesus but Lazarus too, because of his influential testimony about God's Son. Lazarus may very well have still been alive at the time that Mark was written, as were many other primary eyewitness members of the young Christian church. Mark, therefore, may well have been trying to keep them as safe as possible. John though, writing the last Gospel account, penned it most likely after many of these people were then dead. So, he was able to safely name them without fear of retribution or persecution.

So, the proven timeline, as Wallace documents it, is that Jesus died in AD 33. Mark wrote his gospel between the years of 45 to 50, while Luke's Gospel was penned between 50 and 53. Paul's letters quote Luke in the years 50 to 64, and Luke wrote Acts between 57 and 60, with the deaths of James, Peter, and Paul occurring between the years 61 to 65. The Jerusalem siege began in 67 and ended with the temple's destruction in 70.

This timeline is extremely well-supported by the substantial evidence here. Therefore, while many skeptics may try to claim that the Gospels were written many years after the eyewitnesses had died, the evidence verifies the exact opposite. It supports the statement that Mark, Matthew, and Acts, at least, were written between twelve and twenty-seven years from the actual events of Christ's death and rising!

Therefore, the evidence firmly backs up the New Testament. This argument is the strongest and most probable position, much more than any skeptic positions can demonstrate. Additionally, through Wallace's law enforcement insight, he makes the excellent forensic claim that the Gospels and eyewitness reports are even more believable exactly because they are not exact carbon copies. This is what one would expect in real life, with different people telling the same story. If these were exactly the same (or very nearly so), they would be suspicious and likely fakes! As he notes, different persons see and remember different things and will thus describe events differently. So, if there were no differences between these multiple witness accounts, that would suggest forgery and fakery.

Further, as we discussed earlier, Wallace notes how non-Christian eyewitnesses abounded as well, including the Romans Josephus, Thallus, Tacitus, and Phlegon. All these men wrote about Jesus, his death, and his reported rising, as did the rabbis who wrote the Jewish Talmud. They also referenced Jesus and his death. Jesus, therefore, as we discussed earlier, was a historical figure. He lived here on our earth, died by crucifixion, and rose to life again. He was not some mythical creation of a human mind!

Also, regarding archaeological proof for the historicity of Jesus and scriptural accounts, we had discussed some of the more important confirmatory archaeological finds earlier. In his book, Wallace makes mention of Quirinius, the governor of Syria, who ordered the census at the time of Jesus's birth. His name was found on a coin from that era as well as upon a statue. He was reported to have held office from 11 BC until the time of Herod's death, which was after the death of Christ. Further, Lysanius, who is named in Luke, was a tetrarch of Abilene. Inscriptions have been discovered with his name upon them, which also date from AD 14 to 37. These finds place both men exactly within the timeline described by the Gospels.

We earlier discussed the Bethesda Pool at the Sheep Gate, which in 1888 was found with its steps and five porticos as described in the Bible. Skeptics had long stated that no such place was known to have existed in Jerusalem. Also, the Siloam Pool, which is documented in scripture was finally excavated in 2004 as well.

Further, the existence of a real magistrate named Pontius Pilate was also greatly debated, even though he was noted by Tacitus, the Roman historian. Nonetheless, many still doubted Pilate was ever a real person until in 1961 a limestone piece with his name on it was found in Caesarea, which was a provincial capital during his rule from AD 26 to 36. Also, as I discussed above, the more recent Pilate ring discovery undeniably evidences his existence as well.

Skeptics also proposed that a crucified victim such as Christ would never get a proper Jewish burial. They said he would have instead been thrown into a mass grave per the typical documented Roman methods of dealing with the corpses of the crucified. However, in 1968, a proper Jewish tomb was found with a single crucified victim's remains within. So, a crucified victim, if he had enough friends, influence, or wealth, could have had his corpse released for a proper burial despite his execution style.

Wallace makes the valid conclusion against all criticism that the Gospels were written early enough, are corroborated by enough hard evidence, and accurately reflect eyewitness testimony. Thus, as he concludes, they are much more likely to be true than untrue.

***

Okay, then what about how these accounts were passed on in writing and orally? This gets us back to the Muslim comment about Scripture being passed down orally in a kind of phone call that might introduce major alterations into the Bible over time.

In response to arguments such as this, Wallace reveals some excellent history. He states that the oldest complete New Testament copy we have, called Codex Sinaiticus, was written in approximately the year AD 350 by students of the apostle John, as well as those of Paul, Peter, and Mark. It was then passed on in a specific, appropriate, and documented manner, which to me appears to have been an excellent chain of custody. By this I mean a regimented and supervised preserving of the material exactly as it was in its original form. Just as in the law enforcement profession, chain of custody is something I have also dealt with in the medicolegal realm, for instance, when performing autopsies. This basically means that each issue is documented and logged appropriately so that there are no errors or contamination of evidence as a case is being formulated.

Wallace, using specific examples, documents how John passed the information to Ignatius and to Polycarp, who then passed it to Irenaeus before it was then passed to Hippolytus. Paul, meanwhile, passed information to Linus and to Clement, who then passed it to Evanistus, who next got it to Pius and Justin Martyr and then to Tatian. Peter, in his circle, gave the information to Mark, who then passed it to Ananias, Kidron, Primus, and Justus. It then passed to Pantaemus and then to Clement, then to Origen on to Pamphilus and then on to Eusebius. Each man represents a duration of time, from a decade or two up to a full generation. By being carefully preserved in this manner, these latest students' writings would still reflect those of the primary teachers who were eyewitnesses to Christ's claims and deeds!

***

Another question that arises here is: what about those who copied the original texts in order to preserve and to pass them on? How do we know that they did not make copying errors, either intentionally or unintentionally?

Wallace describes how Hebrew copyists and scribes were extremely precise, meticulous, and careful, to put it mildly. They were extensively trained to copy ancient documents of theological nature. They were extremely careful because they viewed the text as God's Holy Word, and they did not want to be responsible for any erroneous or misleading copy. Further, the Jewish Masoretic scribes followed an extremely strict set of rules set up to guarantee that each fresh copy was an exact reproduction of the original. They did word and letter counts partway through the documents and then at the conclusion. So, if there was an addition or omission, it would be discovered and corrected, thus avoiding any bad copy from being sent out. There, indeed, was a solid and reliable system of checks and balances in place with all the copyists.

As we discussed earlier, consider the Dead Sea Scrolls found in 1947. The scrolls included a complete copy of Isaiah dating from about the year 700 BC. It was thus written about one thousand years before the earliest Masoretic Isaiah copy. When compared side by side, the older Isaiah, although copied a millennium earlier, was word for word identical with our standard Hebrew Bible to more than 95 percent of the text. The 5 percent differences were minimal and represent mostly cultural spelling changes, as in favor versus favour, or mild grammar differences or an occasional added word for clarity. But none of these differences changed the meaning of the original text whatsoever!

Therefore, as Wallace concludes, it is readily apparent, if one will look at this issue with an open and unblinded mind, that these strict text preservation traditions are definitive proof that the first Christian writings were preserved and multiplied in a consistent and accurate manner within the Masoretic tradition, one that closely guarded and protected these eyewitness accounts from corruption.

This is what I like to think of as being a method similar to a legal chain of custody over these early centuries, prior to these documents being made official canon by the church. Therefore, the Gospel writers Matthew and John were, as Wallace states, present as eyewitnesses for the events that they describe. Their accounts are corroborated by hard evidence. And further, we have proof that they were exceedingly and particularly accurate.

However, one last issue he brings up is the question: were they biased? As we discussed earlier, there can be many motives for self-ish gain. But what would the Gospel writers have to gain? In fact, they had nothing to gain. These people left everything they had for Christ, including their families, homes, wealth, and inheritances. They were persecuted, imprisoned, and killed. Yet they never denied their writ-ings or their beliefs in the Lord Jesus. There is, thus, simply no mere human motive here, no bias, no falsehood, nor any forgery or faking![9]

***

Lastly, regarding how the books to be included in the Bible were cho-sen, councils of early-church elders were able to recognize those texts which had been written under God's authority by true godly men. They examined how each book correlated with accepted Christian doctrines as well as with the rest of the accepted Scriptures. And they looked to see if the document positively affected audiences in the way you'd expect from a life-changing message from God. Anything that did not meet these criteria was thrown out. The entire Bible was initially compiled by AD 95, quite soon after the events of Jesus's life, and settled on completely by the church by AD 300.

***

In summary, the Bible itself is its own best proof. If you will only study it with an open mind, diligently, while asking to be shown the truth, and if you spend time in it appropriately, you will see its divine nature, its validity, its truthfulness, and its trustworthiness. It has changed many, many extremely intelligent yet initially skeptical modern minds in these past two hundred years alone. The more time spent in it, the less doubt you will have. The greater your confidence will become that it is what it claims to be, the written Word of our holy Father, which he has given to us for our benefit!

Thus, as God's own words, the Bible is fully consistent, non-changing, and infallible, having been inspired by the Holy Spirit, with each word directly chosen by him. Yes, it was written by men. But they were holy men who, being holy, were thus on the same spiritual wavelength as God. They were men who were in tune with his mind and his will. Thus, the Bible's contents are also referred to as plenary, a term that acknowledges the fact that it consists fully of the revelation of God from cover to cover without exception or error.

In conclusion, we must always remember this clearly stated truth from our God: "Heaven and earth shall disappear, but my words stand sure forever" (Mark 13:31).

3. Miracles versus Science

"The heavens are telling the glory of God; they are a marvelous display of his craftsmanship. Day and night they keep on telling about God. Without a sound or word, silent in the skies, their message reaches out to all the world. The sun lives in the heavens where God placed it and moves out across the skies as radiant as a bridegroom going to his wedding, or as joyous as an athlete looking forward to a race!" (Psalm 19:1–5)

Many people tell me that they primarily believe in science, meaning that they, for whatever reason, place their trust in some nebulous-yet-glorious, all-saving entity rather than believing in God and his Bible. They believe only in the natural world and its workings. They trust in only what they can see, touch, hear, smell, or taste. And in so doing, they separate God and the Bible from his science by implying, first, that God and the scientific world are mutually exclusive and, second, that the Bible is not scientifically accurate.

I, however, disagree strongly. The Bible, when one takes the time to delve into it, reveals God's science by clearly describing this world's divinely created nature. It states many scientific laws of the grand nature that God created. It accurately describes facts about the world, which he keeps functioning. Consider Job, said to be the Bible's oldest book. It was written between 700 and 400 BC and includes descriptions of the water cycle and also reports the world as being round as a sphere. Isaiah also talks about the circle of the earth, yet it was not until 1492 that Columbus verified the world as a being a globe, and it was even later when the water cycle finally became known!

Just consider the fact that the world's best and brightest minds generally confessed that the world was flat until only five hundred twenty-eight years ago! Before then, the possibility of a round world was scoffed at and vehemently denied by the best and brightest scientific and mathematical minds for many centuries until this long-held falsehood was finally disproven.

The knowledge of our world's water cycle, similarly, was also greatly flawed. Men had false ideas about it even into the Middle Ages until more modern study methods brought its true workings to light. How much more, therefore, of what we consider generally to be wrong today will we instead learn to be truth in future years, as science continues to play its catch-up game with revealed truth?

As a physician and a scientist myself, I have peered into the mysteries of life and death on a daily basis for more than a generation. I have examined all the workings that occur over the time interval between the beginning and end of natural life. In so doing, it is completely inconceivable to me that our scientific world, with all of its intricacies and minute details, could ever have evolved by chance, let alone that it would continue running in such perfect order over thousands of years, if there were not a divine Creator. Thus, not only was such a divine Creator necessary for it to start, but also, in my view, he must still be continually involved. He is pushing buttons, so to speak, and keeping his creation in appropriate motion!

Even if one is an atheist, can a supernatural explanation ever be completely ruled out? If you are open-minded, honest, and non-prejudiced, how could you ever definitively (not to mention arrogantly) rule out this possible option, O man of human mind?

This premise can logically be extended to state that, if we cannot fully rule out miracles (and thus the existence of the supernatural), how then could we ever completely rule out the possibility that God exists? Conversely, if you believe in God, or will at least grant that he may exist, then it follows that it is not unreasonable to believe that miracles could occur! Consider:

"The Lord says: Cursed is the man who puts his trust in mortal man and turns his heart away from God. He is like a stunted shrub in the desert, with no hope for the future; he lives on the salt-encrusted plains in the barren wilderness; good times pass him by forever. But blessed is the man who trusts in the Lord and has made the Lord his hope and confidence. He is like a tree planted along a riverbank, with its roots reaching deep into the water—a tree not bothered by the heat nor worried by long months of drought. Its leaves stay green, and it goes right on producing all its luscious fruit." (Jeremiah 17:5–8)

***

A scientist myself, I am, with age, constantly in ever-increasing awe of our Creator God as I learn and experience more and more medical developments and knowledge over the three decades I have practiced medicine. Yet it remains plainly clear to me that we are still just barely scratching the surface!

Consider all our world's intricacies and complex, interdependent parts. When I look at even the medical world in isolation, I see how small and insignificant I really am! God did create (and maintains) all this world's living things, including their environments and realms here on earth!

Further, just as Jesus healed miraculously, I feel we today should similarly view the evolving modern miracles of medicine and science as gifts of divine beneficial knowledge as well, gifts that help us to heal also, in their own ways. We have amazing artificial limbs, devices and surgeries, procedures that extend lives and can bring sight and sound to many blind and deaf persons, respectively, much better seizure control, and treatments for diseases like multiple sclerosis, stroke, and parkinsonism, to name a few. All these advances have markedly improved quality of life, as well as extended the lifespan, in patients afflicted by these conditions, as I have witnessed in just the past thirty-plus years over which I have practiced the specialty of neurological medicine.

For instance, we now have clot-busting medications for strokes, which at times will completely resolve what would have otherwise been severely paralyzing and often fatal events. As a result, blood clots in the brain are often resolved within minutes to hours. I vividly remember the case of a sixty-three-year-old woman who presented to my ER completely paralyzed on one side, unable to speak at all, and having lost significant vision. Within just ten minutes of receiving this medication, she was completely normal, walking and speaking about wanting to go home. Without this agent, she almost certainly would have followed the course of most untreated strokes, which I have seen over my career. She would have been permanently disabled and unlikely to ever be independent or to walk again, perhaps never being able to speak well either for the rest of her days.

I have been greatly privileged and supremely blessed to have been able to care for many similarly critically ill persons, seeing many go from being either cardiopulmonary dead or just on the threshold of death's door to full health. I have electrically shocked dead and dying hearts back to life, intubated persons who had stopped breathing, and successfully treated infectious illnesses like meningitis and sepsis (blood poisoning), which were about to claim their victims' lives, as well as preformed many other life-saving interventions. Yet, I give up any and all praise for such actions to God. While I may diagnose and treat, I am absolutely convinced that it is he who guides my head and my hands, thus it is ultimately he who heals, not myself. I serve solely as his conduit.

As an example of the progress of medical knowledge, consider my Parkinson's disease patients. When I first began working in this field, I saw that having parkinsonism reduced one's lifespan by at least two years because of limited treatment options. People would gradually become (as all who had family members with parkinsonism in the 1980s or earlier will recall) more limited and immobile, reaching a generally contracted state at which time they could walk no more. Being bedbound, they then became susceptible to pneumonia and bedsores. One of these two infections would then typically claim the life of a parkinsonian person, who had also in most cases experienced an extremely poor quality of life during the years before their demise. Today, however, in my neurological opinion, having parkinsonism does not reduce one's life span whatsoever. This is because there are now many, many more excellent treatments available for this disease process. So, while I certainly prefer not to have to give one this diagnosis, I tell my patients with the disease how I routinely see that we can keep people going much better now, allowing a long-term, quality life with their families despite the diagnosis.

While we do not yet have a cure for Alzheimer's disease, there are still some excellent treatments now that, in my experience, will usually improve the memory in at least 40 percent of these persons. And in the other 60 percent, in almost every case, treatment will at least stabilize one's memory by markedly reducing the rate of memory decline. Prior to these medications' development, its cognitive decline was much more rapidly progressive when I first began practicing in the late 1980s and into the mid-1990s. It would be worse and worse each time I saw the patient back in the office before these newer treatments became available.

As another dramatic example, consider multiple sclerosis, which certainly carries an extremely dire connotation in its name and is typically thought of by laypersons as being in relatively the same category as Alzheimer's or Lou Gehrig's disease or even cancer. However, dramatically better treatments, which first became available in the mid-1990s, have revolutionized the therapy and prognosis for these persons. Now, even two decades or more after diagnosis, many are still working, and I no longer see the great majority of young people with MS becoming so disabled that they require wheelchairs due to an inability to walk. People no longer become completely dependent on their families or require nursing home placement while still in the early primes of their lives. Unfortunately, I routinely saw this disease ravage the bodies and minds of so many in their teens, twenties, and thirties from the 1980s up into the mid-1990s. But miraculously, this rarely happens in today's patients, given the divine knowledge that God has granted us in the form of multiple, multiple excellent treatment options to slow down this disease process and thus minimize disability secondary to it.

When I first went into neurology, it was a rarely chosen specialty because of the many chronic conditions such as those above, for which we could do very little besides offering symptom management. These diseases were usually managed poorly at best back then due to our limited treatment options. This resulted in most persons not doing well at all. I, therefore, feel amazingly blessed to have been able to practice neurology on both sides of the spectrum of these new treatments, both before and especially after these improvements were discovered and developed.

I daily discuss with patients whom I diagnose and treat for these diseases the revolutionary changes and dramatic improvements in care and treatment, which have optimized disease prognosis and quality of life and have extended survival times. I clearly see the dramatic difference in their outcomes in today's medical era. I too repeatedly realize that the only way in which I can honestly express my thoughts here is that there absolutely must be a divine origin for such, as God is over time imparting more and more of his knowledge to us for our benefit!

Decades ago, I was told by a neuroscientist whom I studied under that every two years, in the complex and rapidly evolving study of the brain and nervous system, half of what we think we know for certain becomes obsolete or is discovered to have been either partly true or completely in error!

In summary, to my perception, personally experiencing all the accelerating discoveries, facts, and advances of today makes it harder not to believe in a God than to believe in him, as I routinely and continually see how these developments allow us to better believe in his miracles.

***

Perhaps my best personal experience with a real miracle was a man named Evo whom I met on a mission trip. Evo was a Bulgarian gypsy who worked as a common laborer, a stone mason with little formal education. Yet, this man had just recently learned the complex Turkish language extremely well in only three weeks so he could translate Turkish to Bulgarian for a church congregation that had lost its translator. He told me the story of how he had asked God for that gift so that he could translate from the minister's Turkish tongue to the Bulgarian language of his fellow church members. My friend, the minister, was a missionary from Turkey, and in relating this story, he agreed that this, indeed, was a miracle. He said that when the man first offered his services and declared that he would learn Turkish, he had tried not to laugh, as the task to this Turk seemed impossible. He stated that even a language scholar could not learn Turkish as well as this man had if given three full years, let alone three brief weeks! There is no other way to explain this, other than this being purely mediated by God for his glory. In him and through him, all things are possible! To him be the glory, forevermore!

* * *

Next, consider the major discovery of splitting the atom. Modern-day science now understands that breaking an atom into its parts causes a huge nuclear explosion. It works by the scientific principle of entropy, in which all matter wants to become less organized (or more disorganized, like this atomic example). It is a principle that is recognized as one of our world's main driving physical and universal forces. But what then is the counterforce, or that which holds all these atoms together into our highly organized human bodies as well as into animals, trees, rocks, and everything else? This simply must be the work of a Creator God, as what else could rationally explain the presence of such an organizing force, one that runs directly counter to the disorganizing force that science clearly recognizes throughout our natural world?

* * *

Let us next discuss the fossil controversy. While we will look at evolutionism in more detail later, suffice it to say that many modern scientists hold that the fossil record first appeared about four hundred thousand years ago. They present this as an argument regarding the earth's age, which, in all likelihood, in looking specifically at the Bible, is most likely just six to ten thousand years old.

What! How is this explainable? Well, to my mind, projecting human or even ape-like forms back hundreds of thousands (or, as some do, even tens of millions of years) seems a huge stretch. It does not make logical sense. Consider how long one million years is and then look at the progress that humanity has made in the past hundred years alone. It seems highly unlikely that such life-forms could or would exist for such a long time without adapting and showing more rapid progress. And if true, we should find at least some degree of documentation for such within the fossil record. Such fossil evidence has never been discovered.

The fossil record appears at a single specific point in time. It is consistent with one major event, such as a great flood or other natural disaster. One event killed and deposited organisms together at one point in time instead of along a general, random, and progressively layered process. The latter is what one would expect if organisms had serially died and layered out over hundreds of thousands or even millions of years.

Also, how did the entire fossil record suddenly start with so many varied species within it at one common point in time? Again, fossils all seem to localize to relatively the same exact time period!

Further, does it really seem possible, let alone plausible, that, as modern science proposes, our planet could support our type or even lesser species for millions and millions of years? This probability seems quite unlikely given our vast consumption of resources.

And is it not possible that a day in Genesis could be a different time duration than the twenty-four-hour days we know presently? Our scientists were not there, yet they project modern-day processes and restrictions onto God's original supernatural work. This does not give me any reassurance whatsoever that this comparison can be accurately and reliably made! Consider Amos 6:13: "And just as stupid is your rejoicing in how great you are when you are less than nothing—and priding yourselves on your own tiny power!"

Further, while evolutionists and naturalists will say that there has been a gradual change from original single cells progressing over millions or billions of years into our current mammalian and human life-forms, does this seem logical and more likely than the alternative? Even if such were true, then where did that first living cell come from?

Nothing in our sciences has ever shown that life can come from non-life. How, therefore, could even a single living cell emerge from some type of primordial, non-living soup to then form amoebae, molds, fungi, or whatever else is suspected to have been floating about in that evolving soup so many proposed millions or billions of years ago? There is no way to explain this based upon reason, neither scientifically nor logically. Look again to God's Word:

> "How can men be wise? The only way to begin is by reverence for God. For growth in wisdom comes from obeying his laws. Praise his name forever." (Psalm 111:10)

> "For the reverence and fear of God are basic to all wisdom. Knowing God results in every other kind of understanding." (Proverbs 9:10)

I meet many people who tell me, "I believe in science and the things all around us, so I believe in nature but not in God." Yet, did not God create all these things? Can you not see this? Anyone who says this worships the creation rather than its Creator!

As a scientist myself and in studying and employing science for four decades now, I have seen many medical miracles, the miraculous workings of the human body, our chemistry and physics in action, and also how all of the physical world is held together by very tenuous, yet also extremely strong, workings. My mind's conclusion from all this is that there simply must be a benevolent Creator. To my scientifically trained mind, there is no doubt that there is an absolute 0 percent chance that this world's science, matter, and overall design within such complex patterns could have initiated by chance!

But what do some of our modern-day, great scientific minds think about this? Consider what Thomas Edison, one of the world's most brilliant modern scientific minds, the man who invented the light bulb, the phonograph, and the motion picture camera, concluded: "When you see everything that happens in the working universe and in the world of science, you cannot deny that there is a 'Captain on the bridge.'"

Two of the greatest thinkers of all time, Galileo Galilei, a scientist, physicist, inventor, and astronomer, and Sir Isaac Newton were solidly convinced Christians as well.

But if still not convinced, consider the brilliant scientific and mathematical mind of Blaise Pascal, who developed not only the probability theory but the first calculator (computer) model as well. In 1654, he humbly submitted to Jesus Christ. He realized that God was so much more than our mere scientific knowledge!

Further consider these three quotes from the great astronomer-scientist Johannes Kepler, who discovered the principles of planetary motion:

a) "These laws of nature are within the grasp of the human mind; God wanted us to recognize them by creating us after his own image so that we could share in his own thoughts."

b) "I am merely thinking God's thoughts after him."

c) "Science is simply learning to think like God."

I also like this quote from G. K. Chesterton: "Truth appears stranger than fiction, because we have fiction to suit ourselves."

Mark Twain also said, "It's no wonder that truth is stranger than fiction. Fiction has to make sense."

I cannot speak for you, but if these seven amazing minds (among so many others!) came to the realization that God and Christ are supreme, then the truth of the gospel is worth serious thought and investigation.

In conclusion, believing in science does not contradict or disallow a belief in God. The two go hand in the same hand, simply because God created science!

4. Evolution versus Creationism

"You made all the delicate, inner parts of my body and knit them together in my mother's womb. Thank you for making me so wonderfully complex! It is amazing to think about. Your workmanship is marvelous—and how well I know it. You were there while I was being formed in utter seclusion! You saw me before I was born and scheduled each day of my life before I began to breathe. Every day was recorded in your book!" (Psalm 139:13–16)

As a scientist, I believe that a firm belief in evolution requires a belief in miracles. Consider devices such as a toaster, a watch, or an airplane, each taken apart and thrown into a bag. No matter how often you shake the bag, could any of these have a realistic chance of coming together into a functional, working device?

To believe it could makes absolutely no sense. This belief position then is held only by a pridefully arrogant human mind, one that is trying to make up its own answers for what happened with creation rather than giving credit to the true Creator God.

Just look around you, wherever you may be. Is there anything in the room you are in now, let's say a table, book, light, rug, or chair that has been created without purpose? No, each of these was created by human beings for a specific purpose.

So, are we supposed to believe that human beings, the most intricate things in this entire world, so much more detailed and complex than the simple inanimate objects we named above, have come to be by random chance without any purposeful creation? To believe this seems extremely nonsensical, does it not?

***

The fossil record again shows a sudden appearance of nearly all phyla at one specific time. No missing link has ever having been found to verifiably document our proposed evolutionary development from primitive forms at some time in the distant past. Further, all the animal fossils look fully formed in the fossil record, without any trace of individual evolutionary ancestors.

It is very interesting for me to read the end of Darwin's *Origin of Species*, where he, in his later life, admits that evolution is not a likely explanation. He reportedly regretted what he had written in his evolutionary theories. I would invite you to read those last pages. I believe you will clearly discern his emotions and attitude for yourself.

Unlike Darwin in his later and apparently wiser years, the evolutionists and naturalists of today continue to deny that there is a divine Creator. They state that nature and science are all that is true. Therefore, the Bible and anyone who believes in a God-created world are wrong and are a threat to our freedoms and laws, which they say should be decided on by each individual per their own preference. If there is no Creator, as they posit, then there is no universal moral code, no reason for our being here, and no life after death.

Naturalistic minds today state that humanity either possesses or can obtain all the answers to everything. Theology, therefore, is useless, just a false and intruding ideology. They state that evolution is the real truth and that this process is ever continuing. Some even state that all creatures continue to evolve. Because naturalism rejects moral boundaries, moral relativists encourage each person to develop their own personally gratifying lifestyle. These souls, quite sadly, will never find their true purpose for being here, nor will they have any positive future past their deaths. They are living lives without hope and apart from God.

To counter evolutionary thought, let's scientifically look at the complexity of creation, starting at ground zero with its tiny building block, the DNA molecule. If one single person's DNA were removed and placed end to end, it would stretch a distance farther than to the sun and then back several times!

Now, could intricate complexity of this magnitude happen by chance? Consider the minuscule odds of a primordial, non-living soup suddenly becoming active with living cells. We know that simply could not happen spontaneously, as we again have never, ever witnessed or achieved, even with all our modern science and technology, the production of life from non-life. The existence of complex life, therefore, makes a strong argument for the existence of a Creator and not at all for life forming by random chance!

Consider those who research and study the DNA molecule itself. Francis Collins has been a lead DNA researcher for decades and headed the Human Genome Project for genetic disease mapping. He now is the current director of the National Institutes of Health. After all his years of work in this field, Collins remains firm in his belief of God as Creator of life![10] Now let me ask you, have you done investigatory work to a volume anywhere near to Collins's degree? Does he not have an authoritatively expert viewpoint—certainly, one worth at least considering and investigating further?

Consider too the fact that there are more than forty-six miles of nerves in every human body! Also, did you know that the average human heart beats about one hundred eight thousand times per day! Even more amazingly unbelievable is the fact that each child's body contains more than sixty thousand miles of arteries, veins, and capillaries. And each adult has about one hundred thousand miles of blood vessels, which is enough to encircle the globe four times!

Science, if you know it well (especially in my areas of expertise of medicine, genetics, and medical research), does not rule out or take away from faith. Rather, it bolsters it! As we discussed above, the entities of science and faith go hand in hand. Science says if you doubt it, then study it! You are meant to strive to understand it better so that your eyes will be opened to the truth!

***

Let's look further at the amazingly brilliant DNA molecule itself. There are 3.1 billion data pieces per strand of human DNA. Surely this argues for intelligent design. Random chance could never set such a life process into motion.

Further, if you would like a real shock, look at drawings or photos of laminin, the basic protein that provides the foundational network for most of our cells and organs. Its arrangement is trimeric; it is cross shaped. Can this be merely another coincidence—honestly!

Again consider biogenesis, the fact that life has only been found to arise from other life, and that no scientist anywhere has ever derived life from non-life. This is thus a basic, underlying law of our world's biology: life simply cannot come from non-living matter! Therefore, it follows that DNA can only be produced from other life. So how then could DNA have spontaneously occurred in a primordial, inorganic, non-living soup?

Fred Hoyle, a top mathematician who wrote the *Mathematics of Evolution*, calculated that the chance of life arising as such is the same as the probability of rolling the same number on a dice five million consecutive times![11] And we are asked to believe this? Certainly, it is more reasonable, considering such extreme probabilities, to believe in the divine Creator God! Consider,

> "God made the earth by his power and wisdom. He stretched out the heavens by his understanding. When he speaks, there is thunder in the heavens, and he causes the vapors to rise around the world; he brings the lightning with the rain and the winds from his treasuries. Compared to him, all men are stupid beasts. They have no wisdom—none at all!" (Jeremiah 51:15–17a)

Look once more at the law of entropy, the second law of thermodynamics for our universe, which states that all matter is constantly moving from a more-organized form to a more-disorganized state, moving downward not upward in its progression. How then could evolution claim the opposite? It violates the natural world's own established entropic principle! Such an evolutionary process has never been evidentially shown to occur in our world, no matter how much one tries to believe or to debate this!

So, in summary, we do not observe evolution in the fossil record or in our natural world in which we have become so technologically precise with our modern scientific investigations. Would you not expect that at least one of our brilliant scientific minds would have discovered perhaps a thread of solid evidence for evolution by now? Yes, one would. But they have not. Therefore, evolutionism is a theory that exists only in the minds of narrow-thinking evolutionists.

Yet, unfortunately, since being taught that we have all come from slimy algae, which somehow formed from non-living swamp water, rather than being created by a loving God with a purpose, we are now seeing its results: a generation with very poor self-esteem constantly searching for meaning in life. They do not know who they are, where they are from, or where they are going.

**

Let us also talk about theistic evolution, an invalid belief that states that God used evolution to create the world. It is a form of progressive creationism. Theistic evolution denies any worldwide flood and dates the universe at older than 15 billion years, because it states that the farthest thing we can see in space is a quasar located 15 billion light years away. The idea is that its light took at least 15 billion years to reach our eyes so that we could see it. Yet, could not a Creator God, one who forged DNA and all else, make starlight immediately visible to us no matter how far away its star may be?

God is transcendent. He is not part of creation but, rather, is its Creator. Yet, he remains immanent, actively involved and concerned about his creation. He is immense, unbound by space, and eternal, meaning that he is not bound by time. Could such a God be limited in any way?

**

Rise and Soar

Let's compare, in chart form, biblical creationism and the evolutionist or naturalist positions:

BIBLICAL CREATIONISM	EVOLUTIONISM/ NATURALISM
LIFE CAME FROM: LIFE, & GOD CREATED IT	NON-LIFE, SOMEHOW
ANIMALS WERE: ALL CREATED AT SAME TIME, ABOUT 6,000 to 10,000 YRS AGO OR MORE	ALL DESCENDED FROM COMMON ANCESTOR, 10,000 to 3.5 B YRS AGO
ALL CHANGES: INVOLVE TRAITS ALONE, NOT TYPES	ALL CAN MUTATE INTO ENTIRELY NEW FORMS/ KINDS
FOSSILS: SUDDENLY FORMED, BY FLOOD	FORMED OVER MILLIONS OF YEARS, GRADUALLY
LIFE & DEATH: HAVE MEANING, IN CHRIST	ARE MEANINGLESS PROCESSES, IN THE BIG SCOPE

Look at these contrasted views side by side and ask yourself which one seems more likely? Do you believe in a grand designer or, instead, that a random event, an unexplained explosion or fusion, somehow set life on this planet, with all its great intricacies, into motion?

The latter theory is, as we have shown, against all known rules of our universe. Chaos never breeds order, and non-life has never been shown to produce life from itself. I believe in a God who, as Creator, spoke this world into existence. And it follows naturally that, if he can do such, what is there that he cannot do?

* * *

If you ever get a chance, I strongly recommend visiting Ken Ham's Creation Museum and his Ark Encounter in northern Kentucky. These present visible examples and thought-provoking arguments that make a very strong case for the Creator God while also exploring the evolutionist position.

I visited recently with my family, and in addition to the many things that I learned, evidence was presented there that in 1993, 1997, and 2005, fossilized dinosaur bones were found with soft tissue and red blood cells still present within them. These findings strongly support the hypothesis that dinosaur fossils are more recent, that is, only thousands of years old rather than millions, and that they were very suddenly killed by a catastrophic event, likely the biblical flood described in Scripture. This would also explain how all fossils everywhere were formed suddenly, about four thousand three hundred fifty years ago, as these creatures were suddenly buried by debris and mud from the flood. Soft tissues and red blood cells do not last millions, let alone billions, of years. These findings shed serious doubt upon evolutionist doctrine! This result of the flood is evidence and testimony of God's existence, not merely proof of his judgement!

Further, Ham presents evidence that most dinosaurs by the fossil record appear to have been sheep or pony-sized, compared to the larger ones we typically imagine from watching modern movies. It appears that there were at least fifty to eighty different types of dinosaurs, as

Ham proposes, upon Noah's ark. Therefore, some dinosaurs appear to have lived after the flood. The flood did not eliminate their kind from the earth. The theory that baby, smaller tyrannosauruses, brontosauruses, and other representatives of the larger species were brought on board also seems sensible and credible looking at the data and logistics presented at the Ark Encounter. I strongly recommend a visit here to help you clarify and understand these issues in your own mind, no matter which side you belong to at the present.

***

Okay, so perhaps now, you may be considering changing your mindset over to the creationism side. Where should you start? Firstly, read Genesis. You must believe that this book and its creation account are the absolute and inerrant truth. Why? Because God says it is such. It is his own God-breathed message to us, his instruction manual for life on this planet, which he knows will best fulfill, protect, and save us until he eventually gathers us unto himself into eternal paradise forever.

You cannot continue trying to disprove God's Scripture with science. This is erroneous thinking, as these two entities are not mutually exclusive! One cannot try to apply mankind's minuscule amount of accumulated knowledge to God's biblical truths.

In my field of neurology, for example, nearly half of what we know becomes obsolete every two years! Things that we think are factually definitive regarding our treatments and diagnosis of diseases are constantly changing. This demonstrates how, in the medical arena of the brain and the nervous system, we are only scratching the very surface of knowledge! Now, extrapolate from neurology to imagine the incomprehensible vast degree of infinite knowledge in the entire universe.

Or look at the multiple organisms in our world. There are so many intricacies and complexities within each solitary species, not to mention the differences between these innumerable species themselves! This is extremely mind-blowing for me! So I ask, how could we ever presume to definitively know even a small part of this by ourselves? You instead must start with belief in our Creator God and Father and then get into his Word. You will soon see how your life changes once you have gained true peace, joy, fulfillment, and, ultimately, rescue. These are his gifts to you.

Surely these facts must make nonbelievers realize they must search thoroughly to be certain that their position is correct rather than simply continuing onward in their blindness, as they go merrily along with their little, fleeting lives on this planet. How can this life be the only thing? How can human beings, we hyper-complex organisms and intellects, merely die and turn to dust? Consider these verses from our Lord:

> "How stupid can they be! Isn't he, the Potter, greater than you, the jars he makes? Will you say to him, 'He didn't make us'? Does a machine call its inventor dumb?" (Isaiah 29:16)

> "Woe to the man who fights with his Creator. Does the pot argue with its maker?" (Isaiah 45:9a)

> "Are you so ignorant? Are you so deaf to the words of God—the words he gave before the world began? Have you never heard nor understood? It is God who sits above the circle of the earth. (The people below must seem to him like grasshoppers!) He is the one who stretches out the heavens like a curtain and makes his tent from them. He dooms the great men

of the world and brings them all to naught. They hardly get started, barely take root, when he blows on them and their work withers, and the wind carries them off like straw. 'With whom will you compare me? Who is my equal?' asks the Holy One. Look up into the heavens! Who created all these stars? As a shepherd leads his sheep, calling each by its pet name, and counts them to see that none are lost or strayed, so God does with stars and planets!" (Isaiah 40:21–26)

5. Mysteries

"We can see and understand only a little about God now, as if we were peering at his reflection in a poor mirror; but some-day we are going to see him in his completeness, face-to-face. Now all that I know is hazy and blurred, but then I will see everything clearly, just as clearly as God sees into my heart right now." (1 Corinthians 13:12)

Mysteries. Secrets. They hold a deep allure for us. There is a strong attraction when we hear or think of such things. We think of finding hidden treasures, going on secret adventures, and discovering, seeing, or experiencing things that no one else has ever done before. Our human minds enjoy these things that we do not yet know.

Nevertheless, when it comes to the mysteries of God and his workings, these perplexities are often presented by critics and skeptics as reasons not to believe, simply because they cannot understand them with their very intelligent-yet-merely-human minds. Just because we do not completely understand something, does that mean we should throw it out the window, ignore it, avoid it, or even worse, defame and decry it?

With worldly mysteries, we tend to do the opposite. We eagerly research, explore, and try to delve deeper. We attempt to learn all we can about what puzzles our minds. I challenge you to approach the mysteries of our heavenly Father with the same curious, investigative intrigue. If you do so, you will not be disappointed in your adventure.

***

Let us start with a major mystery, one that has baffled the human brain since it was first presented: that of the Trinity. I would never pretend to know its full explanation, but a major initial point must be made, especially when religions like the Jehovah's Witness and Islamic faiths say that belief in the Trinity is polytheistic or that it is blasphemy and denies their view of a solitary, singular God. However, the truth is this: our triune God is still one Lord, only with three separate characters or persons. While not an ideal example, a single person may function in different spheres simultaneously: as a parent, a child, a sibling, an aunt or uncle, a grandparent, a coworker, or a friend. Having these multiple roles doesn't split us into multiple people. We remain one person. These attributes are parts that make up an individual, yet we remain a single person.

So, he is one God in three persons.

I counter the doubters by stating that just as we function best with several roles at a time, our triune God is even more perfect. Or, if you are more a scientist than a people person, consider the atom, with its three separate major particles, namely the electron, proton, and neutron. These three parts make up one whole atom. Taking one part away will cause the atom to cease to exist. Also, considered geometrically, any three-sided figure, such as a triangle or a tripod stand, has no opening or weakness. It has strong support from all three sides. It

Rise and Soar

is thus much more difficult to push over or to overcome than it would be with a single or two-legged stance. This is exactly why a third leg, such as a cane, is so commonly used by the elderly or disabled. It adds support and protects from falls.

Similarly, a triune God is your perfect stronghold, your walled city. He is one who can easily protect you. He is Jehovah God. And he is also one who intercedes for you, as Christ. And he remains immanent, involved and helpful throughout your life. And he mediates for you with his Father! The Holy Spirit, meanwhile, enlightens and guides you throughout your life. I like to think of the Trinity as God drawing a protective triangle around his own, so strongly secure that nothing evil can penetrate such. We must get into and remain in the middle of this triune Godhead, protected and surrounded by our God.

Many critics will say that there is no proof for the Trinity in the Bible. I disagree, although they are correct in that the exact term is not specifically noted in the text. Still, references to the Father, the Son, and the Holy Spirit abound in Scripture. For example, consider Genesis 1:2: "The Spirit of God was hovering over the surface of the waters," or even more so, Genesis 1:26: "Then God said, 'Let Us make man in Our image, according to Our likeness'" (HCSB).

In John 10:30, Jesus states that he is one with or the same as God, as he says, "I and the Father are one."

Also, consider 2 Corinthians 13:13, where all three are mentioned at once: "The grace of the Lord Jesus Christ, and the love of God, and the fellowship of the Holy Spirit be with all of you" (HCSB).

Even more convincing to me is Jesus's Great Commission in Matthew 28:19: "Go, therefore, and make disciples of all nations, baptizing them in the name of the Father and of the Son and of the Holy

Spirit" (HCSB). If each were not divine, why then would Christ mention them all in the same breath in this, his final command before his ascension?

No matter how intelligent we may presume ourselves to be, take a step back for a moment and think about this, openly and honestly: can you expect any man to be able to even come remotely close to the intellect and understanding of our divine Creator and heavenly Father?

There are going to be things we will never fully understand in this life. But we should rest assured that he will give us all these answers in our next life if we are with him! We cannot control everything and cannot know everything. This is part of the dependence that God wants us to have upon him. He wants us to be at a point where we communicate with him about our questions, with our concerns, and with our lack of understanding. Bring these to him! Ask him to give you a mental peace with this, and he will! We must leave our wonderings upon these his great mysteries to him for the present time:

> "This plan of mine is not what you would work out, neither are my thoughts the same as yours! For just as the heavens are higher than the earth, so are my ways higher than yours, and my thoughts than yours." (Isaiah 55:8–9)

> "I praise you, O Father, Lord of heaven and earth, for hiding these things from the intellectuals and worldly wise and for revealing them to those who are as trusting as little children." (Luke 10:21)

> "Oh, what a wonderful God we have! How great are his wisdom and knowledge and riches! How impossible it is for us to understand his decisions and his methods! For who among us can know the mind of the Lord? Who knows enough to

be his counselor and guide? And who could ever offer to the Lord enough to induce him to act? For everything comes from God alone. Everything lives by his power, and everything is for his glory. To him be glory evermore." (Romans 11:33–36)

6. Proofs for Jesus's Divinity

The only way to truthfully answer this query is to go directly to the Scriptures, into God's Holy Word, which we have already established as being solely and persistently truthful. Let us look at biblical references that identify Jesus as God.

"If you believe that Jesus is the Christ—that he is God's Son and your Savior—then you are a child of God. . . . Loving God means doing what he tells us to do, and really, that isn't hard at all; for every child of God can obey him, defeating sin and evil pleasure by trusting Christ to help him. But who could possibly fight and win this battle except by believing that Jesus is truly the Son of God? And we know he is, because God said so with a voice from heaven when Jesus was baptized, and again as he was facing death. . . . And the Holy Spirit, forever truthful, says it too. So we have these three witnesses: the voice of the Holy Spirit in our hearts, the voice from heaven at Christ's baptism, and the voice before he died. And they all say the same thing: that Jesus Christ is the Son of God. We believe men who witness in our courts, and so surely we can believe whatever God declares. And God declares that Jesus is his Son." (1 John 5:1, 3–9)

"Jesus told him, 'I am the Way—yes, and the Truth and the Life. No one can get to the Father except by means of me.

If you had known who I am, then you would have known who my Father is. . . . Anyone who has seen me has seen the Father! . . . Don't you believe that I am in the Father and the Father is in me? The words I say are not my own but are from my Father who lives in me. And he does his work through me. Just believe it—that I am in the Father and the Father is in me. Or else believe it because of the mighty miracles you have seen me do." (John 14:6–7, 9–11)

Here, Jesus definitively stated in no uncertain terms and beyond any doubt that he indeed is God. Naturally, it follows that to know Christ is to know God and vice versa, that to know God is to know the Son as well. Consider these further references:

"I and the Father are one. . . . Don't believe me unless I do miracles of God. But if I do, believe them even if you don't believe me. Then you will become convinced that the Father is in me, and I in the Father." (John 10:30, 37–38)

"On the way across he lay down for a nap, and while he was sleeping the wind began to rise. A fierce storm developed that threatened to swamp them, and they were in real danger. They rushed over and woke him up. 'Master, Master, we are sinking!' they screamed. So he spoke to the storm: 'Quiet down,' he said, and the wind and waves subsided and all was calm! Then he asked them, 'Where is your faith?' And they were filled with awe and fear of him and said to one another, 'Who is this man, that even the winds and waves obey him?'" (Luke 8:23–25)

"The home was filled with mourning people, but he said, 'Stop the weeping! She isn't dead; she is only asleep!' This brought scoffing and laughter, for they all knew she was dead. Then he took her by the hand and called, 'Get up, little girl!' And at that moment her life returned and she jumped up!" (vv. 52–55)

These and Jesus's many other miracles fulfilled the predictions of the Old Testament prophets as well as those of John the Baptist. Jesus fulfilled their messages just as they had proclaimed he would! Christ satisfied these biblical prophecies. Against incredible odds, he fulfilled all of them! As one brief example, look to see how the prophecy of Isaiah 53:4 was fulfilled in his healing of the sick and expelling of demons:

"That evening several demon-possessed people were brought to Jesus; and when he spoke a single word, all the demons fled; and all the sick were healed. This fulfilled the prophecy of Isaiah, 'He took our sicknesses and bore our diseases.'" (Matthew 8:16–17)

Jesus fulfilled many prophecies, including more than sixty major prophecies throughout the Bible. Yet, the odds of any one person fulfilling even just several of these is amazingly low!

Mathematics professor Peter Stoner calculated the odds of one person fulfilling even just eight of these sixty-plus prophecies, which came out to be 1×10 to the 21st power, which translates to trillions on the long scale used in much of Europe or sextillions on the short scale used in countries such as the United States. In America, such would come after the millions, and then the billions, followed by trillions, quadrillions, and quintillions, before ultimately getting to the sextillions!

Now, it is easy to throw numbers like this out there, but exactly what numerical amount are we talking about? To explain this better, Stoner used this example illustration: "First, blanket the entire Earth land mass with silver dollars one hundred twenty feet high. Second, specially mark one of those dollars and randomly bury it. Third, ask a person to travel the earth and select the marked dollar, while blindfolded, from the trillions of other dollars." Of note, the American Scientific Association reviewed his work and then verified it, stating, "The mathematical analysis… is based upon principles of probability which are thoroughly sound, and Professor Stoner has applied these principles in a proper and convincing way."[12]

Please realize that this again is only the probability of just eight of those sixty-plus major prophecies being fulfilled, not to mention the Bible's three hundred-plus lesser prophecies, which he satisfactorily fulfills as well. It seems impossible to imagine the probability of such, yet Christ did indeed do so!

In summary, there has been no other historical figure whose ancestry, birthplace, life, work and teachings, initial acceptance followed by rejection, crucifixion and death, and resurrection have been so clearly foretold by so many different authors of the Old Testament. Certainly, no other religion has such amazing prophetic fulfillment in its writings!

If these prophecies have all come true, then look to the still-pending conclusion of God's Word, in his Holy Bible! Do you really wish to take a chance that these foretellings about Jesus's second coming and judgment are not going to happen?

**

There further are many other proofs in Scripture for the divinity of Christ, including:

"Jesus took Peter, James, and his brother John to the top of a high and lonely hill, and as they watched, his appearance changed so that his face shone like the sun and his clothing became dazzling white. Suddenly Moses and Elijah appeared and were talking with him. . . . a bright cloud came over them, and a voice from the cloud said, 'This is my beloved Son, and I am wonderfully pleased with him. Obey him.'" (Matthew 17:1–3, 5)

"He was God, as shown by the fact that he rose again from the dead." (2 Timothy 2:8b)

"We all are witnesses that Jesus rose from the dead." (Acts 2:32b)

"God's Son shines out with God's glory, and all that God's Son is and does marks him as God. He regulates the universe by the mighty power of his command. He is the one who died to cleanse us and clear our record of all sin, and then sat down in highest honor beside the great God of heaven." (Hebrews 1:3)

Can human words add anything to these scriptures? Human words cannot come close to the clear affirmation of these scriptures that Jesus is God Almighty!

7. Proofs for Jesus's Rising from the Dead

If Jesus did not rise, then the Christian faith itself is based upon a fallacy. But is there any hard and true evidence for the resurrection, or are we solely asked to believe it on faith alone?

As discussed previously, the oral and written traditions surrounding Jesus's resurrection are not what would be expected were mere men conspiring to create a myth or a fairy tale. Portraying an epic literary savior or hero, a character meant to be worshiped and followed, as a criminal killed by being nailed to a tree is atypical and unlikely to be successful in that day or any other. Very few sane readers or listeners would be likely to believe such a tall tale. Certainly not the great multitudes who converted, unless it was the truth verified by reliable eyewitnesses!

Further, an appearance of this risen hero to women first, in that time, rather than to his own leading men themselves would certainly not be a theme that would be used or even considered by the Jewish culture of that day. Additionally, would such a story ever be written in the manner where his fearfully secluded main men, his disciples, were so initially skeptical of the women's report of a resurrected Jesus?

We have also discussed the conversion of Jesus's skeptic brothers, namely James and Jude. Would a fabricated hero's family members doubt him during his life but then suddenly, after his death and resurrection, begin declaring him to be what they had previously denied? No, they would more likely support him before and after death, were such a story being created for optimal effect.

Further solid evidence of course is the more than five hundred eyewitnesses who saw Jesus alive again after seeing him die. These people saw proof enough that they threw away their Jewish traditions of one thousand five hundred years, including inheritance and family ties and property claims, to follow this Messiah Christ! Certainly, without definitive evidence, no sane human person would ever do such, let alone the many thousands of Jews who did! These people not only gave up everything in their physical worldly life, but vast multitudes also surrendered their lives for this belief in the risen Christ. They chose to go to their graves for their firm declaration of faith in Jesus and his resurrection. They did not recant even at the point of the sword, a stoning, the wild beasts of the arena, or multiple other forms of injury and death.

One more extremely convincing piece of evidence is the empty tomb. Jesus's dead (not partially dead) body was definitively placed in a hewn-out tomb. We historically know this per the records of the day. But then, his body disappeared, and to date, no one has ever been able to produce it. Neither the Jews nor the Romans could produce the corpse of Jesus. That's why they could not quell the growing belief in the testimony of the five hundred-plus eyewitnesses. Nor could they suppress the witness of Jesus's disciples and other followers who, after his rising, spent forty days in frequent and close physical contact with Christ. They could touch Jesus, speak to him, and eat and drink with him.

Therefore, as Matthew says, the Jews had to create a lie. They created a cover-up that Jesus's corpse had been stolen. However, their account does not explain how the extremely large tombstone was moved by a ragtag group of men and women so frightened that they had locked themselves away for fear of the Jews. And this done at a site being strongly guarded by elite Roman troops as well as Jewish temple guards. In the Roman legions, any guard who fell asleep and let prisoners escape knew he would be executed. So, they would not have stood by while the disciples moved the stone. Finally, it does not explain how this poor, uneducated group suddenly changed from their frightened, cowering, and grief-stricken state into a band of fearless evangelists for Christ, converting three thousand Jews on the very first day that they went out to preach, followed by five thousand the next day.

These remarkably altered men and women refused to recant their belief in Christ to the point of death. Why would anyone in their right mind do this for a confabulation, lie, or fallacy? There is no reason that satisfactorily explains their actions and convictions other than the obvious: they were so certain of Jesus's resurrection that they could not deny it!

Consider yourself attempting, when asked at the point of a sword or a gun, to deny that your nose or your mouth was a part of your face. This would plainly be difficult to do. In the same way, these new Christians were so convinced of all that they had seen and heard from this risen Jesus that trying to deny him would have been as hard and as unnatural as it would be to deny one's own body parts.

Further, we have modern-day evidences for Christ's resurrection. Take the continual growth of the Christian church throughout the world despite steadily increasing persecution. Without real truth being present in the resurrection, how could one explain how the fledgling church survived such extreme persecution apart from the risen Christ empowering and growing it?

Consider also how the Christian faith has become the world's largest religion. Why is this? The only logical answer is its being the one true faith in Jesus Christ, the true Lord God.

Further, one can look at the survival of the communion sacrament, which commemorates Jesus's death for us. When he was eating with his disciples on the night before he went to the cross, Jesus commanded them to eat bread and drink wine in memory of him. If he had not risen, why would this rite be performed at the command of a dead man, being celebrated repeatedly and increasingly year after year all over the world? Such would make no sense either.

As contrary examples, look at some of the founders of false faiths and cults who have died. For example, is there any celebration for Jim Jones and his Peoples Temple cult forty years after his death or for any others like him? No, because none of these are like Christ, who visibly changed and still changes the life of every single person who reaches out to seek him and learns to know and to trust him. This transforming power from God is still available today, even as it was in New Testament times!

These evidences for Jesus's resurrection are irrefutable. There is no other logical explanation. There is no stolen body. Nor did Jesus swoon. Critics claims that Jesus was taken off the cross still alive. They suspect a wounded Christ and suggest, despite torture and mutilation, that Jesus was able to push aside his immense and heavy tombstone to escape. Thereafter, he grabbed a red-eye flight to India or to wherever else other legends and myths suggest that he went.

In conclusion, please look at this logically. There is no other likely explanation. In all probability, Jesus's resurrection is more likely to have happened than not. The evidence exceeds the legal burden of proof, even if one considers the five hundred-plus eyewitnesses alone!

It is thus incredulous and amazing that some people today, many of them extremely intelligent, will blindly continue to neglect and deny the possibility of Jesus Christ rising from the dead. We all therefore need to open our eyes so we can understand exactly what he did in performing this resurrection miracle for us!

8. Why Did Christ Come to Our World?

If Jesus Christ really is God, then why did he come here? Why didn't he stay up in heaven in all his glory? Did he come to spoil our fun? No, not at all. He came out of God's love for us in order to save us. And in saving, he came to give us the privilege of entering a perfect relationship with him. It begins here and continues into an eternal relationship in heaven with he and his Father forever. Jesus's coming to earth is the full and true testimony of God's pure and unchanging love for us!

Now, imagine that you are a parent and that you are asked to give up your only child for someone else. Even if you loved that someone else, how difficult would this be? Certainly, it would be extremely difficult. What about for somebody that did not love you back, or somebody who had been mean to you and your child and whom you knew would mock, torture, and eventually kill your child? We would never give our own child for someone who was so murderous and defiant.

This, however, is exactly what God did for us and for all people by giving his Son, even for those who crucified him that day upon Calvary. How amazing, then, is this love that God has for all of us? It is so amazing that our minds cannot fully comprehend it in our current world. We can never fully understand this!

Our job is to trust him, to realize and to believe that this love is indeed available for us, to accept his free gift of this love, and then to follow his plans for our life, as we express this great love to others in our deeds and in our words. We too will become like Christ, like God's love. We will become his hands, his feet, and his mouth to others. This is the plan that God wants for each of us. And it is the only thing that will ever make us feel fulfilled and complete in this lifetime here upon this earth.

Rather than mere human words, I believe the best way to answer why Christ came is to go directly to Scripture. Consider first, in Luke 19, the story of Zacchaeus, the sinful tax collector whom Jesus simply greeted. Then note how, without any pressure at all (Christ simply told Zacchaeus he would be eating at his house that day), just the presence of Jesus was enough to cause this sinful man to repent. Jesus's response to this was, "I, the Messiah, have come to search for and to save such souls as his" (Luke 19:10). Next, consider:

"I have come into the world to give sight to those who are spiritually blind and to show those who think they see that they are blind." (John 9:39)

"For only I, the Messiah, have come to earth and will return to heaven again. . . . I must be lifted up upon a pole, so that anyone who believes in me will have eternal life. For God loved the world so much that he gave his only Son so that anyone who believes in him shall not perish but have eternal life. God did not send his Son into the world to condemn it, but to save it. There is no eternal doom awaiting those who trust him to save them. But those who don't trust him have already been tried and condemned for not believing in the only Son of God." (John 3:13–18)

"I must fall and die like a kernel of wheat that falls into the furrows of the earth. Unless I die I will be alone—a single seed. But my death will produce many new wheat kernels—a plentiful harvest of new lives. If you love your life down here—you will lose it. If you despise your life down here— you will exchange it for eternal glory. . . . that is the very reason why I came!" (John 12:23–25, 27b)

"Jesus shouted to the crowds, 'If you trust me, you are really trusting God. For when you see me, you are seeing the one who sent me. I have come as a Light to shine in this dark world, so that all who put their trust in me will no longer wander in the darkness. If anyone hears me and doesn't obey me, I am not his judge—for I have come to save the world and not to judge it. But all who reject me and my message will be judged at the Day of Judgment by the truths I have spoken."' (John 12:44–48)

"It isn't your sacrifices and your gifts I want—I want you to be merciful. For I have come to urge sinners, not the self-righteous, back to God." (Matthew 9:13)

"And I, the Messiah, came to save the lost." (Mathew 18:11)

"And if you want to be right at the top, you must serve like a slave. Your attitude must be like my own, for I, the Messiah, did not come to be served, but to serve, and to give my life as a ransom for many." (Matthew 20:27–28)

Finally, as described here in Luke 4, consider how Jesus opened his public ministry at his hometown synagogue in Nazareth. He read Old Testament verses from Isaiah 61:1–2, officially announcing that he is the long-awaited Savior of mankind:

"The Spirit of the Lord is upon me; he has appointed me to preach Good News to the poor; he has sent me to heal the brokenhearted and to announce that captives shall be released and the blind shall see, that the downtrodden shall be freed from their oppressors, and that God is ready to give blessings to all who come to him. . . . Then he added, 'These Scriptures came true today!'" (Luke 4:18–19, 21)

9. Only One Way?!

"I am the way, the truth, and the life. No one comes to the Father except through Me." (John 14:6 HCSB)

Hear this clearly! This is not just my opinion. I am telling you what God's Word clearly says, in no uncertain terms, because I care about you—I love you—and you must know that if you deny or doubt his Word, then I am very worried for you!

I am not oppressing you with my Christian talk. No, I am humbly telling you the truth. I am reporting the news of the best gift in all the world! It is so amazing that I simply must share it—I have to! Would you keep a cure for Alzheimer's, ALS, cancer, or some other fatal disease a secret if you had the cure? No, you would gladly tell it and save others.

Also, logically, if you will not let me express my belief, then aren't you oppressing me? Yes, if you believe something differently from me and tell me your belief emphatically yet refuse to hear or even consider mine whatsoever, are you not oppressing me?

I tell you this good news in the hope that you will seek God, your true Creator Father, and that he will show you his truth so that your eyes will be opened for the salvation of your soul as well as for a better life here in this world, one filled with God's peace, true joy, fulfillment, and his rescue.

Therefore, what God has asked me to tell you cannot in truth be considered as arrogance. Every single religion or belief system, be it Islam, Hinduism, Buddhism, or other systems, claims exclusivity and, therefore, necessarily denies all other religions. It is not solely Christians who claim a single way to salvation!

Therefore, Christian concepts and truths are not arrogant, although some Christians may be. Yet they are not how the Lord Jesus Christ wishes them to be. He would never act as such, were he physically here today speaking with you face-to-face. Therefore, do not let such persons turn you off, resulting in your throwing your life away!

***

Real truth is singular and exclusive by its very nature. Consider the laws of physics, chemistry, and mathematics. Using examples such as 4 + 4 = 8, 1 + 1 = 2, and 2 x 3 = 6 or the fixed boiling, melting, and freezing points of water and other substances, each of these has only one single solitary answer, never multiples. If a proposed truth does not exclude falsities, it then follows that such truth cannot be held as fact; rather, it is exposed to be mere subjective opinion. Truth must exclude its opposites and errors. Pluralism is impossible with genuine truth. Many different truths to the same question or issue are not possible.

So, if there is just one true God, does it not make logical sense that there would be just one way to him? And if it is true that there is this one single path to our God and his salvation, then this is simply true, no more and no less.

No religion today teaches the same things as the others, nor do any in their alternative doctrines describe the existence of multiple ways to God. One path alone is the doctrine with each and every one! Each professes distinct and very mutually exclusive doctrines. Each points out a different road to their perceived divine being or end state, which is described as their final reward or paradise or heaven. Yet, if there is indeed just one path to this goal of reaching the one real God, then these many varied paths, by truth's definition, cannot all be true! No indeed. Only one can be!

If only one path is the correct course, then to decide which is really the true faith, one must then look at the evidence underlying the foundations of each belief system. Looking at the evidence objectively,

Christianity is the only faith with a firm supporting base if you employ our world's legal proof system for such evidence. Simply review and contemplate it with your intelligence and with an open mind! God has gifted you with that intelligent brain, yet it is also necessary for you to open it in order to consider and investigate his truth!

This sole truth is externally separate from man's thoughts and feelings. It has always existed, and will forever continue to do so, whether we choose to believe it or not!

So, no religion is tolerant or universal. Yet, Christianity is certainly more tolerant than the others in that it does not persecute other faiths. With a few rare exceptions, all the other religions do persecute other faiths—especially Christians! Yes, Christianity does seek to convert others in bringing Jesus's good news to them. Yet, it respects everyone's right to choose his or her own destiny.

Christians absolutely share Christ's good news because it is the real and verified truth and because some may not yet have heard it. It is so good and so saving that we absolutely must share it! It is not meant to be kept inside! Think of a time you heard some good news. How hard was it to keep that to yourself? What was your first reaction? For most of us, it is that we want to express it to someone!

Further, while Christianity is exclusive in that you can only come to salvation by knowing Jesus through his cross and the sacrifice that he made for your sins, Christianity is also actually completely and universally inclusive when it comes down to who may come to God. This is wholly unlike Buddhism and Hinduism, with their caste systems and untouchables, or the Jehovah's Witnesses, who exclude people who smoke or have other unbroken bad habits, or Mormonism, where only some of their number are allowed to actually go to temple.

Rather, Jesus and his gift are open to anyone who will accept and believe on him! He came for sinners, and therefore he came for all of us so that all may be forgiven and enter into a perfect relationship with him.

Yes, you can only be saved through Jesus. We have just discussed the need for real truth's exclusivity. However, this one true way is also inclusive, meaning that salvation is available for anyone who will believe. There is no one who cannot be saved!

Consider a story of two restaurants. First, picture an exclusive restaurant. You need to be dressed appropriately for admission. Then, you are required to pay before you can come in and eat. And perhaps you must also do something else after you have eaten, such as wash dishes. Contrast that with an all-inclusive, open door type of restaurant, such as a rescue mission, where all are openly invited and welcome to come in and eat. There is no fee. Your appearance doesn't matter, nor does your wallet size, or your social status. Which eatery would you rather attend?

***

Unfortunately, many people still believe that there being only one way is arrogant and narrow-minded. But once again, how can many different ways to one truth or one state ever be true if you think about this objectively with an open mind? Yet we commonly hear people say, "All religions are pretty much the same."

That fallacy is exactly what the world and its devil want us to believe. It gives one a vague, semi-comfortable assurance. Yet it is a myth that will keep one locked within its trap until that critical last moment—unless one delves into and then explores the true facts for oneself. Therefore, do not delay! Begin this journey today!

To better clarify this point, let's look at some of the basic differences between these religions. While Eastern religions believe in an impersonal god, Islam, Judaism, and Christianity all believe in a personal God. Yet if we look at their doctrinal beliefs regarding Christ, the latter three, however, each claim something fundamentally different. For Muslims, Jesus Christ is seen as a great prophet of Islam, while in Judaism he is seen as a good and wise rabbi (a teacher). And of course, in Christianity, he is seen as God and Savior. Similarly, Islam says that Jesus did not die but swooned (fainted) on the cross and was taken to heaven by Allah, while Judaism simply denies he rose from the dead. Christianity not only says that he rose but that he reigns, ascendant, from heaven. How could one ever rationalize these differences and claim that they are all concurrently correct? Such reasoning is invalid.

Simply step back and think. Claiming that all three of these faiths say the same thing makes no sense! Obviously, one of these must be correct and the other two false. And if two are false, then are not those two religious belief systems also highly suspect, if based upon a false premise?

So, whether you like it or not, there is only one true faith and one true way to God. If there is one true God, it makes sense there would only be one true religion. Christ strictly taught, as God incarnate, that no one comes to God except through him: "I am the way, the truth, and the life. No one comes to the Father except through Me" (John 14:6 HCSB).

Further, Christ clearly stands far above all other religious founders by proving his authority to claim exclusivity! He alone died for our sins, and therefore, only he can forgive them, and only he can save us. Also, Christ's rising from death shows that only he has the keys to eternal life.

Only Jesus gives proof of God forgiving us and granting us full assurance that we also will rise into an eternal heaven with God when we die, just as Christ did, if we will only believe on Jesus!

No other religion offers full assurance of salvation without requiring specific works be done in order to earn it. Only Christ, through his resurrection, answers and solves the sin problem that every person has. And only Christ has conquered death. Therefore, he alone is the way to salvation and to God and to our eternal life! "Salvation is found in no one else, for there is no other name under heaven given to mankind by which we must be saved" (Acts 4:12 NIV).

***

Let's now look deeper into the evidence for the doctrines and viewpoints about Jesus's death and resurrection taught by the above three religions. Which has the best supporting evidence? Again, we must look to the facts: to archaeology, to history given by eyewitnesses, and to science itself. Consider a human body beaten to within inches of death and then hung up to suffocate and die, while also being pierced not just in his distal limbs but also through his very heart! Obviously, the Christian view that Christ died makes logical sense. Other views about his survival from the cross are very, very unlikely. While we must concede that they cannot be absolutely ruled out, it is clear that the Christian view is much more probable than the other two. Judaism and Islam do not and cannot explain away the historically documented reports of the actual physical death of Christ and of the internment of his corpse in a tomb. These other faiths cannot explain the empty tomb. They cannot say why his body was never produced or discovered.

As I discussed above, had his corpse been found, a great spectacle would have been made by the Jews and Romans to disprove this new

Christian view that was spreading. Further, if there was a conspiracy by body snatchers, it would be extremely unlikely that the conspirators would all, to a soul, remain forever true to their secret without spilling the beans when faced with death by persecutors!

Therefore, any claim, view, or doctrine that is put forth must have enough evidence to support it. This is the only way to evaluate whether it is clearly true and logical. Evidence must accurately support all its points and doctrines, rather than simply offering an alternative mythical and illogical system of folly undocumented by facts! Only Christianity has such a claim. Only Christianity backs up its doctrines and beliefs with appropriate eyewitness (that is, historical) truth as well as scientific and archaeological evidence.

***

In summary, Jesus's resurrection is indeed a historical event. It is impossible to deny that Jesus rose from the dead. And so, it is impossible to deny the Christian gospel. It is the truth! What other faith has such historical and eyewitness proof to confirm it? As we will see below, none of the other religions possess this.

Do not take my mere word for it. Check this out for yourself! Is this not the most important question you will face in your lifetime? Is it worth taking a chance on your being wrong? Also, what if you are wrong? Consider these verses:

> "Don't you see that I alone am God? I kill and make live. I wound and heal—no one delivers from my power. I raise my hand to heaven and vow by my existence, that I will whet the lightning of my sword! And hurl my punishments upon my enemies!" (Deuteronomy 32:39–41)

"Let all the world look to me for salvation! For I am God; there is no other. I have sworn by myself, and I will never go back on my word, for it is true—that every knee in all the world shall bow to me, and every tongue shall swear allegiance to my name." (Isaiah 45:22–23)

Christ clearly and blatantly declares that he is the way, the truth, the light, the vine, and the life—that he is God. And he backs this up solidly in his Gospels through his words and by the deeds he performed while he was here in our world. Review these in his Holy Bible, and you shall see for yourself! Besides perhaps the founders of a few short-lived cults, what other founder of a world religion has ever claimed such divinity and power?

How well we live or how morally good we are is not important. We will never be able to live up to God's standard. Therefore, we absolutely must have his grace for our salvation. We can never do this alone. This is the single most important truth: we absolutely need God for salvation, and he, in his great love and concern for us, has given us his Son, Jesus, who has already lived up to God's standard for us! In conclusion, all we need do is simply believe that he has done so and then accept his free gift of forgiveness. We must always remember Jesus's statement here: "The highway to hell is broad, and its gate is wide enough for all the multitudes who choose its easy way. But the Gateway to Life is small, and the road is narrow, and only a few ever find it" (Matthew 7:13–14).

10. Aren't All Religions Basically the Same?

No, each religion is exclusive. This is the clear answer to any objective examiner who takes the time to compare one to each other. He will conclude that they absolutely and definitively are not the same. While many like to conveniently say that we all worship the same god, only Christianity proclaims that Christ is God and that he too is a loving God, so loving that he is the one who died to save us!

All other religions, in total, say that Jesus was just a created man, including Judaism and Islam. Therefore, every other faith system denies the deity of Christ. And in many of these, such as Islam, there is never any mention of a loving god-figure in their writings.

Let's look briefly at our current world's ten largest religious groups, to demonstrate scale and global membership, on the next page.

We discussed some basic differences in the prior section. I will now present further evidence that provides overwhelming proof that each of these religions is in fact extremely unique in their doctrines. They are clearly not the same. In statement of fact, no two faith systems are alike.

Whenever someone repeats this common opinion to me that all religions are basically the same, my response is, "Okay then, name even one religion that says we are all basically the same in our beliefs." Although some of its laypeople may do so, not one single religious denomination claims this officially, were you to approach its clerics and scholars with this question. Each faith has very different claims and doctrines.

The bottom-line difference between Christianity and the others is that all those other faiths each deny that Christ was God made flesh who died so that our loving God could save all of us from death in our sins! Regarding this Jesus, Acts 4:12 tells us, "There is salvation in no one else! Under all heaven there is no other name for men to call upon to save them."

TOP 10 WORLD RELIGIONS

(as of 2018, per "World's Top Most")

RELIGION	FOLLOWERS	% of TOTAL POPULATION
CHRISTIANITY	2.3 Billion	32%
ISLAM	1.6 Billion	23%
HINDUISM	1 Billion	15%
BUDDHISM	400 Million	7%
SIKHISM	30 Million	0.4%
JUDAISM	20 Million	0.3%
BAHAISM	8 Million	0.15%
CONFUCIANISM	7 Million	0.1%
JAINISM	4.5 Million	0.06%
SHINTOISM	4 Million	0.01%

***

So, what is meant by the term religion?

In many discussions about Christianity and our Lord Jesus, people try to stop me by saying, "Whoa there, I'm really not religious." My response of late has been, "Well, I don't consider myself religious either." I then state that, in my view, religions consist of men seeking a divine power or god-state. Religions are the too-numerous-to-count ways in which mankind over the ages has sought a divine being or beings to see if such exist or to please or appease such gods. And how interesting that their imaginary deities always fit their lifestyles, their cultures, and their societal norms.

I then compare these religions to Christianity. It is so different. Its one true God reaches down to humanity rather than humanity reaching up for him. I believe this to be a very important distinction, as it helps us to see and to explain a fundamental difference between Christianity and all other faith systems.

Think about this open-mindedly: how could a single divinity, the one true God, ever fit into all these different perceptions of him? Could they all be right? I believe the best answer to that is to ask another question: is there ever more than one single truth to any given query? While some may feel there can be, this is simply illogical. Consider again science and mathematics: does 2 + 2 ever equal anything but 4? No! 2 + 2 can never be said to sometimes equal 5, 6, 28, or any other number. Consider how the freezing points of water and all other substances, as well as their melting and boiling points, are solitary, fixed, and specific. They do not ever vary. Given these unchanging rules of our universe, why would we expect the supreme Creator God, he who designed our world, to potentially be so many different things to so many different belief systems? It is not common sense to suggest it.

***

Another thought I often have regarding these varied faiths is this: why has there, almost to the point of exclusivity for the past two thousand years (save the exceptions of the recent Hindu persecution of Muslims in India and the two Muslim factions, Sunnis and Shiites, which engage in conflict), only been persecution of the Christian religion? I believe it is because Christianity is the one true and absolute faith, because it is God's truth!

There are an estimated six hundred million Christians being persecuted at this time across the world. I believe Satan attacks essentially just Christianity and its members because it really is the true faith. He ignores all those other belief systems, letting them distract and grow as much as they will because their members are all his enslaved children who have fallen into and are blindly entrapped within his developed falsehoods.

Yet despite Christianity's persecution, it now, as in the days immediately after Christ rose, continues to grow stronger daily, and I firmly believe that it does so only because it is truly from God. Remember Gamaliel, the Pharisee, who spoke to the Jewish Sanhedrin council about the early Christians. His wise advice was to no longer persecute them but to let them be. He correctly reasoned that if faith in Christ was something from man alone, then it would soon die out on its own. However, he also stated that if it was from God, then there was no way that man could ever squelch or stop it, and they would not be wise to go against it.

***

You may ask, what of those who believe alternative doctrines that say Jesus is not God or a Savior? In Mark 16:14–17, Jesus rebukes the disciples for their unbelief. Therefore, we must also understand how great the sin of unbelief truly is!

As we begin, please understand that I have a true heart for nonbelievers. I have spoken with many, many of these persons over the years. And the great majority are extremely good people, trying to be good here so they can gain eternity or paradise or some other type of divinely granted reward based on their beliefs and actions. Many of these people have amazing energy and well-intended zeal in their attempts to please their perceived divine being. But make no mistake about it, they are misguided. Any belief system that denies Jesus Christ is God's Son and, therefore, God himself, and that denies Christ is the risen Savior, the very means of our salvation, is indubitably wrong.

I sadly feel that many of these people are walled off and blinded in their faiths. They live in traditions passed down through their families. They read varied alternative religious texts and follow lost religious leaders.

If you belong to one of these belief systems, I ask you, first, rather than being offended and tuning out, to please step back, no matter what your parents, friends, mentors, books, or religious leaders tell you. Try to step back mentally, put aside for a moment prejudices and prejudgements, and read these words: Let your God-given, amazingly intelligent human brain ponder these issues with an open mind. You need to make this decision for yourself. Do not simply rely on what you have been told or what you have read. Make certain your beliefs are correct! Do not blindly accept what is presented to you, unless you yourself have also researched this thoroughly, because this is without doubt the most important issue that you will ever decide on in your lifetime here on this planet!

In addition to being open-minded, I ask you to pray to God and ask him to show himself to you. I strongly believe that if you pray to him and get into his authentic, living and breathing Word, the Holy Bible, you will without doubt reach an understanding of who he is: your loving Creator Father. This relationship is exactly what he desires for you. So, make an effort to seek him now. You will never regret it. The blessings he will heap upon you, your family, your friends, and all whom you meet will be beyond your understanding and belief!

God says he will reveal himself to those who earnestly seek him. He is not trying to hide from you. You simply need to remove your blinders, become open-minded, and seek the truth. Once again, pray and ask the one true Lord to reveal himself to you. Over the past two millennia, thousands of brilliant minds have tried to disprove Christianity. Nevertheless, history, archaeology, science, and the survival and continued growth of the Christian faith itself all present a solid case, which no skeptic, no matter how brilliant, has ever been able to definitively disprove!

Consider also your specific belief system, whatever it may be. Each religion has its own written doctrines and books to read: the Koran for Islam, the Hindu and Buddhist writings, the Jewish Torah and the Talmud, the Book of Mormon, The Watchtower Bible, and so on. All exist for a single reason: to bring human beings closer to a god-like state, whether by trying to know, to communicate with, or to contact a divine entity in some manner or, in some cases as with the Mormons, trying to become a god oneself.

Yet, look again at the wide diversity of religions spread across our globe. Does it make sense that there would be so many radically different pathways to the same goal? I realize that yes is the politically and culturally correct statement. But step back and think. Does this make logical sense?

Again, if you are in one of these other belief systems, why would you not at least look into and adequately investigate the claims of Christianity, the faith that has the firmest foundation in history, science, archaeology, and from eyewitness testimony? Why would you blindly continue your course without checking out the one faith system with the best supporting evidence?

Jesus Christ is the only religious leader who not only declared he was the Way (in fact, the sole way), but who also had the credentials to back it up. He fulfilled Old Testament prophecy, he performed miracles, he lived a life of integrity and purity of character (documented by eyewitnesses Peter and John), and he rose from the dead and into the heavens.

Jesus, through the evidence and his Bible, asks you to accept an objective truth, one that is clearly confirmed by this wealth of overwhelming archaeological, historical, legal, and scientific evidence. All other religions ask you to accept errors they falsely claim as true without any supportive evidence. They ask seekers to discover their truths by experiences and unsubstantiated faith, while Christianity declares its truth in the currency of historical and legal facts, data which are fully disclosed, available, and open to human investigation by any and all!

No real evidence exists for the claims of Islam, Hinduism, Buddhism, or any other non-Christian religion. Subjective experience, tradition, opinion, and blind allegiance may bring one comfort, but that proves nothing. If there is only one God, and if Christianity is the only true religion, then one should not expect any solid evidence to exist for any other faith.

In summary, only Christianity meets this burden of proof. Its impressive evidence supports its claims as being true. Therefore, Jesus is indeed the only way to salvation, as no one looking at this evidence objectively could honestly deny it. Christianity has been thoroughly investigated. And it has passed the tests!

***

If you do not yet believe, what is your reason for not believing? If you disbelieve, it is most likely because you have refused to even consider believing in him.

Open your mind and at least say something to yourself like, "Well, okay, Christianity might be true, so let me further check this out." If you do so, I know that the Spirit of God will convict you and convince you that the evidence is true. Remove your blinders, and you will realize how the large body of substantial evidence for the belief in a risen Christ is so much greater than any proposed evidence against it.

So, are you ready to consider this? Let's look at some Bible passages that are pertinent here:

> "Many false prophets will appear and lead many astray." (Matthew 24:11)

> "Don't always believe everything you hear just because someone says it is a message from God: test it first to see if it really is. For there are many false teachers around, and the way to find out if their message is from the Holy Spirit is to ask: Does it really agree that Jesus Christ, God's Son, actually became man with a human body? If so, then the message is from God. If not, the message is not from God." (1 John 4:1–3a)

On this scriptural cue, let us next discuss the fulfillment of biblical prophecies. Such predictions occur in all but four of the sixty-six books of the Bible, which again were written by more than forty different authors over approximately one thousand five hundred years. Theologians have proven that these prophecies were written prior to their fulfillments. No one can argue that these were made up later as an attempt to fit events that had already occurred.

As Scripture tells us, only God can accurately predict the future. And he has done so convincingly in his Bible, which he gives to us as solid proof. No other sacred book of any other religious tradition contains so much fulfilled prophecy!

Comparing the Bible with other religious texts, there is a glaring difference. There is clearly a lack of any significant Koranic, Mormonic, Buddhist, Hindu, or Jehovah's Witness/Watchtower Society prophetic fulfillments.

A very reliable prophetic reference is *Science Speaks* by Peter Stoner and Robert Newman, which lists sixty major and two hundred seventy lesser biblical prophecies fulfilled by Jesus during his lifetime.[13] These include the fact that Micah had foretold Jesus's birthplace to be in Bethlehem and Isaiah's foretelling that he would be born of a virgin mother, as well as references to his piercing and crucifixion centuries before this method of execution was invented. Additionally noted is the fact that the Messiah would be contemporary with the Jerusalem temple, as well many others. The authors then state that the probability of Jesus fulfilling even eight of these sixty major prophecies is one in ten to the seventeenth power or one in 100,000,000,000,000,000. To give a concrete perception of this truly astronomical numerical value, they make an excellent reference to the fact that this many silver dollars would cover the entire great state of Texas if stacked two feet deep. I myself decided to stack a few of these. Eighteen silver dollars were required for every two inches. Doing the math, this equals two hundred sixteen coins for every two-foot stack! Consider how amazingly low the odds are of randomly picking out the single correct coin, the one that represents the chance of fulfilling these prophecies! So, the odds are astronomical even for just eight of these prophecies to be fulfilled by one man. The significance of this cannot be denied or minimized. Now—to truly blow your mind—consider that the chance of fulfilling all sixty major prophecies is greater than seven times this already astronomical number!

Therefore, we must realize that since Christ has fulfilled all the Bible's prophecies to date and rose from the dead, he cannot be anything but the prophesied Jewish Messiah, the one who is the Savior of the entire world! Being sinless, he was not and could not lie or deceive us but could only proclaim the truth, as he always does in his Scripture.

In Islam, no messiah is expected, and to suggest such is considered blasphemy by Muslims. Hinduism and Jainism have some concepts that suggest incarnation, gods appearing in the flesh. Yet, no religions besides Judaism and Christianity have the actual expectation of a Messiah or Savior, although the Jews still deny that Jesus was their expected one. Yet Christ is, as we have shown, the only way to salvation and the only true incarnation of God!

Consider this: If we place our bets upon God and he does not exist, have we lost anything upon our death? But if we bet against God and he does exist, we will suffer an infinitely immense loss forever! Why, therefore, should we not bet on him here in this life, especially since we have great evidence to support him? If we look at this openly and honestly, the best-case scenario is that we win everything. And, even at worst case scenario, we would lose nothing and our lives would go well for us, as Proverbs tells us will occur if we can keep our hearts and minds set upon him. Doing that, we limit our heartbreaks and sufferings and secure his support and comfort through those misfortunes and trials we do encounter!

Further, more than one thousand eight hundred verses in twenty-nine biblical books foretell Christ's return, which is yet to come. So, this prophecy has the same chance of being fulfilled as did all those other biblical prophecies: 100 percent!

If you are in one of those false religions that claim to be following the true God with zealous and often overzealous, even violent, actions and works, let me ask you this: I see you are very intelligent and have a great zeal for doing what you believe your god desires of you in order to earn your salvation and eternal happiness. But how can you truly know 100 percent absolutely guaranteed and for certain that your path is the correct one? Is it because your family or a religious leader in your faith or a perhaps a friend told you so? Or is it because you read it in your religion's own text or doctrines? Or perhaps it works for you? Or is it because you have a blind faith, perhaps just following the family traditions? Alternatively, might it instead be that you feel certain in your highly intelligent human mind that your course must be the true and correct one?

If you answer yes to any of these questions, I fail to see how you, or anyone else for that matter, could honestly and comfortably know with absolute certainty and be peacefully and completely reassured. If, however, you still feel that you are, then please explain to me how one human mind can, absolutely and definitively, ever know all truth! Are you smarter than the divine mind, more brilliant than the divine power?

One thing I am certain of is that no matter how you outwardly respond to these questions, I believe that you do have moments of doubt. While you may never admit it to any living person, there are times when you inwardly question your current path or lack thereof. I know so, because this occurs in all of us.

And why are these doubts occurring? These are pricks of your conscience, attention-getting attempts from the true God and his Holy Spirit, who are continually attempting to reach you and to turn you toward Jesus before it is too late!

In trying to help you, I present my request as a challenge. Read at least one chapter of the Christian Holy Bible daily, starting with the New Testament Gospel of John, for at least thirty days. Read with an open mind. And ask each time you begin, "Oh, my Lord and God, please show me your true self, so that I may know the real you and be therefore saved and united with you. Then, here in this world, I will finally know who you are and be certain that I am doing your will as you have commanded, thereby fulfilling all of your plans for my life!"

He will answer this prayer. He says you will find him when you seek him, if you look for him in earnest. And in Isaiah, he also says he hears your prayers when you pray.

To Muslims specifically, do not pray this prayer using the name Allah but rather, pray, "Oh, my Lord," or, "Oh, my God." As for Jews, Mormons, Jehovah's Witnesses, atheists, cult followers, and the like, you should refer to him as either God or Lord or even Yahweh or Jehovah. All are equally fine ways to address him in your prayers.

***

While you may perceive that you do zealous works for your god, as humbly and as gently as I can say this, I am extremely worried and afraid for you. Your doctrines wall you off. They are a master trick of the great deceiver himself, Satan. For example, the Muslim's Koran specifically forbids associating with Christians or Jews and exhorts Muslims to keep with their own kind. This walls them off and makes it difficult for them to hear the gospel. They may never have an opportunity to even consider the possibility that their way is incorrect!

Yet, why should you not hear your options and decide for yourself? This is not what Satan wants. He desires for you to continue blindly believing his lies right up until the day you die or the day when Christ returns. At that time, it will be too late for you if you have died. Or, if you are still alive at his return, you will have to endure a very difficult time of tribulation even if you should realize his truth, as multitudes will at his return finally see and understand that Christ truly is Lord and God of all!

Pray to him and then read his Holy Bible, as I challenged above. Ask God to please show you his truth. Then you will no longer have doubts or misgivings. You will finally be certain of your salvation! Doesn't that sound amazingly awesome, to have complete and permanent reassurance from him that you are his forever!

Why would you ever delay doing this? Don't be afraid. The true God wants you to seek him. Therefore, you should not be fearful of instigating his anger by asking this. Whether you presently believe that the divine entity is Jehovah-Yahweh and his Son, Jesus, Allah, or some other divine being or force, certainly any human seeking and asking for truth and communication will never be frowned upon or punished by the one God who is truly divine, don't you think?

So why not give this a try? What do you have to lose? Everything will be lost if you are wrong and do not realize it or correct your ways! Yet, what is there to gain? Everything is to be gained: peace, joy, and fulfillment in this world as well as rescue from the messes of this place, then ultimately, salvation and rescue into his eternal presence and paradise, into his heavenly world to come. Look to these verses:

"At the name of Jesus every knee shall bow in heaven and on earth and under the earth, and every tongue shall confess that Jesus Christ is Lord, to the glory of God the Father." (Philippians 2:10–11)

"[You] become slaves once more to another poor, weak, useless religion of trying to get to heaven by obeying God's laws? You are trying to find favor with God by what you do or don't do on certain days or months or seasons or years. I fear for you." (Galatians 4:9–11)

"Christ is useless to you if you are counting on clearing your debt to God by keeping those laws; you are lost from God's grace. But we by the help of the Holy Spirit are counting on Christ's death to clear away our sins and make us right with God. . . . all we need is faith working through love." (Galatians 5:4–6)

***

What then about these so-called wise men, these scholars, these brilliant debaters of this world's other religions? God says that he will make them all look foolish. He will show their wisdom to be useless nonsense. For God in his wisdom saw to it that the world would never find him through human brilliance, yet he then stepped in and is saving all those who will believe his message, which the world calls foolish and silly. It seems absurd to other faith systems because they want a sign from heaven as proof that what is preached is true or, too often, because they believe only what agrees with their philosophy and seems wise to them.

Therefore, when we preach about Christ dying to save them, some may feel offended and scoff that it's all nonsense and foolishness. But God has opened the eyes of all those called to salvation, allowing them to see that Christ is really the loving and mighty power of God sent here to save them. Christ is the center of God's wise plan for their salvation. This so-called foolish plan of God is far wiser than the wisest plan of the wisest man, and even God in his sole moment of weakness—in Christ dying on the cross—is far stronger than any mere man!

***

In summary, here is my big question: do you know what Christ has done just for you? Did Allah, Buddha, or any other religious deity-figure or founder, besides Jesus Christ, ever come down here, give up his god-state for you, and sacrifice himself out of his great love for you so that you might live forever with him? Alternatively, does your religion and its leaders ask you to do this and to do that, to pray this specific way, to go there, to give here, and so on, until it is only about what you can do? They ask you to perform certain duties, giving you veritable hoops to jump through and boxes to check off. Yet the Christian God, the one true God, has already done all the work for you. He has completed the task of perfect holiness for you, and he has perfectly borne the cross of sinfulness for you. All that is required is your belief in him to ensure your salvation and thus your entry into eternal paradise! He frees us by giving us no other specific tasks that we must complete in order to earn his favor, besides having belief in Jesus!

We make the biggest mistake ever if we don't acknowledge and accept God's gift. Such refusal and disbelief are what he sees as the biggest sins that there are. We should not blindly blow past his offer, busily living our lives as a "proud man, frail as breath, a shadow," as Scripture very appropriately describes us.

We, at the very least, need to seek, to investigate, and to research the true Christian God before we decide against him. Why not give him a chance? If a doctor diagnosed you with a fatal disease yet offered you a guaranteed cure, how many of us would simply refuse, ignore, walk away, or merely put it out of our thinking? Would you not, even if skeptical, research it or even get another opinion so that your life was not merely thrown away or ended prematurely?

As God says, "Seek me and you will find me." He wants us to look for him and promises that we will find him. I strongly urge and plead with you to begin this process today by asking him for help to reveal himself to you. Pray to the true God and ask him to reveal himself and his will for your life. Then investigate him in that perfect guidebook that he has left for us, his Holy Bible. This is the most important decision that you will ever face in your lifetime. Please do not let it slip by! Consider this scripture, which describes how we can receive accurate and perfect enlightenment about the one true divine power in our universe:

> "This veil of misunderstanding can be removed only by be-lieving in Christ. . . . But whenever anyone turns to the Lord from his sins, then the veil is taken away. The Lord is the Spirit who gives them life, and where he is there is freedom from trying to be saved by keeping the laws of God. But we Christians have no veil over our faces; we can be mirrors that brightly reflect the glory of the Lord. And as the Spirit of the Lord works within us, we become more and more like him."
> (2 Corinthians 3:14b, 16–18)

11. Why Choose Jesus?

"We're not going to make it!"

I will never forget this statement, uttered in a blinding snowstorm by my expert and usually stoical Arctic guide who was now wide-eyed and doubting the outcome of our attempted trek home across the frigid polar ice pack.

Imagine Lewis and Clark or any other wilderness explorer. Where would they have been without their guides and their trailblazers? Yes, they may still have accomplished their missions without these help-ers. But imagine how much more difficult it would have been. Imagine how much longer it would have taken, not to mention all the miser-able days of wandering lost, backtracking after getting cliffed out, and enduring harsher conditions with less food and water, as well as less-appropriate shelter.

Having spent many moons in the wildernesses of the American and Canadian west and northwest, I have sometimes been alone. At other times, I have had a professional guide. Unfortunately, not all my guides were worth following (tales for another time). When I had a good guide, my travels went markedly smoother, with much less risk, danger, and hardship.

Jesus is the best wilderness guide you could ever enlist for your trip, your mission here in this world. He will get you through that deep forest, down that sheer cliff face, across that fast-moving and deep river, and over that high mountain pass with as little trouble as is possible here in this crazy world.

Take him as your guide, as your trailblazer. Without him, we can never expect to go through these difficult places as adeptly or to come out as well in the end! If you don't have him, as humbly as I can say it, you will not make it.

Ask him in. Enlist his expert skills. If you have never employed his guide services, if you have never known or trusted him, ask him now! You may be the first on your team or in your family or office or within your circle of friends to choose him. In such a case, you will also become a trailblazer among your company of life explorers, and you will all be amazed at his results!

***

Why exactly one should choose Jesus is always a major question. Everyone wants to know what benefit they will get from following him. Consider this verse: "Choose to love the Lord your God and to obey him and to cling to him, for he is your life and the length of your days." (Deuteronomy 30:20a).

We talked about the peace, the joy, the fulfillment, and the amazing rescue that comes from knowing him throughout one's lifetime in this crazy world. These gifts are given to all who seek and come to him earnestly. By giving us these, he makes our lives into what they are meant to be.

However, you will never know these positive benefits until you check him out, just like going to a good concert or watching a waterfall or the waves crashing upon the beach, or perhaps experiencing a gorgeous sunset. You must get into it and experience it, both seeing and feeling it! Employ the Bible and regularly use prayer, church, a small group, and other Christian media such as books and songs to help you get into the appropriate mindset.

But what about all of God's laws and rules? Do they not take away our fun and make life boring? No, they do not. Not only are they the best things for us, but they also reflect his nature. These rules are given out of his desire for our protection so that things will go well with us. He states these out of his love for us as a Father who is protecting his own!

These commands are God's laws. He in essence says, "Follow them so as to know me, as these are me." Originally, American values were based closely upon on God's values. Now, however, much of our country is continuously looking for new value systems and alternative moral standards. This is plainly and sadly obvious if you look at our society today!

Many think they can be good without God. But what they do not realize is that true goodness and morality always reflect the very God who exemplifies these qualities. He is their perfect portrait! So even if an atheist follows the Ten Commandments or the second of Christ's two greatest commands about loving his neighbor as himself, he unknowingly is reflecting the very God whom he denies, because this good nature, this moral standard that he follows, actually derives from God.

So, where do our values, our good and bad, come from? They are classified as good or bad solely in comparison to God's moral standard, and our God is good, yes, the one and only source of all goodness.

***

Another way to look at this question about why to choose Christ is, "Why do I not choose Jesus?" Many will even say, "If Jesus is so great, why don't more people choose him?" There are six reasons that I have come up with, from speaking to many people and asking myself this same question over the years.

The first reason to not choose Jesus is because of your human pride. Christ calls you to die to yourself, violating one's own personal autonomy and power. This is very difficult for many people to give up.

Second, many of us feel we are too smart to be fooled by Christianity. We think that we, in our small human minds, are all-knowing in and of ourselves. What grounds me personally here in this situation and concerns me about those who claim such great intelligence is the biblical example of wise King Solomon. Solomon was likely the wisest man who ever lived. Yet, even with his great gift of wisdom from God and all of his wealth, women, and possessions, Solomon still fell because he took his focus off God and began trusting worldly things. And this even though Yahweh appeared to and directly communicated with him! I don't know about you, but God has never appeared to or directly spoken with me. So, if even with such advantage Solomon still messed up, how can we ever be certain that we are absolutely correct in trusting our mere human intelligence alone? We cannot be blindly overconfident or complacent but must rather be constantly upon our guard so that we can avoid Solomon's fatal mistake!

Third, we may be afraid of giving up or losing things, such as activities and interests that seem fun. However, what is gained when we commit to Christ is so very much more. The things we are afraid to give up or lose are often the exact things that are not healthy for us. God, through his instructions, is trying to save us from them and keep us from making poor decisions that will lead to disastrous consequences.

Fourth, many people say they are too busy with all the craziness in this world. Unfortunately, that craziness lasts only for the brief duration of your lifetime. What happens thereafter? Is this life and this world all that there is—a place where you continually run around your whole life putting out fires until, one day, you die and go into the ground? Does that make logical sense? I think not.

Fifth, I have discovered that some people seem to like the pain of going through a godless life for a myriad of selfish reasons, as strange as this may seem.

Last, we may be afraid of judgment. Perhaps we feel guilty, or dirty. Many feel or say that they will come to God once they have cleaned up their lives. However, we do not need to be cleaned up before we come to him. He will clean you. He will remove the guilt you carry. Ask yourself, are you a bigger or better judge than God? You say you are when you judge your sins too great for forgiveness or if you believe they prevent you from coming to God.

We, instead, must actively seek our God in his Word and in prayer with an open, unprejudiced mind. We must ask for his help, and then, we should test the Word's truth. If we step out in keeping with it, we will realize and be forced to admit that this is the one true path. As he says, seek and you will find me (Matthew 7:7).

Consider these two statements by Christ: "Unless you believe that I am the Messiah, the Son of God, you will die in your sins" (John 8:24b), and "How earnestly I tell you this—anyone who believes in me already has eternal life! Yes, I am the Bread of Life!" (John 6:47–48a)

So, why do you still resist Christ? Why not accept him right now? If you don't, you waste your today just as you have wasted your life's other years to date by missing out on his blessings.

For me, no treasure is worth my giving up one hour or even one minute of having Jesus as my friend, my Lord, and my Savior. With him, you get his peace, joy, fulfillment, and rescue. You indeed waste progressively more of your life the longer you wait. When you see who and what he is, you will agree with my statement that I would still be a Christ-follower even if there were no heaven and nothing beyond this world. I would follow just to have the benefit of him in the here and now, helping me through this world's craziness!

It is important to remember that your heart hardens the longer you wait, as described in Hebrews 3:7. The longer you resist him, the better you become at doing so, as your heart becomes dry and hardened ground, resistant to the gospel's seeds. These seeds then cannot enter, nor can they grow. Instead, they bounce off and blow away.

If you are still a nonbeliever, think back to the first time you heard the gospel. Did it not touch you then in a deeper way than it does when you hear his invitation today? Isn't it easier than before to refuse and say no to Jesus?

Therefore, open your heart today, asking for his assistance. Then repent and return to him, and he will, without doubt, welcome you!

12. Is Jesus Really Coming Back for Judgment?

Scripture plainly answers these questions with strong and affirming proclamations:

"There is going to come a day of wrath when God will be the just Judge of all the world. He will give each one whatever his deeds deserve. He will give eternal life to those who patiently do the will of God, seeking for the unseen glory and honor and eternal life that he offers. But he will terribly punish those who fight against the truth of God and walk in evil ways—God's anger will be poured out upon them. There will be sorrow and suffering . . . But there will be glory and honor and peace from God for all who obey him." (Romans 2:5b–10a)

"Fear God . . . and extol his greatness. For the time has come when he will sit as Judge. Worship him who made the heaven and the earth, the sea and all its sources." (Revelation 14:7)

"The nations of the world will see me arrive in the clouds of heaven, with power and great glory. And I shall send forth my angels with the sound of a mighty trumpet blast, and they shall gather my chosen ones from the farthest ends of the earth and heaven." (Matthew 24:30b–31)

The date of Jesus's coming to judge all people and to make all things right and just, is close at hand. It is near. When will this be? As Jesus said, only the Father knows the day and the hour. What is certain is he will return. And the time of his return is closer now than it was last week, or yesterday, or even a minute ago. Jesus will return, as Revelation states, to judge and to justify.

We again can only reference good or bad in our fallen world in comparison to his measure of holiness. As discussed above, God allows sinful choices and their bad consequences. Yet he will turn all evil toward some ultimate good. He is always merciful and loving and sovereign. He remains in charge of all that happens, all of the time. As Saint Thomas Aquinas said, "God's infinite goodness is that he uses evil to bring forth good."

The cross provides the best example. It is the greatest evil ever committed, as Christ was the sole innocent man unjustly killed by evil men. Ultimately, just as such immense goodness and grace for all people came from his death, some good will come from every degree of pain and from every suffering we endure in this world.

So, God allows some suffering because it shapes and perfects us. It keeps us focused on him. Just think, can you say that your best communications and prayers with God were in your best of times? I believe that for most of us the opposite is true: optimal communications are much more likely to occur when things are going badly.

Again, Christ is coming back, and there is no question about this. The rest of the Bible, as we have discussed, has already come true, including his first coming, his death, and his resurrection, in his fulfillment of many prophecies. Therefore, we must take Revelation's prophecy, that is, Jesus Christ's warning, at its very word, as well: "These words are trustworthy and true: 'I am coming soon!'" (Revelation 22:6)

Think about this: why would the last book of the Bible not come true when the others (besides the end-time prophecies in Daniel and Ezekiel) already have! God cannot lie. There will be trumpet blast, just as Christ says, and he will come. And then all who know God and have therefore received his grace and forgiveness will be taken up to him into eternal paradise, while the others will not.

In the meantime, as commanded in Matthew 28 and Acts 5, our instructions are to tell others about this good news! We all must repent and realize the need for him to save us in order to make us right with God! Consider more of God's counsel here:

"Has the Lord as much pleasure in your burnt offerings and sacrifices as in your obedience? Obedience is far better than sacrifice. He is much more interested in your listening to him than in your offering." (1 Samuel 15:22)

"But when I, the Messiah, shall come in my glory, and all the angels with me, then I shall sit upon my throne of glory. And all the nations shall be gathered before me. And I will separate the people as a shepherd separates the sheep from the goats, and place the sheep at my right hand, and the goats at my left. Then I, the King, shall say to those at my right, 'Come, blessed of my Father, into the Kingdom prepared for you from the founding of the world. For I was hungry and you fed me; I was thirsty and you gave me water; I was a stranger and you invited me into your homes; naked and you clothed me; sick and in prison, and you visited me.' Then these righteous ones will reply, 'Sir, when did we ever see you hungry and feed you? Or thirsty and give you anything to drink? Or a stranger, and help you? Or naked, and clothe you? When did we ever see you sick or in prison, and visit you?' And I, the King, will tell them, 'When you did it to these my brothers, you were doing it to me!' Then I will turn to those on my left and say, 'Away with you, you cursed ones, into the eternal fire prepared for the devil and his demons. For I was hungry and you wouldn't feed me; thirsty, and you wouldn't give me anything to drink; a stranger, and you refused me hospitality; naked, and you wouldn't clothe me; sick, and in prison, and you didn't visit me.' Then they will reply, 'Lord, when did we ever see you hungry or thirsty or a stranger or naked or sick or in prison, and not help you?' And I will answer, 'When you refused to help the least of these my brothers, you were refusing help to me.' And they shall go away into eternal punishment; but the righteous into everlasting life." (Matthew 25:31–46)

So, upon which side will you be? How does one avoid being grouped with the evildoers and cast away from the presence of God forever into eternal misery? This classification and the decision as to which group you are in is not established by your works alone, nor by your perception of how good you are, as Christ states. Many people do multitudinous good works, but if they do not know Jesus, their works are not done in his name and count for nothing.

Again, we can never save ourselves. We must realize that we absolutely require Christ and his sacrifice in order to be saved! Therefore, it is our relationship with him, through our faith in him, that determines whether we will be among the sheep or among the goats at that day of judgement.

The question to you now is this: do you have faith in Jesus Christ? Have you specifically chosen him as your Savior, the Lord of your life? And do you therefore believe that he sacrificed himself to save you, has forgiven all your sins, and that only through him can you be saved? Do you realize that you cannot ever achieve salvation by your own merits or goodness?

We all fall and make mistakes. And while this does not make such mistakes okay, we still should be able to see a degree of progress in our lives. This again is a process called sanctification. It means personal growth in holiness. When you fall, do you continually repeat the same sin, staying away from God, being angry, or being bitter? Or do you realize the sin, repent of it, and return to God, all the while becoming more and more Christ-like, for example, more loving, more humble, and more caring of others? Do you stay in his Word and in his commands as well as in prayerful conversation with him, getting to know him better and better as time goes on? This is exactly how you know that you are bound for Christ's heaven.

***

So, we know that he is coming back. Exactly when this will be, no one knows other than the Father. We do know, however, that at his return "every eye shall see him" (Revelation 1:7). All will see Jesus Christ as the true God, including everyone who ignored him, despised him, mocked him, and denied him. We also know that in his mercy and great love for us, he is delaying his return and postponing his judgment, allowing more sheep into his fold.

> "He isn't really being slow about his promised return, even though it sometimes seems that way. But he is waiting, for the good reason that he is not willing that any should perish, and he is giving more time for sinners to repent. . . . He is giving us time to get his message of salvation out to others." (2 Peter 3:9, 15)

***

Finally, consider what I call the realization. At Jesus's second coming or at your death, whichever is first, would you not prefer to be in the group that already knows he is God and is, therefore, saved by faith in him? Imagine the deathbed alternative: suddenly seeing and hearing him and, in that moment, realizing that Christ Jesus is the one true God, not your logic or your science or Allah or any of the other false deities of other religions. Then, in that moment, you will realize how great your sin of disbelief has been and that you are subject to his wrath eternally. Your opportunity has passed—forever!

Alternatively, if you are still alive when he returns as judge, you will have a chance to profess belief in him, although this will need to occur during what will be an extremely difficult time of trial and tribulation for all who remain upon the earth, something that would be best avoided, if at all possible.

Knowing these facts, how can you continue arrogantly and blatantly ignoring his offer of salvation without at least exploring it and asking for God's enlightenment about himself and his Son, Jesus?

Do not delay! This is the most important decision you will ever make, for he is coming!

13. What of Those Who've Never Heard Christ's Gospel?

Okay, what about unreached people, those who never hear of Jesus Christ before they die? Consider the multitudes who existed before Jesus. Or think of the native tribes now who have never heard, like the most-isolated Sentinelese people in the Andaman Islands. Will they be condemned for lack of knowledge alone?

No, according to Scripture they will not, though they are responsible for knowing that there is a God, a divine Creator, through the witness of nature and their consciences.

The natural world all around us and our consciences as well bear witness to God's existence. Nature declares his existence and his glory. Our consciences tell us when we violate God's laws, helping us to be righteous in obeying his statutes for living godly lives.

Therefore, even in distant millennia past, those persons who realized the divine from the natural world and who followed their consciences to live rightly will be saved by grace according to God's Word.

> "He will punish sin wherever it is found. He will punish the heathen when they sin, even though they never had God's written laws, for down in their hearts they know right from

wrong. God's laws are written within them; their own conscience accuses them, or sometimes excuses them." (Romans 2:12–14)

As Scripture repeatedly emphasizes, God's power and deity are revealed to all persons through his creation. He also puts his law into our hearts in the form of our consciences so that we will seek him, our loving heavenly Father, find him, and then follow him.

God maintains control always, therefore we must remember that even those who have never heard of Jesus specifically have been placed, each into their individually unique and specific place and time in history, into a position where each is able to seek, and to find, God.

As Scripture states, all who earnestly seek him will find him (Matthew 7:7–8, Acts 10:34–35; Hebrews 11:6). This means each person is internally aware of God and sees enough truth in their lifetime to respond to him, no matter one's society, culture, setting, or degree of isolation from others.

So those who have never heard Christ's name are not necessarily lost. Imagine the millions who were undoubtedly saved from those early eras well before Christ was born!

14. What's So Great About Heaven Anyway?

"I mean, certainly heaven's activities list and its video games cannot be as great as what we have here! I really like the food here, and just what are the chances that the pizza, burgers, and soft serve are as great in heaven as they are down here? And what about our sports and our cuddly pets? Also, I hope they have my comics and these great TV shows there!"

How often do we say (or at least think) things like this?

My impression is that heaven cannot be boring. Do you think being in the presence of the Almighty God and Creator Father would or could ever be boring? Could it get old and tiresome? Did John or Moses or Daniel or Ezekiel or any of the other biblical characters who physically visualized and experienced God and his heaven seem at all bored in his presence?

To our minds, Revelation's constant worshiping and singing to the Almighty God may remind us (unfortunately) of some of the longer and slower church services in our lives. Yet I believe there is absolutely no way that heaven will compare to our worldly perceptions. Being in the presence of the Almighty God, our loving Father, and worshiping him are going to be ever so markedly and exponentially better than having a new Christmas day in this world, with all its trappings, every single day of our life!

God states in Isaiah and in Revelation that he is making all things new. Consider Isaiah 65:17–18: "I am creating new heavens and a new earth—so wonderful that no one will even think about the old ones anymore. Be glad; rejoice forever in my creation." The odds of God placing us into an eternal paradise to do repetitive, unstimulating, and boring things day after day for the remainder of eternity simply makes no sense!

Scripture discusses the amazing gold and gems in the appearance of heaven's structure as well as the amazing food of heaven. But, even better, it foretells the extreme happiness and joy that we will have in our eternal paradise.

Therefore, I believe that every day, every hour, and even every second will be so amazing and so completely different that heaven will outshine our grandest perceptions. It will be greater in comparison than, say, taking a never-ending, super-fast airplane tour over this entire world's most beautiful, scenic, and joyous places complete with whatever companions, snacks, and entertainments we desire along the way!

Think of what you enjoy doing the most: travel, sports, the beach, family time. Then imagine it being done in an exponentially enjoyable manner without a repetitious event or moment! We will never become tired of or bored with what is happening there, as our joys will never cease. As God says, our minds cannot begin to comprehend, not one bit, even a small amount of what great things he has planned for us! Consider Revelation 21:5: "And the one sitting on the throne said, 'See, I am making all things new!'"

Unfortunately, none of us will ever know the sheer magnificence and joy of heaven until we get there. Yet, in my view, paradise cannot ever be a boring place. Therefore, it is indeed worth striving for and so much so that it should be of the utmost importance in our lives to do so! We need to trust God on this point.

15. Is There Really a Hell?

Put aside your gut feeling on hell, whatever it may be and whether you agree with the concept or not. Instead, consider whether the existence of a hell is both morally right and necessary, like a quarantine facility you would use in an Ebola or coronavirus outbreak.

Clearly, God did not form a hell with his first creation. No, he needed to make hell when some of his angels rebelled against him. Think of early American society as a loose comparison. There were no prisons here when America was first settled, but sadly, prisons became necessary as society changed.

I am often asked, for example by someone who does not believe in God or by someone whose dead or dying family member did not or does not believe, about whether a person will be going to hell.

Per our Scriptures, if you are a nonbeliever in Christ as God and your Savior, then the correct answer here is an unfortunate yes. Yet, explaining this using our modern legal system greatly helps others to understand this fact rather than giving a point-blank affirmative reply. That often hinders further communication or even loses your audience altogether.

You instead can first ask, "Should criminals be punished for their crimes?" Most will agree that the answer here is an affirmative yes. Then, ask if they themselves have ever done any bad things. The answer here will certainly be yes also. Then ask, "So we both agree. But this is worrisome because we sinners are under pending judgment for our wrongs by our loving yet also holy Father who, like any good father, has to deal with the errors we have made!"

Then ask them to imagine themselves on trial for all the wrongs done over their lifetime, with (as per their admittance) no option but to plead guilty. Next, ask them to imagine that the judge, instead of sentencing them, offers them the free pass of a pardon. And then he goes a step further and exchanges places with them so that he transfers their blame onto himself. How would that make them feel? Also, why would one not accept such an offer?

This, I explain, is exactly what God and Christ did. And this is how they offer us a full pardon if we will only believe and accept it! I then explain how we can never be good enough. And since we are all guilty, we all need a save or a pardon and a savior who is Christ the Lord!

***

Some ask if God tortures people in hell. He does not ever enjoy doing or seeing torture. But hell is a punishment. We must realize that it is one that has been self-chosen by each person who goes there. God has given everyone in that place their own personal choice, which they have made throughout their worldly lives. Their choice was to live for themselves rather than for him, not choosing him, not knowing him, and not fulfilling his purpose for them. Therefore, after their death here in this world, they are granted their choice and separated forever from the most beautiful being ever.

Hell is a permanent exclusion from all things of value, a state of being separated from all things that matter. Imagine a rather poor comparison from our world: What if you were completely cut off from, and for a prolonged duration kept apart from, all that mattered to you and which made you happy, for instance, your family, friends, pets, favorite activities and hobbies, foods, or nature. Then, imagine that as you longingly dreamed of being reunited with all of these, you were told that you had in fact been permanently cut off from any future contact with these comforts and joys!

Further, if heaven really is, as God tells us, so much grander than our world here, consider how much worse you would feel then, knowing that you had deliberately and willingly forfeited, and thus would never have access to, such great joys and blessings? The torture becomes the fact that you realize how you continually, throughout your life, refused to acknowledge God's power, refused his gift of grace through Christ his Son, and that you refused to live for his purposes, which he made you for.

So therefore, if you go to hell, you are put away for all eternity. If you chose against God in your life, you may well choose against being with him in heaven as well, don't you think? Why would you expect to suddenly change your attitude at that time? You have shown no interest in being with God nor with those who love him. You never exhibited this desire during your lifetime. Therefore, even after death, God would not be the choice you would make. As Voice of the Martyrs founder Richard

Wurmbrand so aptly noted, "Hell is to sit alone in darkness remembering the evil you've done."

Once again, God in his fairness and love grants you your wish, giving each either heaven or hell based on their life choice. He allows you your selected preference, conceding to your soul the life you have chosen, for eternity.

Yet God, our loving Father, does not wish for one single soul to go to hell's judgement! You must realize he does not send anyone to hell. If you do go there, it is through your own choice made of your own free will. Consider 1 Timothy 2:4–6a, "He longs for all to be saved and to understand this truth: That God is on one side and all the people on the other side, and Christ Jesus, himself man, is between them to bring them together, by giving his life for all mankind."

***

Some will also ask about the possibility of children being condemned to hell. I believe Scripture is very clear upon this. Children are not old enough to make valid choices for themselves. Therefore God, in his great fairness and mercy, would in truth never sentence any child to an eternity of agony.

***

"Well," some will ask, "why doesn't God make or force everyone to love him so that no one will go to hell?"

God does not want a world of blindly adoring robots, forever mindlessly repeating, "I worship you. I worship you." How would you feel if you only received forced affection and forced love from your spouse, friends, and family? What if they loved and cared for you not because they wanted to but because you forced them to? Could this ever be a true relationship?

Nevertheless, many still ask, "Why doesn't God love us enough to forgive us all our sins anyway, like our earthly fathers do? Does he not love us?"

This is an excellent question. Yes, many earthly fathers do forgive their children of most transgressions, but a good father will go one step further and correct his errant child. He wants to save them from poor choices and disastrous consequences in the future! That is the best example of a loving and guiding father figure: he loves his children so much that he not only corrects them but does all he can to protect them from harm!

God loves us so much more than we could ever imagine. And he proved this beyond any doubt by sending his Son to take our punishment for us. Because of this love for us, God genuinely endured hell himself, by separating himself from his Son, when he laid it squarely on Jesus's lovingly broad shoulders. His intervention is a guaranteed forgiveness for all our sins. However, we must accept his forgiveness before, and so that, we can enter our holy God's presence! We should never doubt his affection for us, his children. He loves us so much that he gave up his own child for us (John 3:16)!

***

Also, in response to people (such as the Latter-Day Saints) who say that there is no hell (or to any other non-Scriptural variation of final judgment that one tries to imagine or construe), we must remember that our human hearts will try to make up a god that we want, one that fits with our lives, our desires, and our lifestyles. Our gods provide a spiritual arena upon which we can rationalize that we are good and are doing God's will, when in truth we are not.

Also, some persons have been wrongly misled into believing that God has certain non-Scriptural features and attributes. They will often say things like, "I don't believe in a God who judges or sends people to hell." You can respond, "Well, I do not believe in that type of god either," and then help them understand the true God and Father using his Word as your correcting reference.

For instance, when one says, "I do not believe in a God who punishes sinners in hell," or "My God (or a good God) would not send anyone to hell just because one does not believe in his Son, Jesus," we can respond lovingly by saying, "You are right, your god would not because your god is not the real God!" As we have shown, our God is a holy Lord, and if we are to place our trust in him, is this not exactly the way he should be? Shouldn't he be wholly unable to be near the presence of sin? And if he is such, can you see now how he, unfortunately, had to make a hell to appropriately deal with sin? It is a problem that is not his fault. It is the result of humanity's poor choosing.

***

Many ask, "Well, doesn't the Bible say that there are flames, worms, and gnashing of teeth in hell?" Yes, it does. The flames symbolize God's judgment. For example, in Revelation Jesus is reported to be returning with his fiery sword on his day of judgment.

Regarding the worms: Located outside of Jewish cities in those days were garbage dumps, ugly and unclean places replete with the flies, worms, and other insects that typically infest such sites. When Jesus talked about "the worm that never dies," he meant that hell is even worse than that unclean worldly place. It is a powerful image that would have been extremely meaningful to any Jew of that era.

The gnashing of teeth comes from the intense anger, frustration, and regret the damned experience as they realize their great loss. Therefore, it may well be more a mental and spiritual anguish, far beyond any physical pain. Remember, Jesus also says that hell has been prepared for Satan and his angels. They do not have physical bodies that could be tortured by fire or worms, although once again, with God all things are possible. Just because we cannot wrap our minds around these concepts, we should not get caught up in the semantics. We simply need to take Jesus and God the Father at their Word, just as they have given it to us in our holy Scripture. God's Holy Bible says there is a place of judgment, and that it is a terrible eternity for anyone sent there, forever and ever after.

***

Another question people often have is, "Do all people suffer the same in hell?" They imply that since there are bigger sinners and smaller sinners, shouldn't punishments be adjusted to one's individual degree of sinfulness?

The Bible does say that there are degrees of separation, of emptiness, and of isolation. There are varied degrees of punishment in hell. People are indeed sentenced according to their lack of faith and according to their sinful actions. For example, in Sodom and Gomorrah, and also in Tyre and Sidon, Scripture states that the people of these cities (which have long since been completely wiped off the map by God for their great evils) will still have it better than the Jewish cities that refused Christ after hearing his message. Similarly, Scripture also reports different degrees of reward in heaven, which appear to be allotted per your faith and your secondary works done in his name.

***

"Well, I am a good person, so I will be okay with God, as I believe God is okay with me." How often do you hear someone say this? How often do we think this about ourselves? Remember Galatians 2:21: "I am not one of those who treats Christ's death as meaningless. For if we could be saved by keeping Jewish laws, then there was no need for Christ to die."

Think about this: If a person could be saved by being good, then Jesus's brutal death on the cross was unnecessary. If we can earn salvation, why would God have sacrificed his only Son, a very part of himself, a member of the triune Godhead? That makes no sense.

In God's sight, our self-perceived righteousness is as filthy rags (Isaiah 64:6). We can never be good enough, given our human hearts. We must open our eyes to this realization! Our good works can erroneously give us a false sense of self-righteousness. But our works cannot save us, no matter how much good we may do.

Christ's righteousness is the only way to forgiveness, and only God's Holy Spirit can help you understand this. If we believe on Christ, then our faith alone gives us true righteousness. Yes, it is a hard concept to grasp, so ask God to help you to understand and believe it.

We can never be good enough for our God. He is fully perfect. Even one single sin in isolation would condemn us, should we still believe that our own personal works and righteousness can earn us a trip to heaven. Once again, if we by ourselves could do it, then Christ did not need to suffer and die.

In summary, if we believe his firm redeeming promise, we receive God's peace, joy, and fulfillment as well as his rescue, both here in this world and, ultimately, in paradise. But on the other hand, if we do not believe, our judgment is coming. Christ has already won. The outcome has been determined. He is coming to our world once again. This time he will judge the nations. The only question now is when. If you will only believe and accept his gift of eternal life, his blood then draws a protective circle around you, as you are righteously clothed in his royal robes, which he has exchanged for your dirty rags, your sinfulness and meager attempts at self-righteousness. You need to believe, to accept his cloak of holiness, and to trust him, thereby giving your life over to him for his purposes.

A very pertinent prayer for persons at this stage would be: "Lord, I realize I am a sinner, fully unable to save myself. I am sorry for all my sins. Please give me your help so I may do these sins no more. I believe that you sent your Son, Jesus Christ, to cover my sins with his blood sacrifice. And today I confess my faith in him as my Lord, my Savior, my friend. Thank you for giving me your righteousness and for allowing me to finally step from my blinding darkness into your everlasting light. I, here and now, accept, trust, and love you, Jesus!"

16. Why Does There Have to Be Eternal Punishment?

These are both reasonable questions. Consider what Jesus states in John 16:9: "The world's sin is unbelief in me." A lifetime of ignoring and denying Christ, living for oneself, is the ultimate sin, the one that is worthy of ultimate punishment.

The Bible states that the only unforgivable sin is blaspheming the Holy Spirit: continually denying him and thwarting his continued attempts to make himself known to you throughout your lifetime. "I solemnly declare that any sin of man can be forgiven, even blasphemy against me; but blasphemy against the Holy Spirit can never be forgiven. It is an eternal sin" (Mark 3:28–29).

Besides this one sin, Jesus assures us that any other sin can be forgiven if we will bring it to him and endeavor to do it no more. Even this blasphemous, unforgivable sin can still be forgiven if one repents before it is too late, before death.

Therefore, God does give us more chances. Consider what Christ says in the passage about the woman caught in the act of adultery in John 8:10–11: "Jesus asked her, 'Where are your accusers? Didn't even one of them condemn you?' 'No, sir,' she replied. And Jesus said, 'Neither do I. Go and sin no more.'"

***

Some will ask, "Why can't God send everyone to heaven?" As we discussed, he respects human freedom of choice, namely our free will, and would never attempt to force himself on those who do not want to be with him. How unloving would it be for someone to force another to do something they did not want to do? As Jesus said, he stands at your door and knocks (Revelation 3:20). He does not arrive at the door with an axe, a hammer, or a battering ram. As we discussed above, forced love can never be true love.

However, because of God's holiness, while still constantly loving us, he can never be associated with sin. So, he needs to be a just judge and deal with our sins appropriately.

Consider a worldly example: What if a judge in our justice system indiscriminately let everyone walk because he decided to be merciful to all? Would justice be served? What would our world be like? Would not this inaction be unmerciful to many, including those criminals who would never reform and those whose justice was denied, in addition to the innocents who will be hurt by the released evildoers' future misdeeds?

Also, regarding the possibility of God giving second chances: he gives us second, third, fourth chances and so on. In fact, we have many, many chances over our lifetimes because he is trying to bring as many people as possible into heaven with him. Even now he continues deferring judgment for as long as possible. But there is coming a time when no more chances will be given, or when one's heart becomes so hard that it will never choose God.

***

Further, some believe in the existence of purgatory, a holding place where the dead go temporarily. Purgatory is neither heaven nor hell but a place where sins unforgiven at death are paid for. And this payment can be assisted by others still here on earth who are praying, tithing, and doing works for the benefit of the departed soul. Purgatory is not found in Scripture, so it is an erroneous belief. One must not ever rely on it!

While it is mainly Roman Catholics who hold to a belief in purgatory, I have met Muslims who believe similarly. My question is just this: why would anyone rely on a potentially bad plan that vaguely suggests a possible acceptance into heaven?

Not being biblical, the doctrine of purgatory was created by people who realized that, due to bad lives and evil deeds, they might not be saved. So, they contrived this system to reassure themselves. It is related to the Catholic practice of selling indulgences. This doctrine holds no merit and may not be relied on for eternal salvation! It is an imaginary safety net that will never catch you as you tumble!

***

Another question some ask is, "Why doesn't God just snuff out people bound for hell in order to end their misery?" It is because we are made in God's own image with God's gift of free will, which he will not overrule. He cannot simply kill anyone, as this would be contrary to his character of being a good and loving Father.

***

So, ask yourself, are your concerns and questions on hell because you fear it or because you fear God your Father? If one is afraid of God and fearful of what he will do to him, this shows that such person is not fully convinced that God really loves them. If we have accepted his gift of Christ, then we must not fear one who loves us so perfectly. We must not fear what he might do to us, because his loving mercy is extended to all who believe upon and know him. Consider:

> "We need have no fear of someone who loves us perfectly; his perfect love for us eliminates all dread of what he might do to us. If we are afraid, it is for fear of what he might do to us and shows that we are not fully convinced that he really loves us. So you see, our love for him comes as a result of his loving us first." (1 John 4:18–19)

17. Do All Suicides Go to Hell?

Unfortunately, many of us, myself included, have dealt with a suicide attempt or a completed suicide act in our friends' families, or with co-workers or patients, or even in our own families. I have had to wrestle with this issue in my immediate family as well as in patients with severe and chronic medical conditions.

After an attempt or the completed act of taking one's life, friends or family will often ask, "Don't all suicides go to hell?" Many feel that killing oneself violates God's sixth commandment, thou shall not kill.

I have thought, prayed, and wrestled with this question. But in the end, I am always reassured by Scripture that the answer is not a guaranteed affirmative yes if the victim knew the Lord Jesus. The Bible states that the only unforgiveable sin is blaspheming the Holy Spirit, denying God and his Christ over a lifetime. This does not include suicide.

So, what about the commandment thou shall not kill? Yes, killing yourself does violate this commandment. This is Old Testament law. So, although we are commanded to obey it, it predates the new covenant God made with us through the cross. For those who know him, the blood of Jesus covers all sins.

Therefore, I believe that if any person, though they commit suicide, knows and is one with Christ as their Lord and Savior, then, per the gospel, Jesus's blood covers all sins, suicide included—all besides blasphemy toward the Holy Spirit.

Also, from dealing with this issue medically for decades, as well as in my family situation, I have not seen a single suicide attempt (or death) in which the person who attempted it was mentally and physically in control of their emotions and decision-making. I highly doubt that anyone who makes the choice to harm themselves is at that point fully sane.

There are significant mental and physical issues that arise that may exceed the victim's control and limits, be it mental illness or a cancer progressing inexorably to an end state that one can see coming, or perhaps severe and intolerable chronic pain that continues and persists without respite, as well as severe guilt or grief. Put yourself into the

Rise and Soar

mind of a person afflicted in such a way. Do you feel you would be fully in your right mind, dealing with such day after day?

We can think of the suicide victim as a person with dementia (severe memory loss) or a debilitating psychiatric condition, such as schizophrenia or severe depression. Their soul may not be mentally able to stop putting their thought of suicide into action. I believe that the term victim is very appropriate. It connotes a lesser degree of personal responsibility for the suicide act, similar to how we describe motor vehicle accident or homicide fatalities as victims.

To take one's own life is, I believe, a desperate act that comes only from an extremely unnatural, altered mindset. Therefore, in my view such persons will not be fully held to blame for their action by our all-knowing, merciful, and loving Father, especially not if they know him and his Son.

While we can never fully know the answer here, these arguments reassure me as I examine what Scripture says. Thus, I feel comfortable using its authority to discuss with family, friends, and patients, that if a person is altered in their mind enough to consider, attempt, or unfortunately complete the suicide act, then they were in a mental state for which they are in greatest likelihood not culpable or blameworthy in the view of our loving God.

18. Do I Have to Be Baptized to Go to Heaven?

"John . . . taught that all should be baptized as a public announcement of their decision to turn their backs on sin, so that God could forgive them." (Mark 1:4)

While baptism is not absolutely necessary for salvation, Jesus strongly recommends that we as his followers take this step, if we have not already, and that we do so as a conscious choice, rather than as an infant who has none.

Why? First, because Christ did it, therefore demonstrating its obvious importance. Second, he commanded that we do so because baptism is the Christian's public demonstration of repentance and of their new relationship with Christ.

> "Your old sin-loving nature was buried with him by baptism when he died; and when God the Father, with glorious power, brought him back to life again, you were given his wonderful new life to enjoy." (Romans 6:4)

> "So look upon your old sin nature as dead and unresponsive to sin, and instead be alive to God, alert to him, through Jesus Christ our Lord." (v. 11)

> "For the wages of sin is death, but the free gift of God is eternal life through Jesus Christ our Lord." (v. 23)

Okay, so what is actually said at baptism? The baptizer will say something such as: "I baptize you in the name of the Father, and of the Son, and of the Holy Spirit. You are buried like Christ (on submersion), and now risen with Christ (on coming up again), renewed to live a brand-new life in him."

Okay, then what happens after baptism? Let us look to the Scriptures for this and for how we are to act postbaptism:

> "For in baptism you see how your old, evil nature died with him and was buried with him; and then you came up out

of death with him into a new life because you trusted the Word of the mighty God who raised Christ from the dead." (Colossians 2:12)

"Awake, O sleeper, and rise up from the dead; and Christ shall give you light." (Ephesians 5:14)

"Since you became alive again, so to speak, when Christ arose from the dead, now set your sights on the rich treasures and joys of heaven where he sits beside God in the place of honor and power. Let heaven fill your thoughts; don't spend your time worrying about things down here. You should have as little desire for this world as a dead person does. Your real life is in heaven with Christ and God. . . . Away then with sinful, earthly things; deaden the evil desires lurking within you; have nothing to do with sexual sin, impurity, lust, and shameful desires; don't worship the good things of life, for that is idolatry. God's terrible anger is upon those who do such things. You used to do them when your life was still part of this world; but now is the time to cast off and throw away all these rotten garments of anger, hatred, cursing, and dirty language. Don't tell lies to each other; it was your old life with all its wickedness that did that sort of thing; now it is dead and gone. You are living a brand-new kind of life that is continually learning more and more of what is right, and trying constantly to be more and more like Christ who created this new life within you." (Colossians 3:1–3, 5–10)

"Throw off your old evil nature—the old you that was a partner in your evil ways—rotten through and through, full of lust and sham. Now your attitudes and thoughts must all be constantly changing for the better. Yes, you must be a new and different person, holy and good. Clothe yourself with this new nature." (Ephesians 4:22–24)

"Since we believe that Christ died for all of us, we should also believe that we have died to the old life we used to live. He died for all so that all who live—having received eternal life from him—might live no longer for themselves, to please themselves, but to spend their lives pleasing Christ who died and rose again for them. . . . When someone becomes a Christian, he becomes a brand new person inside. He is not the same anymore. A new life has begun!" (2 Corinthians 5:14b–15, 17)

19. What About Those "Bad" Christians and Churches?

Unfortunately, we all can probably think of examples in this category. However, my initial response to those raising this objection is that any person who does evil while stating that they are doing their deeds for God or Christ is not acting as Jesus Christ would. Rather, they mislead and manipulate both his name and his character to gain power, wealth, or to commit impure acts. I instead ask people to look to the Jesus Christ of the Bible. This is where we are given the true example of Jesus, which is meant to be followed and which should be exhibited by his followers in this world.

None of us are, nor can we ever be, perfect as was Jesus Christ. Being human, one can never hope to more than scratch the surface of manifesting a true Christ-like character in word, thought, and action. Yet there are many, many of his followers who do this very well. This does not include anyone who does evil while claiming the name of God and Christianity. So I tell persons with this complaint, "Yes, what they did was wrong, but don't blame Christ, and don't throw yourself under the bus because of them, and don't let another's bad mistakes make you lose your salvation as well."

I ask people to open their eyes and see Jesus by meeting with him in the Scriptures and through prayer. And I reassure them that he then will reveal himself to them, and they will see all the perfect goodness that he is. They will clearly realize the difference between him and any of those false, so-called Christians.

Unfortunately, there are hypocrites everywhere, not just in Christianity and in the church. But we don't avoid our workplaces, ballgames, restaurants, or other places where hypocrites may exist. So, hypocrisy is not a valid excuse to avoid attending church. It is, instead, a tool of Satan to keep you from hearing the Word of God and from fellowshiping with other Christians. Satan is, as the Bible describes, a roaring lion looking to devour us. Satan seeks to take us out one person at time, never a whole flock or herd simultaneously, as such is much more difficult!

We must get past this stumbling block and view bad acts and actors as unfortunate, yet rare, errors and anomalies in what is otherwise the one institution that has made more positive contributions than any other in the history of this planet. We should not look at the church as power-hungry, violent, or exploitative.

Admittedly, we can easily call to mind rare evil examples, such as some of the Crusades, the Inquisition, the Salem witch trials, some missionary exploitations, Hitler's labeling of his Nazi movement as "Christian," and anti-Semitism elsewhere, as well as the oppression of women, Southern slavery, and sex scandals. Nevertheless, I propose that those who perform such evils and enact these heinous crimes are cultural Christians. They are not acting as true Christians as they primarily possess worldly intent and designs. They are pseudo-Christians.

Therefore, it is not valid to accuse and attack real Christianity. Cultural Christianity and authentic Christianity are vastly different!

Not all that is done in Christ's name should be attributed to Christianity. Sinful men use Jesus as an excuse for their greed and bloodlust, as they do things that are totally contrary to Christ's real teachings. So, it is not Christ who is at fault but those who have strayed from his laws of loving our enemies and caring for others, to instead seek self-gain!

Do not let evil pseudo-Christians cause you to throw away your own salvation. They do not practice true Christianity any more than Satan does. While it is difficult to forgive sins, God does do so, and thus we are called to do so also. Why let another derail you and keep you from heaven after you die and from a relationship with Christ while here in this world? Why let someone isolate you from Jesus's loving gifts of joy, peace, fulfillment, and rescue? It makes as little sense as throwing out all the money in your wallet because some money is counterfeit. Do you never eat eggs again because you find a rotten one in your store-bought dozen? Some of the very best people in this world meet in and make up our churches. Do not deny yourself access to them!

***

Now, let's reverse gears and look at what significant good has come from the church, even in some of the above situations where unfortunate evil concurrently happened. Missionaries overall, we must agree, have done vastly more good than bad. Early Catholic church efforts here, as well as modern Christian mission systems today, have always insisted on the humanity of the unreached or lost people group. They are also made in the image of Christ, with the same basic rights as any other person.

However, through economics and the politics of mercantilism in earlier times, greedy people latched onto this well-intentioned and true Christian endeavor for their own selfish personal gains, contrary to Christ's true teachings.

Yet, many of the native tribes at those early times existed in dire, extremely unhappy physical and spiritual circumstances (and many still do, even in our modern world), until they were greatly helped by the Christian missionaries.

Mission fieldwork continues today, stronger than ever, helped by advancements in technology, health care, transportation, finances, and by Bible translation into thousands of native languages. Scripture is yet only available to many by oral tradition, but every day, more translations are made. These souls are being fully shown Christ's true love in missionary efforts to care for and educate them.

Regarding the Crusades: Pope Urban started the first one, which was a response to Muslim violence against Christians in the Middle East. It had a positive albeit brief effect in delaying by two hundred years Islam's conquest of parts of Europe, such as the capture of Constantinople in 1453.

As for anti-Semitism, Martin Luther did make some anti-Semitic statements. But these were not in keeping with Christ's true teachings. For all the good that Luther did with the Protestant Reformation, he was still a human being prone to mistakes, just as Abraham, David, Peter, and Paul were in our Bible, and just as we all are today.

***

In stark and dramatic contrast to those rare and uncommon unloving acts committed in the name of Christianity throughout history, let us look at the history of our modern and civilized world of today, which is markedly worse. For instance, consider the works of atheists and political or false-religion extremists such as Lenin, Stalin, Hitler, and Mao Tse Tung. Look to the present evil North Korean regime, which is currently imprisoning an estimated thirty thousand souls for their Christian faith, as well as similar acts in Eritrea and other so-called prison nations. Consider the Sudanese government practicing Nuba-mountain area genocide upon Christians, as well as actions in Iraq, Iran, Afghanistan, Indonesia, the Philippines, and parts of Africa by radical jihadist Islamic groups such as Boko Haram, ISIS, al-Shabab, Al-Qaeda, and the Taliban.

These non-Christians butchered an estimated 4,146 civilian human beings in 2018 alone simply for being Christ-followers. This translates to eleven souls per day! This data is from Open Doors USA, which has carefully collected such figures for over sixty years. Its CEO, David Curry, testified to Congress earlier this year. And new data released in August 2019 reports that, in the fifty most persecutorial nations against Christians, they estimate 245 million Christians are presently under persecution because of their belief in Jesus and his good news!

These fifty nations are where persecution primarily occurs now. The worst ten in descending order are North Korea, Afghanistan, Somalia, Libya, Pakistan, Sudan, Eritrea, Yemen, Iran, and India.

In the past one hundred years, it is estimated that 180 million combatants worldwide (that is, military personnel) have been killed in action. Per Worldometers, the current population of the United States is 330 million.[14] So, in just the past century, a population equivalent to over half of the entire American population has been killed in military actions worldwide, not even counting those souls butchered for their Christian faith.

To Christian martyrs and military deaths, add also the vast millions of civilian homicides, as well as those non-Christian civilian deaths from genocides and purges over the past century, for example, Stalin and Hitler's purges of Jewish and other "societally dangerous" persons or the Khmer Rouge's Cambodian killing fields where over one million were slaughtered.

This mortality data's exponentially high figures of slain humans clearly shows that without God, human beings are undoubtedly and completely lost. Therefore, while Christians certainly need to humbly apologize for evils that have been done under the guise of Christianity and do our best to make certain that these do not recur, we must all admit that our world is a much, much better place because of Christianity. It brings the planet God's peace, his joy, his fulfillment, and his rescue. It delivers as well his hope via its missions, its food programs, its hospitals and schools, and the amazing efforts of so many Christian relief organizations.

Consider also how Christianity has given its gifts of higher learning, science, and literacy. The now almost-exclusively secular institutions of Harvard, Yale, and Princeton, which were some of the first universities in this country, were initially Christian-founded endeavors. Christianity's civilizing, God-derived ideals of humanitarianism, liberty, conscience, truth, and humility were prominent in their origins.

In summary, although the Bible is without error, Christianity unfortunately is not. Christians are finite and fallible human beings. Thus, Christianity should be viewed as a system of truth, with some human error, while other religions, looking at these openly and honestly, are systems of complete error.

Why do I say this? It is not just my opinion. The facts speak for themselves. Evidence clearly shows that no other religion whatsoever can come close to matching Christianity in its degree of financial outreach or its hands-on physical labor. Looking at the bottom-line hard numbers, these are benefits that God has bestowed upon the world, both physically in the here and now as well as those we shall gain after our death upon this planet!

Of utmost importance here is the fact that Christianity opens heaven to all people by the Cross of Christ! This is the true message we cannot allow to be darkened or subdued by what are unfortunate yet infrequent misrepresentations of Jesus. Go to the real Christ and let him show you the difference!

20. What If I Have Doubts?

In truth, human beings will have seasons of doubt. That is part of who and what we are. In my view though, these are often positive, as they help to test and to define one's faith and beliefs. Doubts are not something to be ashamed of. Rather, doubts are to be addressed and dealt with.

God our loving Father knows our human hearts possess this tendency to be uncertain at times. Therefore, I believe that he is very understanding when we are in these seasons of questioning.

But, do not merely repress or squelch your doubts. Instead, use your questions as your impetus to further explore, to read, and to pray. Use them to refine and better develop your relationship with God your Father! (See also Chapter XI, Faith, Works, and Doubt.)

21. Why Does God Seem to Dislike Some People?

This first question is usually a reference to the book of Romans:

> "Who are you to criticize God? Should the thing made say to the one who made it, 'Why have you made me like this?' . . .

Does not God have a perfect right to show his fury and power against those who are fit only for destruction, those he has been patient with for all this time? And he has a right to take others such as ourselves, who have been made for pouring the riches of his glory into, whether we are Jews or Gentiles, and to be kind to us so that everyone can see how very great his glory is." (Romans 9:20, 22–24)

As discussed at great length above, under Big Question 1, God allows some evil events to occur for his greater purpose and glory. Nevertheless, people bring these bad consequences about by making wrong choices, not ever by being puppet-like figures forced into evil roles by God's direct choice. What man means to do for evil, God means and ultimately uses for good, as per Genesis 50:20. Only in our minuscule mortal minds does it seem that there might be a contradiction.

We need to avoid being such evil instruments by reaching out to Christ. We need to ask him into our hearts and pray for him to change us. Then we should strive daily to better know him through reading Scripture, in our prayers, and in church and small groups, as well as through Christian media and service to others. Only Christ can change our sinful hearts!

Further regarding this seeming contradiction to our human minds, I like what Charles Spurgeon said in his autobiography: "If, then, I find taught in one part of the Bible that everything is foreordained, that is true; and if I find, in another Scripture, that man is responsible for all his actions, that is true; and it is only my folly that leads me to imagine that these two truths can ever contradict each other. I do not believe they can ever be welded into one upon any earthly anvil, but they certainly shall be one in eternity. They are two lines that are so nearly parallel, that the human mind which pursues them farthest will never discover that they converge, but they do converge, and they will meet somewhere in eternity, close to the throne of God, whence all truth doth spring."[15]

***

This topic provokes the major question of whether God already knows who among us will be going to heaven and who will not. People often respond, "But doesn't he love us all unconditionally?"

This is an extremely difficult question and topic, and to attempt to view it appropriately, we need to look at the two types of loves that God has for people. The first is referred to as benevolent love, which is his general grace, care, and the concern that he extends to all humans. This is the love by which he keeps our lungs breathing and our hearts beating, and through which he gives us good things such as food, family, shelter, clothes, rain, sunshine, and the beautiful natural world that we live in.

However, there is another type of love that is theologically called complacent love. It refers to a more unique affection in which he takes special delight and satisfaction in some people. This is his redemptive, saving love. It is like the love of a good parent for their child. It is a different love than they may feel for a friend, a coworker, or a distant family member. In a similar way, God's complacent love is focused primarily upon Jesus, his Son. And it spills over onto all of those who are renewed in Christ so that they come to share in his glory and will receive the reward that Christ received! This is a very special, fatherly affection for his own people, which he does not have for the remainder of the world that denies and refuses him.

Consider the love and the care of a cattle or sheep owner for his herd or flock versus the livestock of a neighbor. While he certainly may care for and help with those others when needed, he takes a more special and involved responsibility with his very own.

We will discuss predestation in more detail in the next section, but in brief, suffice it to say that God does indeed know what is going to occur, and he also knows your heart. He thus knows the choices that you are going to make on the way to your worldly end. As 2 Timothy 2:19 states, "The Lord knows those who are really his."

Therefore, while we can never say whether another will or will not be saved and go to heaven, God is already aware of the end of all stories and of our personal lives' conclusions, even as he knows the end of our world and his coming ultimate victory over all evil things!

22. What About Predestination?

A legend, quite uncertain as to its validity, is yet told of the atheistic, communist, Russian tyrant Joseph Stalin on his deathbed. After killing and persecuting innumerable Christians and multitudes of others, Stalin reportedly clutched a crucifix and asked for forgiveness and salvation from God in his last moments. Despite all that he had done over his entire evil life, which continued right up until perhaps the very minute before he expired, if his was a repentant, coming-to-Jesus conversion, then Stalin is indeed in heaven, as hard as it may be for us to believe.

***

That God knows all that is going to occur and all who are his is an extremely difficult concept for our human minds to comprehend. To better understand it, let's look at what is meant by the term predestination.

The doctrine of predestination states that God ordains exactly what is going to happen throughout the remainder of history, just as he has all along. Consider how Ephesians states that he chose us before establishing the foundation of the world. This means that he predestined us for adoption: "Long ago, even before he made the world, God chose us to be his very own through what Christ would do for us; he decided then to make us holy in his eyes, without a single fault—we who stand before him covered with his love" (Ephesians 1:4).

That says it all. How can we men of mortal minds ever hope to explain, fully understand, or even attempt to rationalize this? Our human intellect has a very difficult time wrapping itself around this concept.

We have already discussed God's knowing which persons are going to be his, ultimately, at the end of time, and which will not be. Yes, this is extremely hard for us to understand, but we nevertheless should not blatantly assume that God is some unfair, arbitrary tyrant. He does indeed have a plan in choosing certain people to be saved, and such has always been his plan, before the world was ever created! Therefore, God can be viewed as electing those whom he chooses and condemning those who deny him and his free gift of salvation.

Scripture states that predestination is based solely upon God's good will and that he does all that he does for his own glory. His choices are made from his good pleasure, and we know for certain that there is no such thing as bad pleasure in God, as given his nature, he cannot make a bad or evil choice.

Let us also look at what is termed the prescience view of predestination. It states that God's election of his chosen is based on his prior knowledge of what each person will do or not do. So, in eternity past, God looked down the halls of time to see who would embrace Christ and who would not. That's how he knows whom to adopt. Prescience implies that he chooses us because we either have chosen or will choose him at some point. However, this view goes against Scripture, to my human mind, as Ephesians places the initiative with God: because he first chose us, we are then able to choose him.

Consider for a moment how God chose to redeem Jacob and not Esau, Peter and not Judas. He dispenses his grace and mercy however and upon whomever he chooses, and we humans are not able to comprehend why (yet). Esau and Judas received justice, which is what they deserved. They did not receive unmerited evil doled out by God. Jacob and Peter alternatively received grace, which was more than they deserved. So, he does redeem guilty people (who turn to him), although not all. And he is under no obligation to redeem a single one of us. The amazing thing is that he redeems any of us.

But why is he allowed to choose? Is this not unfair? My reply here is to use the amazingly simple yet profound wisdom of a child, as stated so well by my daughter, Lexie, at nine years of age when I posed this same question to her. Her answer was, "Because he is God!" Consider Ecclesiastes 3:11: "Everything is appropriate in its own time. But though God has planted eternity in the hearts of men, even so, many cannot see the whole scope of God's work from beginning to end."

***

Another thought that helps me in trying to understand predestination is that God knows his sheep. Their choice is not an active issue to him. Some people do not care about God and never will. For example, Esau trivialized his birthright, his father's blessing, whereas Jacob actively sought after and ultimately received it from both his natural father, Isaac, as well as from God, his heavenly Father. Human desire and effort reveal the heart: selfishness does not seek God whereas selflessness does.

Further, consider how even Paul in his writings could not reconcile this issue in his mind. He admitted how confusing it is. So how can we, considering Paul's greater scriptural insight, ever be able to come to a true comprehension of predestination?

God wishes all to be elected—and, yes, I do believe in his elect, his chosen ones. But I also believe that the principles behind God's election can never be known or understood in the here and now. Perhaps the only reason we are still here in this world is because God is yet working upon us. I firmly believe we remain here simply because he yet has a plan for us. Thus, we must continually and steadfastly be confident and believe and pray for those lost, being confident that in his timing and in his way, he will save each lost soul that we know and pray for. He is waiting to return to give more time for sinners to repent (2 Peter 3:9). We need to trust God's will, his timing, his grace, and his glory.

***

Thus, we see from Scripture that he chose us first so that we, in turn, can then choose him. We cannot easily understand or wrap our minds around this, as Saint Paul concedes. Another key concept to discuss here is irresistible grace, which means that once we are chosen, we will not be able to resist him forever, even if our surrender occurs on our very deathbed!

In my mind, I believe that God does predestine all men to be saved, while Satan desires all to be condemned. It is then each person in each individual case who casts the deciding ballot, based upon how each person deals with God, and lives his life, and makes his choices.

I like to consider the parable of the good shepherd. The shepherd looks for his lost hundredth sheep in earnest and doesn't give up until he finds it. When he does, he puts it on his shoulders and brings it home. The shepherd symbolizes Jesus's strength and his salvation. He is not satisfied that he has the ninety-nine sheep. He wants them all! In the same way, I believe that God goes after each human during their lifetime, always trying to get every one into his fold. This is a very reassuring thought!

I like to use the Good Shepherd parable to respond to those who say that God is unfair or arbitrary and that God uses people or that he makes some of them bad and some of them good simply to accomplish his goals, with bad examples being Judas, Esau, the Pharisees, Pilate, and others. However, throughout Scripture we see his gift of free will employed by both good and bad persons. Think of the contrasting stories of Judas and Peter and of Esau and Jacob. Consider too the self-absorbed and arrogant Pharisees, scribes, and Sadducees, the many Jewish teachers of law and religion who had the evil roles to play in Jesus's death and resurrection.

Yet, I still believe God pursues each one of us. He wants to welcome all of us into his family. As Jesus states in Luke 13:34, "O Jerusalem . . . How often I have wanted to gather your children together even as a hen protects her brood under her wings, but you wouldn't let me."

Consider the story of Peter's vision: a sheet that came down from heaven with multiple types of food upon it. This represents the fact that God is welcoming all people, not just certain groups, into his kingdom.

Yet, some people willingly choose not to come to God and refuse to give up their selfish pursuits instead of living the real life he intended, in fact, that which he designed for them, for his glory (as well as for their optimal fulfillment). God plainly states that if you cling to idols in this manner, you will not be saved.

In summary, God pursues all people, yet some resist him until either their dying day or until their hearts harden so much that it becomes impossible to hear the Spirit's call any longer. It is not that God gets discouraged and reduces his volume. Instead, we learn better and better how to ignore his voice calling to our hearts by turning him down and tuning him out. Someone who listens to music too loudly will gradually lose his hearing until he cannot make out other sounds. And if the process continues, eventually all sound will stop, as he becomes deaf.

Again, God made us with the option to choose love and goodness over sin and evil, to choose a life with him in it or a godless life. He allows us the choice of the good or the evil.

As Scripture affirms, in his being the all-knowing, timeless God that he is, it seems clear that, while he does know exactly how the ultimate end is going to be with each of us, this is not something that any of us, nor our friends or family, can ever know for certain. We must leave this difficult concept in God's hands, knowing that he is doing what is in his nature, that of being mercifully good to us and continually seeking us up until our very end. Don't keep him waiting. Answer his call now!

And how do we do this? Given today's society, with not only printed Bibles but also online versions at our very fingertips, there is no excuse for any of us. If we want to know who God and Christ, his Son, are, we must step forward to meet and get to know them in their Scriptures. Pray for an open mind as you read. Ask God to show you what he needs to show you for that day and for your life, as per his plan for you. As he states, anyone who asks him earnestly and seeks him honestly will indeed find him!

We can therefore get to know him just as well as did the people who knew Christ when he was on this planet in his human form. It can be as if he was sitting right with us and having a conversation. We have in the Bible his very words, thoughts, and deeds, as well as the words of his closest trusted followers, all easily within our grasp on a daily basis.

Please do not miss this opportunity! It is the most important opportunity of your life, and it will again lead you on an amazing adventure as you give your life over to him and then watch the blessings he bestows upon you and others.

As we do such, another amazing thing we will see is that we become transformed into a Christ-model too, a member of the body of Christ. Then, as a vital part of his kingdom, we ourselves will affect the eternal end state of other people, playing a part in the predestined story of many lost souls. We will be valuable assistants to our Lord in his bringing these lost sheep into his fold, into his family!

Thus, it is not only we who are being changed into our predestined eternal state with him, but we are also helping others to do this as well! What greater sense of fulfillment and satisfaction can there be in this world, relative to knowing Christ as your friend, guide, and savior. What joy there is in being able to help others see who he is, thereby changing their eternities forever!

So, are you still looking at worldly issues, devices, and mere people for your fulfillment? If so, you feel and know that you are still unfulfilled, still perceiving that something is missing. So, why not try the Christ alternative? What have you to lose? Say yes to Jesus today!

***

One further thought on predestination involves this commonly asked question: "If God already knows and has set up everything, and such is going to happen exactly as he has ordained, why then do we ever need to make any plans, or put any human plans into action?"

As discussed above, we humans are expected to do our part, and we are meant to be intimately involved in his plans for his kingdom.

This is worth thinking about, and yes, it can be perplexing. Three Proverbs that best help me in thinking about such plans are as follows: "We can make our plans, but the final outcome is in God's hands"

(Proverbs 16:1), "We should make plans—counting on God to direct us" (v. 9), "Commit your work to the Lord, then it will succeed" (v. 3).

These verses counsel me to, firstly, step out and make plans, realizing that God is ultimately in control. We should ask him honestly for advice and then try to do as he instructs us. Also reassuring here is the promise that if we dedicate our plans and efforts to God, we then have his promise of ultimate success.

23. What Does God Actually Say About _____?

A) What Must We Do?

For God to fully work, both in us and through us, we must put forth an effort rather than sitting back to wait on him.

So, what do we need to do? We must go directly to his Word to learn his actual instructions for us:

> "'Brothers, what should we do?' And Peter replied, 'Each one of you must turn from sin, return to God, and be baptized in the name of Jesus Christ for the forgiveness of your sins; then you also shall receive this gift, the Holy Spirit.'" (Acts 2:37b–38)

> "He has told you what he wants, and this is all it is: to be fair, just, merciful, and to walk humbly with your God." (Micah 6:8)

> "If you love me, obey me." (John 14:15a)

> "'Sir, which is the most important command in the laws of Moses?' Jesus replied, 'Love the Lord your God with all your heart, soul, and mind.' This is the first and greatest commandment. The second most important is similar: 'Love your neighbor as much as you love yourself.' All the other

commandments and all the demands of the prophets stem from these two laws and are fulfilled if you obey them. Keep only these and you will find that you are obeying all the others." (Matthew 22:36–40)

"And so I am giving a new commandment to you now—love each other just as much as I love you." (John 13:34)

"Just believe it—that I am in the Father and the Father is in me." (John 14:11a)

"'Here is your part: Tell the truth. Be fair. Live at peace with everyone. Don't plot harm to others; don't swear that something is true when it isn't! How I hate all that sort of thing!' says the Lord." (Zechariah 8:16–17)

God wants us to recognize him for who he is and then to praise and to honor him accordingly.

"Take care to live in me, and let me live in you. For a branch can't produce fruit when severed from the vine. Nor can you be fruitful apart from me. Yes, I am the Vine; you are the branches. Whoever lives in me and I in him shall produce a large crop of fruit. For apart from me you can't do a thing. If anyone separates from me, he is thrown away like a useless branch, withers, and is gathered into a pile with all the others and burned. But if you stay in me and obey my commands, you may ask any request you like, and it will be granted! My true disciples produce bountiful harvests. This brings great glory to my Father." (John 15:4–8)

Further guidance from our God is as follows:

"If you have two coats . . . give one to the poor. If you have extra food, give it away to those who are hungry." (Luke 3:11)

"Love your enemies. Do good to those who hate you. Pray for the happiness of those who curse you; implore God's blessing on those who hurt you. If someone slaps you on one cheek, let him slap the other too! If someone demands your coat, give him your shirt besides. Give what you have to anyone who asks you for it; and when things are taken away from you, don't worry about getting them back. Treat others as you want them to treat you. Do you think you deserve credit for merely loving those who love you? Even the godless do that!...Love your enemies! Do good to them! Lend to them! And don't be concerned about the fact that they won't repay. Then your reward from heaven will be very great, and you will truly be acting as sons of God: for he is kind to the unthankful and to those who are very wicked. Try to show as much compassion as your Father does. Never criticize or condemn—or it will all come back on you. Go easy on others; then they will do the same for you. For if you give, you will get! Your gift will return to you in full and overflowing measure, pressed down, shaken together to make room for more, and running over. Whatever measure you use to give—large or small—will be used to measure what is given back to you." (Luke 6:27–32, 35–38)

"'If any of you wants to be my follower,' he told them, 'you must put aside your own pleasures and shoulder your cross, and follow me closely. If you insist on saving your life, you will lose it. Only those who throw away their lives for my sake and for the sake of the Good News will ever know what it means to really live. And how does a man benefit if he gains the whole world and loses his soul in the process? For is anything worth more than his soul? And anyone who is ashamed of me and my message in these days of unbelief and sin, I, the Messiah, will be ashamed of him when I return in the glory of my Father, with the holy angels.'" (Mark 8:34–38)

"Ask, and you will be given what you ask for. Seek, and you will find. Knock, and the door will be opened. For everyone who asks, receives. Anyone who seeks, finds. If only you will knock, the door will open." (Matthew 7:7–8)

"Then Jesus came near and said to them, 'All authority has been given to Me in heaven and on earth. Go, therefore, and make disciples of all nations, baptizing them in the name of the Father and of the Son and of the Holy Spirit, teaching them to observe everything I have commanded you. And remember, I am with you always, to the end of the age.'" (Matthew 28:18–20 HCSB)

"Don't copy the behavior and customs of this world, but be a new and different person with a fresh newness in all you do and think. Then you will learn from your own experience how his ways will really satisfy you." (Romans 12:2)

"God has given each of us the ability to do certain things well. So if God has given you the ability to prophesy, then prophesy whenever you can—as often as your faith is strong enough to receive a message from God. If your gift is that of serving others, serve them well. If you are a teacher, do a good job of teaching. If you are a preacher, see to it that your sermons are strong and helpful. If God has given you money, be generous in helping others with it. If God has given you administrative ability and put you in charge of the work of others, take the responsibility seriously. Those who offer comfort to the sorrowing should do so with Christian cheer.

Don't just pretend that you love others: really love them. Hate what is wrong. Stand on the side of the good. Love each other with brotherly affection and take delight in honoring each other. Never be lazy in your work, but serve the Lord enthusiastically. Be glad for all God is planning for you. Be patient in trouble, and prayerful always. When God's children are in need, you be the one to help them out. And get into the habit of inviting guests home for dinner or, if they need lodging, for the night. If someone mistreats you because you are a Christian, don't curse him; pray that God will bless him. When others are happy, be happy with them. If they are sad, share their sorrow. Work happily together. Don't try to act big. Don't try to get into the good graces of important people, but enjoy the company of ordinary folks. And don't think you know it all! Never pay back evil for evil. Do things in such a way that everyone can see you are honest clear through. Don't quarrel with anyone. Be at peace with everyone, just as much as possible. Dear friends, never avenge yourselves. Leave that to God, for he has said that he will repay those who deserve it. Don't take the law into your own hands. Instead, feed your enemy if he is hungry. If he is thirsty give him something to drink and you will be 'heaping coals of fire on his head.' In other words, he will feel ashamed of himself for what he has done to you. Don't let evil get the upper hand, but conquer evil by doing good." (Romans 12:6–21)

"So run your race to win. To win the contest you must deny yourselves many things that would keep you from doing your best. . . . So I run straight to the goal with purpose in every step. I fight to win. I'm not just shadow-boxing or playing around." (1 Corinthians 9:24b–26)

"For God is at work within you, helping you want to obey him, and then helping you do what he wants. In everything you do, stay away from complaining and arguing so that no one can speak a word of blame against you. You are to live clean, innocent lives as children of God in a dark world full of people who are crooked and stubborn. Shine out among them like beacon lights, holding out to them the Word of Life." (Philippians 2:13–16a)

"Stay always within the boundaries where God's love can reach and bless you. Wait patiently for the eternal life that our Lord Jesus Christ in his mercy is going to give you. Try to help those who argue against you. Be merciful to those who doubt. Save some by snatching them as from the very flames of hell itself. And as for others, help them to find the Lord by being kind to them, but be careful that you yourselves aren't pulled along into their sins. Hate every trace of their sin while being merciful to them as sinners." (Jude 1:21–23)

"Worship God alone." (Revelation 22:9b)

"Be strong and courageous and get to work. Don't be frightened by the size of the task, for the Lord my God is with you; he will not forsake you. He will see to it that everything is finished correctly." (1 Chronicles 28:20)

"But watch out! Be very careful never to forget what you have seen God doing for you. May his miracles have a deep and permanent effect upon your lives! Tell your children and your grandchildren about the glorious miracles he did." (Deuteronomy 4:9)

"Be gentle and ready to forgive; never hold grudges. Remember, the Lord forgave you, so you must forgive others. Most of all, let love guide your life . . . Let the peace of heart that comes from Christ be always present in your hearts and lives, for this is your responsibility and privilege as members of his body. And always be thankful. Remember what Christ taught, and let his words enrich your lives and make you wise; teach them to each other and sing them out in psalms and hymns and spiritual songs, singing to the Lord with thankful hearts. And whatever you do or say, let it be as a representative of the Lord Jesus." (Colossians 3:13–17a)

"Dear brothers, warn those who are lazy, comfort those who are frightened, take tender care of those who are weak, and be patient with everyone. See that no one pays back evil for evil, but always try to do good to each other and to everyone else. Always be joyful. Always keep on praying. No matter what happens, always be thankful, for this is God's will for you who belong to Christ Jesus." (1 Thessalonians 5:14–18)

"Fight well in the Lord's battles . . . Cling tightly to your faith in Christ and always keep your conscience clear, doing what you know is right." (1 Timothy 1:18–19a)

"Don't waste time arguing over foolish ideas and silly myths and legends. Spend your time and energy in the exercise of keeping spiritually fit. Bodily exercise is all right, but spiritual exercise is much more important and is a tonic for all you do. So exercise yourself spiritually, and practice being a better Christian because that will help you not only now in this life, but in the next life too." (1 Timothy 4:7–8)

Also consider the Holman translation here:

"But have nothing to do with irreverent and silly myths. Rather, train yourself in godliness, for the training of the body has a limited benefit, but godliness is beneficial in every way, since it holds promise for the present life and also for the life to come."

"Let us strip off anything that slows us down or holds us back, and especially those sins that wrap themselves so tightly around our feet and trip us up; and let us run with patience the particular race that God has set before us. Keep your eyes on Jesus, our leader and instructor. . . ."

"To keep from becoming fainthearted and weary, think about his patience as sinful men did such terrible things to him. . . . Don't be discouraged when he has to show you where you are wrong. For when he punishes you, it proves that he loves you. . . . Being punished isn't enjoyable while it is happening—it hurts! But afterwards we can see the result, a quiet growth in grace and character." (Hebrews 12:1–3, 5–6, 11)

"But ask the Lord Jesus Christ to help you live as you should, and don't make plans to enjoy evil." (Romans 13:14)

"Stop loving this evil world and all that it offers you, for when you love these things you show that you do not really love God; for all these worldly things, these evil desires—the craze for sex, the ambition to buy everything that appeals to you, and the pride that comes from wealth and importance—these are not from God. They are from this evil world itself. And this world is fading away, and these evil, forbidden things will go with it, but whoever keeps doing the will of God will live forever." (1 John 2:15–17)

The following is an excellent overall summary of what God says we must do in these verses from 1 John: "And this is what God says we must do: Believe on the name of his Son Jesus Christ, and love one another. Those who do what God says—they are living with God and he with them. We know this is true because the Holy Spirit he has given us tells us so." (3:23-24)

If we will only do such, his other commands will then be followed as well!

B) Using Our Time and Talents?

Further regarding what we are to do, we are asked to put forth our time and our talents appropriately and optimally for God's kingdom work.

But exactly how are we to do this? Jesus has given us the prime example of how we are to act, speak, think, and serve. We should strive to emulate and to mirror him. With our efforts employed in such manner, it will be difficult for us to go astray or be in gross error or waste our talents and resources.

As we work at our assigned duties each day, whether in the home or out, we should strive to make our work of whatever kind into a form of praise and honor to God, as what we do and are good at is exactly what he has made us for.

Employing the amazing wisdom of our current youngest generation (who seem, to me, to be much further along at much younger ages than we were at their given age), my daughter one day had a unique explanation when I asked her what we are meant to do in our lives for God and Jesus. She replied, "Jesus coming to this world was Jesus Version 1, our model (she meant an initial baseline or template). And now, we are Jesus Version 1.5, as his Spirit is upon us and he and God are in our hearts. So, we are supposed to follow in continuing his work until his return, at which time Jesus Version 2 will be here among us!" I have no words to add to this.

***

I often consider our time remaining here in this world as the timer used in a football or basketball game. The clock is continually running until at one final point it gets down to 00:00. Therefore, each moment, each minute, each day, and so on can only be used once. Then it is gone forever. Frittering away our remaining time is not wise.

This thought helps me stay on course. I think about focusing upon Christ and his kingdom work of serving others in my telescope or in the crosshairs of my spotting scope. We must keep ourselves focused without flinching, shaking, or deviating away. This helps us remain true to his cause and true to the purpose that God intends for each of us to have in this world.

In the wet and cold environments where I often hike and hunt, it is a continuous effort to keep scope lenses, binoculars, and rangefinder optics defogged and dry. Once on a brutally cold Arctic night, after a long frigid hour of lying in the snow, I had finally predator-called (by imitating a wounded deer) a large black wolf to within fifteen yards of my face. As silently as a timber-ghost, he magnificently material-ized from out of nowhere directly in front of me. He was in stalk-mode with head low but ears perked, huge yellow eyes staring at what he thought was a venison dinner. I could see him well against the snow, but despite all precautions, my breath's moisture on the objective lens had frozen thickly. I could see nothing at all through the scope. Not having a shoot-through mount option on this piece, I simply watched him and let him walk, but this lesson was not forgotten.

To avoid this going forward, I routinely employ scope covers, defogging chemicals, and wiping cloths called shammies. In a similar way, we too must keep our lenses from becoming foggy, cloudy, or frozen over so that we can clearly see God's full plan for us.

***

Our ends are coming to us all; death is for certain. At some point in each of our futures, an activity-limiting illness, age, or disease will eventually come calling no matter how much money we have and no matter our jobs, power, connections, or any other accoutrements we may possess.

If you are not a Christian, consider this with respect to time itself: we invest so much time into looking at different job prospects, man-aging our portfolio of investments and our stuff, deciding where we should go or how to spend our family vacation and so on. Should we not at least spend some time looking at our eternal futures to be certain that we are also doing the right things in that realm? Why not research Christ along with Christianity and its claims? Almost every intelligent mind that has objectively done this has ultimately concluded that Jesus is the genuine truth.

Do not to fritter away the days of your life. Do not waste your remaining hours, delaying until the very knife edge of the end! The following scripture I feel best makes the point that God wants us to take stock and obey, regarding the use of our time and the talents he has given us: "Teach us to number our days and recognize how few they are; help us to spend them as we should" (Psalm 90:12).

I don't know about you, but that one always grabs my attention! Also, consider Luke 19:12–26 and Matthew 25:14–30, the parable of the talents, in which money, called talents back then, was given to three separate assistants while their boss left town. One invested it well, making a tenfold return, and another made five times the original amount. When he returned, their boss was overjoyed and rewarded the two men. But the third man did not even try to invest, instead simply hiding his away out of fear of losing it. And because he did not use his gift, it was taken from him. He was also cast out into the darkness. He was judged for his grave error!

Also, consider the words of John the Baptist about his God-given purpose proclaiming Jesus's coming: "God in heaven appoints each man's work. My work is to prepare the way for that man so that everyone will go to him" (John 3:27–28a).

What if we understood that preparing the way for the kingdom of the Lord is our main job, our main duty, no matter where we are or what we are doing in life, whether employed or unemployed, a housewife, in school, retired, disabled, or even bedbound! Wouldn't our lives be radically and wonderfully changed? Look at Jesus's viewpoint in the following verses:

"All of us must quickly carry out the tasks assigned us by the one who sent me, for there is little time left before night falls and all work comes to an end. But while I am still here in the world, I give it my light." (John 9:4–5)

"You are the world's seasoning, to make it tolerable. If you lose your flavor, what will happen to the world? And you yourselves will be thrown out and trampled underfoot as worthless. You are the world's light—a city on a hill, glowing in the night for all to see. Don't hide your light! Let it shine for all; let your good deeds glow for all to see, so that they will praise your heavenly Father." (Matthew 5:13–16)

"'The harvest is so great, and the workers are so few,' he told his disciples. 'So pray to the one in charge of the harvesting, and ask him to recruit more workers for his harvest fields.'" (Matthew 9:37–38)

Also consider:

"Another reason for right living is this: you know how late it is; time is running out. Wake up, for the coming of the Lord is nearer now than when we first believed. The night is far gone, the day of his return will soon be here. So quit the evil deeds of darkness and put on the armor of right living, as we who live in the daylight should! Be decent and true in everything you do so that all can approve your behavior. Don't spend your time in wild parties and getting drunk or in adultery and lust or fighting or jealousy. But ask the Lord Jesus Christ to help you live as you should, and don't make plans to enjoy evil." (Romans 13:11–14)

"There is going to come a time of testing at Christ's Judgment Day to see what kind of material each builder has used. Everyone's work will be put through the fire so that all can see whether or not it keeps its value, and what was really accomplished" (1 Corinthians 3:13)

"Never let it be said that Christ's people are poor workers. Don't let the name of God or his teaching be laughed at because of this." (1 Timothy 6:1)

"However, Christ has given each of us special abilities—whatever he wants us to have out of his rich storehouse of gifts." (Ephesians 4:7)

"So, my dear brothers, since future victory is sure, be strong and steady, always abounding in the Lord's work, for you know that nothing you do for the Lord is ever wasted as it would be if there were no resurrection." (1 Corinthians 15:58)

C) Persecution?

While never easy to think about or to undergo, we must remember that Christ paid a dear price for our salvation. Therefore, we too may be called on to suffer persecution for the salvation that we have been granted through him! I feel we, therefore, should strive to see our persecutions as chances or as opportunities to serve and honor Christ.

We should accept these and welcome all oncoming trials, with hearts trusting God, who is our hope, our joy, and our peace. He has also given his assurance of our ultimate rescue. Consider these verses relative to this theme:

"For no apparent reason, my enemies hunted me like a bird. They dropped me alive into a pit and threw stones at me. Water flooded over my head, and I thought: I'm going to die! I called on Your name, Yahweh, from the depths of the Pit. You hear my plea: Do not ignore my cry for relief. You come near when I call on You; You say: 'Do not be afraid.'" (Lamentations 3:52–57 HCSB)

"Hide your loved ones in the shelter of your presence, safe beneath your hand, safe from all conspiring men. Blessed is the Lord, for he has shown me that his never-failing love protects me like the walls of a fort!" (Psalm 31:20–21)

"But the eyes of the Lord are watching over those who fear him, who rely upon his steady love. He will keep them from death even in times of famine! We depend upon the Lord alone to save us. Only he can help us; he protects us like a shield. No wonder we are happy in the Lord! For we are trusting him. We trust his holy name. Yes, Lord, let your constant love surround us, for our hopes are in you alone." (Psalm 33:18–22)

"God is our refuge and strength, an ever-present help in trouble. Therefore we will not fear, though the earth give way and the mountains fall into the heart of the sea." (Psalm 46:1–2 NIV)

"When I am afraid, I will put my confidence in you. Yes, I will trust the promises of God. And since I am trusting him, what can mere man do to me?" (Psalm 56:3–4)

Looking at these verses, it appears that persecution is something that can be considered a privilege to the right-thinking Christian. We, by our Christ-like examples, must try to get to our persecutors' hearts. We should love them as Jesus would by continually forgiving their misdeeds against us, by sharing the gospel with them, and by praying that they will come to know and serve the true God. We should feel sorry for them despite all their bravado and seemingly self-assured control and toughness, as they are far from Christ. Without Christ Jesus, they are the ones suffering much more than any degree of physical or mental persecution they may heap upon us.

Sabina Wurmbrand, in her book *The Pastor's Wife*, gives an amazing insight regarding ministering to a prison guard who had been persecuting her physically. Her response was to smile at her torturer and to say, "I smile because of what I see in your eyes: as myself, before I learned to love, and also, before I knew Christ! Since then my hands no longer strike out. You look into my eyes and see yourself as God can make you."[16]

Similarly, we too can discuss with our persecutors how we were like them before we knew Christ. We can bid them to see us now as Christ has transformed us and as something they can become.

Still, we cannot persevere on our own strength alone. We must rely on Christ. He is the vine and we are the branches, as he states in John 15. We need to stay firmly attached to him in his Word while displaying his character. We must show our persecutors that we care enough about them to tell them his good news and that we also believe and act out what we profess.

I will tell those who protest my gospel conversations that the reason I continue to tell them about this is because I care about them and because I am convinced that it is true. And so therefore, in my knowing what it can do, I want to tell them for their benefit.

Imagine if you found a cure for cancer or some other incurable disease. Would you ever and could you ever keep it to yourself? No, you would have to tell others. In a similar way, especially because Christ's love and grace so exceed anything else we might try to compare them to, including a cancer cure, we must feel an urgent obligation to profess it to whomever we can.

In other words, if you know him, how can you not tell others? We should develop a mindset within us that constantly states, "I have to tell you of Christ and his saving gift!" Again, I routinely tell protesters that if I do not tell them, then I either do not care about them or I myself do not believe what I am saying about Jesus. This sentence almost always calms even the most agitated and upset among them!

Now, does it sound scary or unnerving to be interrogated or asked to testify about your Christian belief in our Lord Jesus Christ? Yes, on the surface this indeed may seem so, but we must constantly remember that he has promised that he will always be with us in these situations and that he will, through his Holy Spirit, always give us the exact words that need to be said at the very time that such are needed: "But when you are arrested and stand trial, don't worry about what to say in your defense. Just say what God tells you to. Then you will not be speaking, but the Holy Spirit will" (Mark 13:11).

As we grow closer to God, he, by his strength, allows us to continue to endure and to obey him no matter the trial or the cost. We can pray for endurance or even rescue, as per God's will. Yet, we must realize that if such comes, it will be according to his will, in his timing, and for his glory.

Our trials are sent to mold and form us into who we are meant to be so that we can do what we are meant to do here on earth, for God's soon-to-be eternally victorious kingdom. As Jesus says in John 16:33,

"Here on earth you will have many trials and sorrows; but cheer up, for I have overcome the world."

***

Another important aspect of persecution is forgiveness. We need to try to extend forgiveness to our torturers. God's Word tells us we must do so, as hard as it may seem and as long as it can sometimes take us to get there. The act of forgiving is another way we are asked to obey the God who has forgiven and who continues to forgive all who accept his gift through Christ's sacrifice. His example of radical and complete forgiveness, offered even for those who put him to physical death, should be our ongoing model.

Yes, forgiveness is difficult, and our human hearts naturally resist granting it. Only by trusting God and letting him help us with this forgiveness can our injured hearts ever really forgive. We must continue to seek after, to trust, and to obey God for true forgiveness to take root in our hearts, allowing it to replace our bitterness, our anger, and our sorrow.

We should pray to Christ for his help in granting us a spirit of true forgiveness just as he forgave, so that we are able to carry his cross through carrying ours. Then we may assist others with carrying their crosses as well. Remember what Christ says in Matthew 10:38–39: "If you refuse to take up your cross and follow me, you are not worthy of being mine. If you cling to your life, you will lose it; but if you give it up for me, you will save it."

Our lives are not ours to lose, but they are God's, meant to serve his kingdom for his glory. His Great Commission will be accomplished, so why not be a part of it? He will be with you, guiding your thoughts, your speech, your steps, and your actions as you maintain a solid trust in him no matter the circumstances.

Galatians 5:11 states, "The fact that I am still being persecuted proves that I am still preaching salvation through faith in the cross of Christ alone." We discussed above why the false religions are so minimally persecuted worldwide, while those of the Christian faith are so universally persecuted. I believe the reason is because Satan persecutes the true faith in his desire to squash and eliminate it. It is the only one he is worried about.

Open Doors, a Christian organization dedicated to serving the persecuted worldwide, has released recent research that reveals the following: every month, worldwide, 255 Christians are killed, 104 are abducted, 180 Christian females are raped or sexually harassed or forced into marriages, 66 churches are attacked, and 160 Christians are imprisoned without trial. They also compile a list of the fifty most difficult countries to be a Christian in, given the degree of persecution. In just these fifty nations alone, 245 million Christians are reported to be experiencing high levels of persecution. This was again just in these fifty nations. In 2018 alone, the known statistics gathered thus far from these lands include 4,146 Christians killed, 1,252 abducted, 1,020 raped or sexually harassed, and 793 churches attacked, which are staggering numbers. And these are only the known and reported cases!

Their data collection has been ongoing for decades, and Open Door's CEO has testified before Congress. One cannot dismiss these as exaggerations.

***

We need to and should want to preach Christ's gospel simply because so many people are lost. They don't know it or understand it. Even when it is dangerous to do so, we still should not remain quiet nor fearful. As 2 Corinthians 6:4–10 states:

> "In fact, in everything we do we try to show that we are true ministers of God. We patiently endure suffering and hardship and trouble of every kind. We have been beaten, put in jail, faced angry mobs, worked to exhaustion, stayed awake through sleepless nights of watching, and gone without food. . . . We have been kind and truly loving and filled with the Holy Spirit. We have been truthful, with God's power helping us in all we do. . . . We stand true to the Lord whether others honor us or despise us, whether they criticize us or commend us. We are honest, but they call us liars. The world ignores us, but we are known to God; we live close to death, but here we are, still very much alive. We have been injured but kept from death. Our hearts ache, but at the same time we have the joy of the Lord. We are poor, but we give rich spiritual gifts to others. We own nothing, and yet we enjoy everything."

***

I have met Muslims who say, "True Muslims don't pray for Christians." But Jesus, I like to remind them, tells Christians to pray for all people, even our enemies. Isn't this what one would expect the one true God to say? Why would any divine figure, unless he was unloving and solely power-hungry in isolation, ever ask his believers to be evil to or persecute others?

Surely this must prick the conscience of any Muslim as well as those of other faiths if they will take the time to contemplate it. Isn't a merciful and loving figure exactly how you would in all honesty expect the true God to be, that is, eternally forgiving and concerned even for his enemies? This true God loves them despite their evil deeds. And he, in turn, asks us to love them also. Therefore, he asks us to pray for our enemies and to forgive them.

When persecuted, then, we should feel sorry not for ourselves but rather for our persecutors. They are blinded from the truth and lost. Their lives must therefore be a mess, even in those cases when they seem to be very powerful and in control and have everything going well for them.

**

Certainly, fear is going to be present whenever there is a degree of persecution or simply the threat of such. Here, however, remember 2 Timothy 1:7, which states, "For God has not given us a spirit of fearfulness, but one of power, love, and sound judgment" (HCSB).

Consider Richard Wurmbrand's insight on February 29, 1948. While riding in a car with a sack over his head after being captured by the secret police and led off to what would be fourteen years of imprisonment, he recalled comfortingly that the Bible, three hundred sixty-six times, states "do not be afraid." That is once for every day of the year, including even that extra leap year day!

He also said, "Why should we fear those who can kill us or break our hearts? Once we have passed from this life, our foes can no longer harm us. We will be with God."[17]

I too have always admired what Christian General Stonewall Jackson said when asked about his famed composure and bravery under fire. He replied, "My religious beliefs teach me to feel as safe in battle as in bed. God has fixed the time of my death. I do not concern myself with that, but to be always ready whenever it may overtake me. That is the way all men should live, and all men would be equally brave."

Also, recall the profoundly insightful and accurate statement made by Henry Martyn, a missionary to India and Persia and a Bible translator: "I am immortal until God's work for me here is done." Therefore, we must not fear. Instead, we should give ourselves to God's plan for us and thereby allow such plans to be fulfilled! We should consider ourselves invincible and even immortal in this world, until God's plan and work for us here is either finished or is ignored by you for too long of a duration, so that the calling voice extinguishes.

Think more on this great reassurance! God ends your time here, not any evil person or car accident, no cancer or other illness. Therefore, we must not fear persecution or even death. Death will come to all of us, as per our Lord's plan, but only in his timing, in his will, and ultimately for his glory! Worrying about it, as Jesus says, will not add a single moment to our lives. Therefore, cast away all fear. Step out and ask him to show you what he needs you to do every day for him.

***

One further noteworthy thought is this: regarding the millions upon millions who have been killed because of their faith in Jesus Christ, including the estimated 150 million martyred in just the last one hundred years alone (per Wurmbrand's Voice of the Martyrs organization), in their honor and unto their memory each persecution throughout history has been very important. These always have and always will result in the spread of the gospel and growth of Christ's church.

Persecution always has the opposite effect of that intended by the persecutor, beginning with the Roman and Jewish persecutions of Christ's era right up to our modern tyrannical regimes and radical terrorists. Christ's scars, as well as the ones that we sustain in our serving him, remind us always of the price he paid for our salvation!

Always remember, too, in these sufferings that Christ is the only one who will always be right there with you in any and all circumstances. He is the only fully reliable family and friend that you have. He promises to never, ever leave or forsake us. Romans 8:35 says, "Who can separate us from the love of Christ? Can affliction or anguish or persecution or famine or nakedness or danger or sword?" (HCSB). Also, Isaiah 30:19–20 says, "He will answer you. Though he give you the bread of adversity and water of affliction, yet he will be with you to teach you—with your own eyes you will see your Teacher."

Persecution purifies believers and makes them see the true value of their faith. In countries where Christianity is now being persecuted strongly, the faith of our Christian brothers and sisters is amazing to witness. It far exceeds the general faith outwardly evidenced in lands that allow the freedom to practice Christianity openly.

Let us now look at some other helpfully relevant scriptures here:

"Three different times I begged God to make me well again. Each time he said, 'No. But I am with you; that is all you need. My power shows up best in weak people.' Now I am glad to boast about how weak I am; I am glad to be a living demonstration of Christ's power, instead of showing off my own power and abilities. Since I know it is all for Christ's good, I am quite happy about 'the thorn,' and about insults and hardships, persecutions and difficulties; for when I am weak, then I am strong—the less I have, the more I depend on him." (2 Corinthians 12:8–10)

"It will be a clear sign from God that he is with you, and that he has given you eternal life with him. For to you has been given the privilege not only of trusting him but also of suffering for him." (Philippians 1:28–29)

"For God has said, 'I will never, never fail you nor forsake you.' That is why we can say without any doubt or fear, 'The Lord is my Helper, and I am not afraid of anything that mere man can do to me.'" (Hebrews 13:5–6)

"So be truly glad! There is wonderful joy ahead, even though the going is rough for a while down here. These trials are only to test your faith, to see whether or not it is strong and pure." (1 Peter 1:6–7a)

"This suffering is all part of the work God has given you. Christ, who suffered for you, is your example. Follow in his steps: He never sinned, never told a lie, never answered back when insulted; when he suffered he did not threaten to get even; he left his case in the hands of God who always judges fairly. . . . Like sheep you wandered away from God, but now you have returned to your Shepherd, the Guardian of your souls who keeps you safe from all attacks." (1 Peter 2:21–23, 25)

"Dear friends, don't be bewildered or surprised when you go through the fiery trials ahead, for this is no strange, unusual thing that is going to happen to you. Instead, be really glad— because these trials will make you partners with Christ in his suffering, and afterwards you will have the wonderful joy of sharing his glory in that coming day when it will be displayed." (1 Peter 4:12–13)

Paul C. Buechel, M.D.

"But if we are to share his glory, we must also share his suffering. Yet what we suffer now is nothing compared to the glory he will give us later." (Romans 8:17b–18)

"So if you are suffering according to God's will, keep on doing what is right and trust yourself to the God who made you, for he will never fail you." (1 Peter 4:19)

"What happiness it is when others hate you and exclude you and insult you and smear your name because you are mine! When that happens, rejoice! Yes, leap for joy! For you will have a great reward awaiting you in heaven." (Luke 6:22–23a)

"Happy are those who are persecuted because they are good, for the Kingdom of Heaven is theirs." (Matthew 5:10)

"I have given you authority over all the power of the Enemy, and to walk among serpents and scorpions and to crush them. Nothing shall injure you!" (Luke 10:19)

"One night the Lord spoke to Paul in a vision and told him, 'Don't be afraid! Speak out! Don't quit! For I am with you and no one can harm you.'" (Acts 18:9–10a)

"We know that all that happens to us is working for our good if we love God and are fitting into his plans." (Romans 8:28)

"After you have suffered a little while, our God, who is full of kindness through Christ, will give you his eternal glory. He personally will come and pick you up, and set you firmly in place, and make you stronger than ever." (1 Peter 5:10)

In other verses regarding our trials and persecutions, the Scriptures refer to us as commodities such as steel, diamonds, trees, and gold and silver. Each is made stronger and refined by stress, fire, high winds, or other harsh conditions that drive out impurities. Similarly, we are reassured that our hardships will bolster our faith and our basic trust in God, making our bond grow stronger and stronger. But how does God know when enough is enough? How does he know exactly how much we can bear?

He promises that he will never give us more than we can individually handle (1 Corinthians 10:13). Interestingly, a parallel can be drawn to silversmithing. Silver is refined by heating and reheating, which burns off the impurities in the metal. If this process continues for too long, it will ruin the silver. Thus, the silversmith stops the process at one specific time. He stops once he can see himself in the purified silver!

Similarly, I believe God can visualize us taking on more and more of his traits and, thus, more of his character, which greatly satisfies him as we progress through our life's trials. He then stops the trials when we are perfectly refined. And he never carries these far enough to allow our ruin. Consider:

> "Be strong! Be courageous! Do not be afraid of them! For the Lord your God will be with you. He will neither fail you nor forsake you." (Deuteronomy 31:6)

> "No one will be able to oppose you as long as you live, for I will be with you . . . I will not abandon you or fail to help you." (Joshua 1:5)

In summary, we cannot simply give up when we meet the resistance that our friend and Savior has told us will indeed come our way if we are following him. He did not give up in his trial, so neither then can we!

Keep your eyes and soul focused upon him. Trust him. Commit to bringing his salt and light and, thus, his life to this dark world, and he will indeed keep you and fulfill his work through you!

D) Generosity and Giving?

In Chapter VIII, Talents and Time Management, we covered this in detail. However, let's look scripturally at several other things that Jesus mentions about this in addition to what we reviewed earlier:

"Purity is best demonstrated by generosity." (Luke 11:41)

"Sell what you have and give to those in need. This will fatten your purses in heaven! And the purses of heaven have no rips or holes in them. Your treasures there will never disappear; no thief can steal them; no moth can destroy them. Wherever your treasure is, there your heart and thoughts will also be." (Luke 12:33–34)

"Take care! Don't do your good deeds publicly, to be admired, for then you will lose the reward from your Father in heaven. When you give a gift to a beggar, don't shout about it as the hypocrites do—blowing trumpets in the synagogues and streets to call attention to their acts of charity! I tell you in all earnestness, they have received all the reward they will ever get. But when you do a kindness to someone, do it secretly...And your Father, who knows all secrets, will reward you." (Matthew 6:1–4)

"And if, as my representatives, you give even a cup of cold water to a little child, you will surely be rewarded." (Matthew 10:42)

"But remember this—if you give little, you will get little. A farmer who plants just a few seeds will get only a small crop, but if he plants much, he will reap much. Everyone must make up his own mind as to how much he should give. Don't force anyone to give more than he really wants to, for cheerful givers are the ones God prizes. God is able to make it up to you by giving you everything you need and more so that there will not only be enough for your own needs but plenty left over to give joyfully to others. It is as the Scriptures say: 'The godly man gives generously to the poor. His good deeds will be an honor to him forever.' For God, who gives seed to the farmer to plant, and later on good crops to harvest and eat, will give you more and more seed to plant and will make it grow so that you can give away more and more fruit from your harvest. Yes, God will give you much so that you can give away much, and when we take your gifts to those who need them they will break out into thanksgiving and praise to God for your help. So two good things happen as a result of your gifts—those in need are helped, and they overflow with thanks to God." (2 Corinthians 9:6–12)

E) Possessions and Worldly Concerns?

Jesus addresses wealth and worldly concerns many, many times in the Bible. Some of these references include:

"And I'll sit back and say to myself, 'Friend, you have enough stored away for years to come. Now take it easy! Wine, women, and song for you!' But God said to him, 'Fool! Tonight you die. Then who will get it all?' Yes, every man is a fool who gets rich on earth but not in heaven.

"Then turning to his disciples he said, 'Don't worry about whether you have enough food to eat or clothes to wear. For life consists of far more than food and clothes. Look at the ravens—they don't plant or harvest or have barns to store away their food, and yet they get along all right—for God feeds them. And you are far more valuable to him than any birds!

"And besides, what's the use of worrying? What good does it do? Will it add a single day to your life? Of course not! And if worry can't even do such little things as that, what's the use of worrying over bigger things?

"Look at the lilies! They don't toil and spin, and yet Solomon in all his glory was not robed as well as they are. And if God provides clothing for the flowers that are here today and gone tomorrow, don't you suppose that he will provide clothing for you, you doubters? And don't worry about food—what to eat and drink; don't worry at all that God will provide it for you. All mankind scratches for its daily bread, but your heavenly Father knows your needs. He will always give you all you need from day to day if you will make the Kingdom of God your primary concern.

"So don't be afraid, little flock. For it gives your Father great happiness to give you the Kingdom. Sell what you have and give to those in need. This will fatten your purses in heaven! And the purses of heaven have no rips or holes in them. Your treasures there will never disappear; no thief can steal them; no moth can destroy them. Wherever your treasure is, there your heart and thoughts will also be." (Luke 12:19–34)

"Anyone who wants to be my follower must love me far more than he does his own father, mother, wife, children, brothers, or sisters—yes, more than his own life—otherwise he cannot be my disciple. And no one can be my disciple who does not carry his own cross and follow me. So no one can become my disciple unless he first sits down and counts his blessings— and then renounces them all for me." (Luke 14:26–27, 33)

Wow! These are certainly very direct statements from our Lord, which cut deeply into our worldly hearts, into those feelings that make us human. We desire to gain and to hold onto things, even to hoard them, to keep them for ourselves for that potential rainy day.

Personally, I think that we, as his people (or his priests, as he calls us), should strive to be as the Levites were in Joshua 13:33 to whom no land was given. They had no inheritance, for the Lord God was their inheritance. He was all they needed. They took care of God's temple, and therefore he took care of them in other ways. While certainly a difficult shift for many of us in our mindsets, this seems clearly to be what God desires, as many more biblical references to these issues abound:

"'I came naked from my mother's womb,' he said, 'and I shall have nothing when I die. The Lord gave me everything I had, and they were his to take away. Blessed be the name of the Lord.'" (Job 1:21)

"But as for me, my contentment is not in wealth but in seeing you and knowing all is well between us. And when I awake in heaven, I will be fully satisfied, for I will see you face-to-face." (Psalm 17:15)

"As they were walking along someone said to Jesus, 'I will always follow you no matter where you go.' But Jesus replied, 'Remember, I don't even own a place to lay my head. Foxes have dens to live in, and birds have nests, but I, the Messiah, have no earthly home at all.' Another time, when he invited a man to come with him and to be his disciple, the man agreed—but wanted to wait until his father's death. Jesus replied, 'Let those without eternal life concern themselves with things like that. Your duty is to come and preach the coming of the Kingdom of God to all the world.' Another said, 'Yes, Lord, I will come, but first let me ask permission of those at home.' But Jesus told him, 'Anyone who lets himself be distracted from the work I plan for him is not fit for the Kingdom of God.'" (Luke 9:57–62)

"Neither you nor anyone else can serve two masters. You will hate one and show loyalty to the other, or else the other way around—you will be enthusiastic about one and despise the other. You cannot serve both God and money." (Luke 16:13)

"Watch out! Don't let my sudden coming catch you unawares; don't let me find you living in careless ease, carousing and drinking, and occupied with the problems of this life, like all the rest of the world." (Luke 21:34)

"The seed among the thorns represents those who listen and believe God's words but whose faith afterwards is choked out by worry and riches and the responsibilities and pleasures of life." (Luke 8:14a)

Rise and Soar

"So don't be anxious about tomorrow. God will take care of your tomorrow too. Live one day at a time." (Matthew 6:34)

"Jesus replied, 'Let me assure you that no one has ever given up anything—home, brothers, sisters, mother, father, children, or property—for love of me and to tell others the Good News, who won't be given back, a hundred times over, homes, brothers, sisters, mothers, children, and land—with persecutions! All these will be his here on earth, and in the world to come he shall have eternal life. But many people who seem to be important now will be the least important then; and many who are considered least here shall be greatest there.'" (Mark 10:29–31)

"Do you want to be truly rich? You already are if you are happy and good. After all, we didn't bring any money with us when we came into the world, and we can't carry away a single penny when we die. So we should be well satisfied without money if we have enough food and clothing. But people who long to be rich soon begin to do all kinds of wrong things to get money, things that hurt them and make them evil-minded and finally send them to hell itself. For the love of money is the first step toward all kinds of sin. Some people have even turned away from God because of their love for it, and as a result have pierced themselves with many sorrows." (1 Timothy 6:6–10)

"Tell those who are rich not to be proud and not to trust in their money, which will soon be gone, but their pride and trust should be in the living God who always richly gives us all we need for our enjoyment. Tell them to use their money to do good. They should be rich in good works and should give happily to those in need, always being ready to share with others whatever God has given them. By doing this they will be storing up real treasure for themselves in heaven—it is the only safe investment for eternity! And they will be living a fruitful Christian life down here as well." (vv. 17–19)

"Trust in your money and down you go! Trust in God and flourish as a tree!" (Proverbs 11:28)

"Stay away from the love of money; be satisfied with what you have. For God has said, 'I will never, never fail you nor forsake you.'" (Hebrews 13:5)

Therefore, all those things of this world, be they riches, fame or praise, a high position, or any other perishable element, must be seen for what these are. And they must also be kept from being hindrances to our kingdom work as well as to our ultimate entry into heaven.

In breaking all things down to base level, I have always felt that beyond the motives of God's kingdom, the worldly reasons for any and all secularly based acts and decisions are rooted in just four types of motives. They are the reason for any product, work, effort, or thought that the world puts forth. The first is money or reward. The second is power, including pride and position. The third involves trying to please others. And the fourth emanates from a sexual (or some other type of a relational) motivation. We must strive not to be preoccupied with any of such.

Again, all earthly rewards will pass much more rapidly than any of us realize. What seems to be solid earthly wisdom is all too soon shown to be false. The only true wisdom is for one to fully understand the meaning of Christ's cross, which God grants to all who earnestly seek and follow him, through his grace.

F) Humility and Pride?

Biblical references to these concepts abound:

"Pride comes before a fall." (1 Timothy 3:6b)

"Pride ends in destruction; humility ends in honor." (Proverbs 18:12)

"The humble shall see their God at work for them." (Psalm 69:32a)

"For everyone who tries to honor himself shall be humbled; and he who humbles himself shall be honored." (Luke 14:11)

"Your care for others is the measure of your greatness." (Luke 9:48b)

"'Humble men are very fortunate!' he told them, 'for the Kingdom of Heaven is given to them. ...The meek and lowly are fortunate! for the whole wide world belongs to them.'" (Matthew 5:3, 5)

"About that time the disciples came to Jesus to ask which of them would be greatest in the Kingdom of Heaven! Jesus called a small child over to him and set the little fellow down among them, and said, 'Unless you turn to God from your sins and become as little children, you will never get into the Kingdom of Heaven. Therefore anyone who humbles himself as this little child is the greatest in the Kingdom of Heaven.'" (Matthew 18:1–4)

"The more lowly your service to others, the greater you are. To be the greatest, be a servant. But those who think themselves great shall be disappointed and humbled; and those who humble themselves shall be exalted." (Matthew 23:11–12)

"Anyone wanting to be the greatest must be the least—the servant of all!" (Mark 9:35)

"What are you so puffed up about? What do you have that God hasn't given you? And if all you have is from God, why act as though you are so great, and as though you have accomplished something on your own?" (1 Corinthians 4:7)

"As the Scriptures say, 'If anyone is going to boast, let him boast about what the Lord has done and not about himself.'" (2 Corinthians 10:17)

"As for me, God forbid that I should boast about anything except the cross of our Lord Jesus Christ." (Galatians 6:14a)

"And all of you serve each other with humble spirits, for God gives special blessings to those who are humble, but sets himself against those who are proud. If you will humble yourselves under the mighty hand of God, in his good time he will lift you up." (1 Peter 5:5–6)

Pride can certainly be a detriment. Yet, some degree of pride is needed in our lives. I believe that we should exhibit a good and healthy degree of pride in what we do, always putting forth our best efforts and being happy that we are able to work through God's design to help others, as he plans for us to do. This is a non-self-serving, positive pride, which must be distinguished from the negative type, namely that arrogant, selfish pride that always seeks attention, or praise, or other secondary gain. The easiest way to distinguish between the two types is to look at your motives and decide whether they are selfless or selfish.

I have heard some who persecute Christians become infuriated, saying, "How weak those Christians are!" As humble people, we are not actually as weak as the world thinks. As the Bible says, in our weakness, God makes us strong. It often takes a degree of weakness on our part, be it illness, job loss, grief, or something else that drops us down to a very low level, before we realize God's presence with us as well as his great power.

As Christians, we too must guard against being proud because of the wisdom we have been given by God. The Father allows us to learn and understand his gospel in the Scriptures. Yet learning and knowing is only part of the battle. (Even possessing knowledge by itself can lead into a negative type of pride.) Thus, merely learning is not enough. Rather, we must perform as well, following God's instructions. Following his commands to us in the service of others will defuse our negative pride. Service is pride's antidote. But any service done, or used, or thought about erroneously can easily leave us prideful as well if we possess incorrect motives.

Whether at work, at home, or out socially, we should never act as if we are a big deal. Rather, we must repeatedly work to develop the mindset personally, as well as the ability to tell others routinely, that God is the big deal rather than ourselves, and that we are doing all that we do solely for him and his glory! For example, I am very often thanked by patients and families for my medical help. Knowing my place, however, I always point an upraised hand to him, telling them to pass the praise up and onward to him, as I do. Yet, I also tell them that they are welcome, as I am very happy to act as his conduit by using the knowledge and experience he has given me to be able to help others. If you practice this attitude, it very easily becomes a humbling habit, which will keep bad pride from taking root in your heart.

Always remember that God has you where you are not just for any old reason but for his purpose and for his reason. He keeps extending his grace to we undeserving people simply by giving us our next breaths, our next heartbeats, and our next seconds of time. And if he is doing so, he certainly has a plan that he wants us to either start or to continue performing, as humbly as possible. We should take a healthy pride in what we do for him. But we must not let this pride become a negative type of attitude or asset. Consider these verses:

"The Lord says: Let not the wise man bask in his wisdom, nor the mighty man in his might, nor the rich man in his riches. Let them boast in this alone: That they truly know me, and understand that I am the Lord of justice and of righteousness whose love is steadfast." (Jeremiah 9:23–24)

"Oh, that you were not so proud and stubborn! Then you would listen to the Lord, for he has spoken. Give glory to the Lord your God before it is too late, before he causes deep, impenetrable darkness to fall upon you so that you stumble and fall upon the dark mountains; then, when you look for light, you will find only terrible darkness. Do you still refuse to listen?" (Jeremiah 13:15–17a)

Rise and Soar

"Lord, help me to realize how brief my time on earth will be. Help me to know that I am here for but a moment more. My life is no longer than my hand! My whole lifetime is but a moment to you. Proud man! Frail as breath! A shadow! And all his busy rushing ends in nothing. He heaps up riches for someone else to spend. And so, Lord, my only hope is in you." (Psalm 39:4–7)

G) Unbelief / Faithlessness?

As we discussed above, we all have doubts and times when belief grows thin. Even God's greatest saints and apostles went through such times, as is evidenced multiple times in the Scriptures.

But what about gross and complete unbelief, a full and utter faithlessness, a blind ignoring of God and all that he has given us, especially the gift of his Son, Jesus? What does Scripture say about those who completely ignore, refuse, and scorn God's gift right up to the end of their lives here on earth? Let's consider these verses:

"He began to cry. 'Eternal peace was within your reach and you turned it down,' he wept, 'and now it is too late. . . . for you have rejected the opportunity God offered you.'" (Luke 19:41–42, 44b)

"Then Jesus said to them, 'You are such foolish, foolish people! You find it so hard to believe all that the prophets wrote in the Scriptures!'" (Luke 24:25)

"For God loved the world in this way: He gave His One and Only Son, so that everyone who believes in Him will not perish but have eternal life. For God did not send His Son into the world that He might condemn the world, but that the world might be saved through Him. Anyone who believes in Him is not condemned, but anyone who does not believe is already condemned, because he has not believed in the name of the One and Only Son of God." (John 3:16–18 HCSB)

"And all who trust him—God's Son—to save them have eternal life; those who don't believe and obey him shall never see heaven, but the wrath of God remains upon them." (John 3:36)

"The world's sin is unbelief in me." (John 16:9)

"Then he said to Thomas, 'Put your finger into my hands. Put your hand into my side. Don't be faithless any longer. Believe!' 'My Lord and my God!' Thomas said. Then Jesus told him, 'You believe because you have seen me. But blessed are those who haven't seen me and believe anyway.' Jesus' disciples saw him do many other miracles besides the ones told about in this book, but these are recorded so that you will believe that he is the Messiah, the Son of God, and that believing in him you will have life." (John 20:27–31)

In summary, the world says, "Show me, and I'll believe," but Christ says, "Just believe, and I'll show you!"

Please take him at his Word and ask him to help you. Then you will experience his many special blessings for yourself.

H) His Love for Us?

Easing carefully down the pitch-dark mountainside trail, smack in the middle of brown bear-dense southeast Alaska's Baranof Island, I rounded a turn. And suddenly, through the misty blackness, my head-lamp illuminated a pair of big red eyes and then another smaller pair alongside the first: a brown bear sow with cub!

Being just ten yards away, there was nowhere for me to go but off and over the trail edge onto the steep mountainside below. There was no time to think; only time for reflex action. I held my rifle over my head with both hands to protect what might be needed most to get me through this encounter and leapt off over the ledge into the black-ness below.

Now, I had hiked up this same path earlier in daylight, so it was not a purely blind jump. Yet I knew that the slope was steep: about a fifty five-degree angle of pitch and covered with big rocks and boulders. Two of those my knees found by immediately cracking onto them. By God's grace, I did not fall farther or suffer any injuries more severe than deep bone bruises. I clawed my way around the dark mountainside, bypassing the bears, who apparently had continued moseying on down the trail, and none of us came to any further harm. Now, you may ask, why did I do this?

Just two days before, I waded onto a small gravel island in a swollen Alaskan river. I sat down next to a huge fallen tree, which crossed over from the bank onto my island. After an hour, something told me to leave that spot, so I moved about twenty yards down the island into a stand of three-foot-high swamp grass. There I knelt with binoculars, watching for bears in the misty rain from a much more camouflaged spot.

Just minutes later, a huge mother brownie led two cubs from the trees along the riverbank and out across that log. They dropped down onto the island so close that I could smell them. The cubs began root-ing around in the gravel looking for salmon scraps, but mother bear caught my scent and went on instant alert, standing on her hind legs and sniffing the air, with her hackles up, growling and snarling. Frozen in place and still kneeling, I dared not move.

A bear's vision in daytime is similar to a man's, but they pick up movement extremely well. (At night, their eyes are about fifty times better than ours.) Nevertheless, their sense of smell is amazing. They have what is felt to be the best nose of all land animals, estimated at over two thousand times better than a human nose. They routinely travel up to twenty miles to a scented food source. I saw a video in which a helicopter followed a male polar bear sixty miles on a beeline to a female in heat. And some bears have been tracked going over a hundred miles to breed.

Watching this upset and hyper-alert behemoth from such a close range, which knew there was a human nearby, I stayed completely still. That way, she would have much more difficulty figuring out exactly where I was. But if I moved, her nine hundred pounds or so would be on me in an instant. She would have teeth and claws on me even if I were able to get off a point-blank shot. Fortunately, she did not know where I was. When she turned and scanned the other way, I dropped facedown into the gravel, watching her search.

My rifle was at my side, but I did not want to use this on her or orphan her cubbies. And at that range, even with perfect vital organ shot placement, she would be on top of me in seconds and chew on me anyway. One bullet would be unlikely to end her assault soon enough to avoid a good mauling, or worse. According to outfitter friends and guides, the average number of shots required to take down a brownie is eight. I personally know of mortally wounded bears going for ten seconds and even running one hundred and ten yards or more with bullet-obliterated hearts. Even a mortally wounded bear can still do great damage in a short amount of time.

Fortunately for me, after thirty seconds of seeing no definitive threat, she barked orders to the cubs, and they jumped back up onto the log. She ran back to the riverbank rainforest with her two young and disappeared silently into the dense Tongass Forest jungle. Had I not moved minutes prior to her arrival, there would have been a different outcome for either myself, the she-bear, or most likely, for the both of us.

Anyone who has experienced a close encounter with a mother grizzly or brown bear or a mother black or polar sow with their cubs close at hand has seen evidence of the intense love, care, and protection that the mother provides against any presumed threat. Without hesitation and without any consequence or worry about possible harm to herself, a mother bear will fight any and all challengers (even much larger male bears) to the death if need be. She will not stop until the threat is eliminated. Even gigantic males commonly back off when faced with her fury and determination. I have seen this in the wild several times.

Let's consider this wildly fierce yet fully selfless love of a female bear, or the love of a human mother for her young. Multiply that love several million times, if not more, and it still pales in comparison to the magnitude of God's great love and protection for us! How could our human minds ever even begin to understand the depth of his love? It is immense and amazing!

Besides God's great holiness, I believe that his most amazing character trait is his constant and immense love for us. The Scriptures repeatedly echo and reinforce this. Yet most of us still ask, "How can he love me? I have been too bad, and I have done too many evil things." Or we may think, "A bad thing happened to me, and ever since, I am tarnished and dirty. God could never love me."

You must always remember that he does not love you because of what's inside of you or for the duties you do or do not do, nor what you have done or have not done, nor what has been done or not done to you. Rather, he loves you because God is the perfect embodiment of the most perfect love. He is love, so he simply does love us. Love is his very nature, and therefore his loving attitude toward us can never change! Consider Hosea 6:6, "I don't want your sacrifices—I want your love; I don't want your offerings—I want you to know me."

Likewise, once we accept his love, God calls us to mirror his great love to others. He wants us to pass it on so we can grow to love our enemies, those who oppose the gospel, and even the seemingly unlovable. By seeing them through Christ's eyes, they become Jesus Christ. We love Jesus as we love them.

The more we spend time with God and with Jesus in Scripture and in prayer, the more we come closer and closer to achieving this goal, as difficult as it is to do so. Let us look at several of the multiple scriptural examples of God's great love for us, such as John 3:16–17: "For God loved the world so much that he gave his only Son so that anyone who believes in him shall not perish but have eternal life. God did not send his Son into the world to condemn it, but to save it."

Consider as well the example of Luke 15:2–7 regarding Jesus as the good shepherd searching tirelessly for his lost sheep, or also verses 8–9 which describe the joy of finding a lost coin. And verses 11–31 contain the parable of the prodigal son. In each of these, Jesus tells us how overjoyed our heavenly Father is when we finally come to him, we who are lost.

The father of the prodigal son is one of my favorite examples. Even though his Son greatly disrespected him and did many bad things, his father remained continually watching and waiting for him. Then, on the day when the son decided to return to his father and seek forgiveness, the father ran to the boy, threw his arms around him, and blessed him immensely. This shows us that God is always waiting for us, always hoping, continually pleading and desiring for us to return to him and his amazing love.

Consider also John 13, in which Jesus demonstrated his great love as well as the love that we are asked to show to others. He washed his disciples' feet, providing the classic example of loving servanthood. He then told the disciples to do to others as he has done, which is also his command for us today.

Also, let's look at:

> "I have loved you even as the Father has loved me. Live within my love. When you obey me you are living in my love, just as I obey my Father and live in his love. I have told you this so that you will be filled with my joy. Yes, your cup of joy will overflow! I demand that you love each other as much as I love you. And here is how to measure it—the greatest love is shown when a person lays down his life for his friends." (John 15:9–13)

> "And I, the Messiah, came to save the lost. If a man has a hundred sheep, and one wanders away and is lost, what will he do? Won't he leave the ninety-nine others and go out into the hills to search for the lost one? And if he finds it, he will rejoice over it more than over the ninety-nine others safe at home! Just so, it is not my Father's will that even one... should perish." (Matthew 18:11–14)

> "Don't you realize how patient he is being with you? Or don't you care? Can't you see that he has been waiting all this time without punishing you, to give you time to turn from your sin? His kindness is meant to lead you to repentance." (Romans 2:4)

"But God showed his great love for us by sending Christ to die for us while we were still sinners." (Romans 5:8)

"Overwhelming victory is ours through Christ who loved us enough to die for us. For I am convinced that nothing can ever separate us from his love. Death can't, and life can't. The angels won't, and all the powers of hell itself cannot keep God's love away. Our fears for today, our worries about to-morrow, or where we are—high above the sky, or in the deep-est ocean—nothing will ever be able to separate us from the love of God demonstrated by our Lord Jesus Christ when he died for us." (Romans 8:37–39)

"So overflowing is his kindness toward us that he took away all our sins through the blood of his Son, by whom we are saved; and he has showered down upon us the richness of his grace—for how well he understands us and knows what is best for us at all times." (Ephesians 1:7–8)

"God is so rich in mercy; he loved us so much that even though we were spiritually dead and doomed by our sins, he gave us back our lives again when he raised Christ from the dead—only by his undeserved favor have we ever been saved—and lifted us up from the grave into glory along with Christ, where we sit with him in the heavenly realms—all because of what Christ Jesus did." (Ephesians 2:4–6)

"Plant the good seeds of righteousness, and you will reap a crop of my love; plow the hard ground of your hearts, for now is the time to seek the Lord, that he may come and shower salvation upon you." (Hosea 10:12)

"Then I will cure you of idolatry and faithlessness, and my love will know no bounds, for my anger will be forever gone!" (Hosea 14:4)

"God showed how much he loved us by sending his only Son into this wicked world to bring to us eternal life through his death. In this act we see what real love is: it is not our love for God but his love for us when he sent his Son to satisfy God's anger against our sins. Dear friends, since God loved us as much as that, we surely ought to love each other too." (1 John 4:9–11)

"We know how much God loves us because we have felt his love and because we believe him when he tells us that he loves us dearly. God is love, and anyone who lives in love is living with God and God is living in him. And as we live with Christ, our love grows more perfect and complete; so we will not be ashamed and embarrassed at the day of judgment, but can face him with confidence and joy because he loves us and we love him too. We need have no fear of someone who loves us perfectly; his perfect love for us eliminates all dread of what he might do to us." (1 John 4:16–18a)

"Oh, give thanks to the Lord, for he is good; His love and his kindness go on forever." (1 Chronicles 16:34)

God's amazing love for us is so much more than we can ever imagine. Yet Satan in our hearts tells us (and, unfortunately, we often believe) that we are unworthy. We know how bad we really are and how we have messed up. Therefore, we often feel that God can never love the person we really are. And we feel too as if we must earn his love, which places pressure on us, a tension for performance, an anxiety. We feel as if we can never measure up, and we often put ourselves down.

Instead, we must change our mindset, opening our eyes and our minds to see just how very much God loves each of us. He loves us with the same love he has for his own Son. He gave up Christ Jesus out of his great love for us!

Now think, would you give up your only child for a bad person if you did not love that bad soul? Of course not! Consider how difficult it would be to give your child up for even a good person. God has, through this great sacrificial act, clearly proven that he does love each of us. He wants to make us all his very own beloved children and to take us into heaven with him for all eternity!

Step back, see, and realize this fact of God's character. Accept and believe that his love is true. Then you will receive his true peace, joy, fulfillment, and rescue. This lets you enjoy each day in this life, like a vacation day at the beach, relaxed and basking in the light of his love and approval, no longer striving and worrying about earning his favor. Earthly fathers may require such efforts, but our heavenly Father does not. Let him fill you up with his love for you. He is your true Father, so much better than even the very best earthly parent can ever be.

Once you realize, believe in, and accept his love, it pulls you out of your own darkness and into his light! So why be sad, stressed, worried, anxious, depressed, or feel squashed down, controlled, bitter, or angry? Remember that our loving Father God is always with us!

Yet, we are doubting and questioning humans. Where can we get the daily reassurances we all need? God's Word bears witness to the confirming agreement between him and us. There, he declares and promises to always love us because of who he is. It is not by what we've done or not done. His love is not tethered to our being good or not being bad. It is true and forever unchanging. It is not mythology. Try it and you'll see!

Simply tell your heart, your mind, and your soul that God loves you as much as he loves his Son, Jesus. And realize that no matter where you are today, God has a big and special plan for you. If he did not, you would no longer be breathing and no longer living here in this world. You simply need to reach out, ask him to help you, and grab onto his free gift of love. Let it enter into you and take root, becoming your primary guiding and calming force for the rest of your days until your ultimate rescue into his paradise!

An appropriate prayer here is as follows: "Dear Lord, open the eyes of every one of us. Let us all realize the blessings you give us every day, even our very next breath and our next heartbeat. May all people, especially those who do not know you and therefore do not yet believe in you, today be firmly convinced of your great love for them by your Holy Spirit! We ask this in the name of your beloved Son, Jesus, our Christ, whom you sacrificed, giving him up for us as the greatest example and as a perfect guarantee of your unending love for us! Amen!"

May we never forget such!

I) Forgiveness?

As difficult as forgiveness is for our human hearts, what best helps me is to think as such: If Jesus can forgive even his torturers and murderers at his cross, how can we not forgive others? Have we ever been wronged as much as Christ was?

Still, forgiveness is a very difficult thing for us to do. It involves changing our hearts so that we no longer hold grudges, or anger, or bitterness against those who have wronged us. And it allows us to begin to seek forgiveness from those whom we ourselves have wronged, as we both apologize and ask for their forgiveness. Let us look at some important passages from Scripture regarding this concept:

"But anyone who asks for mercy from the Lord shall have it and shall be saved." (Acts 2:21)

"Then Peter came to him and asked, 'Sir, how often should I forgive a brother who sins against me? Seven times?' 'No!' Jesus replied, 'seventy times seven! The Kingdom of Heaven can be compared to a king who decided to bring his accounts up to date. In the process, one of his debtors was brought in who owed him $10 million! He couldn't pay, so the king ordered him sold for the debt, also his wife and children and everything he had. But the man fell down before the king, his face in the dust, and said, "Oh, sir, be patient with me and I will pay it all." Then the king was filled with pity for him and released him and forgave his debt. But when the man left the king, he went to a man who owed him $2,000 and grabbed him by the throat and demanded instant payment. The man fell down before him and begged him to give him a little time. "Be patient and I will pay it," he pled. But his creditor wouldn't wait. He had the man arrested and jailed until the debt would be paid in full. Then . . . the king called before him the man he had forgiven and said, "You evil-hearted wretch! Here I forgave you all that tremendous debt, just because you asked me to—shouldn't you have mercy on others, just as I had mercy on you?" Then the angry king sent the man to the torture chamber until he had paid every last penny due. So shall my heavenly Father do to you if you refuse to truly forgive your brothers.'" (Matthew 18:21–35)

Rise and Soar

"Even blasphemy against me or any other sin can be forgiven—all except one: speaking against the Holy Spirit shall never be forgiven, either in this world or in the world to come." (Matthew 12:31–32)

"Your heavenly Father will forgive you if you forgive those who sin against you; but if you refuse to forgive them, he will not forgive you." (Matthew 6:14–15)

"'Father, forgive these people,' Jesus said, 'for they don't know what they are doing.'" (Luke 23:34)

J) Faith?

Previously, in Chapter XI, we discussed this in much detail, but let's look further at some specific Scripture references to see how Abraham's great and unquestioning faith was so greatly blessed by God:

"I, the Lord, have sworn by myself that because you have obeyed me and have not withheld even your beloved son from me, I will bless you with incredible blessings and multiply your descendants into countless thousands and millions, like the stars above you in the sky, and like the sands along the seashore." (Genesis 22:16–17)

Also, consider what we will gain by remaining faithful:

"This Good News tells us that God makes us ready for heaven—makes us right in God's sight—when we put our faith and trust in Christ to save us. This is accomplished from start to finish by faith. As the Scripture says it, 'The man who finds life will find it through trusting God.'" (Romans 1:17)

"Remain faithful even when facing death and I will give you the crown of life—an unending, glorious future." (Revelation 2:10b)

"Everyone who conquers will be clothed in white, and I will not erase his name from the Book of Life, but I will announce before my Father and his angels that he is mine." (Revelation 3:5)

24. Reaching Others for Christ

I like to consider that every nonbeliever in Christ, each false-faith follower or atheist, has a cover or shell about them. Some are very hard and resistant, while others are softer and more pliable. No matter how hard or resistant their barrier may seem, always remember that Christ's gospel good news is stronger. Even if it does not visibly penetrate their defenses immediately, it still (especially if presented persistently and repeatedly), will sink in and weaken even the nonbeliever's thickest outer layers. The gospel can and does break through any wall, no matter how high or impenetrable it may seem. Let's consider these verses on reaching others:

"How beautiful upon the mountains are the feet of those who bring the happy news of peace and salvation, the news that the God of Israel reigns." (Isaiah 52:7)

"Sing a new song to the Lord! Sing it everywhere around the world! Sing out his praises! Bless his name. Each day tell someone that he saves." (Psalm 96:1–2)

"I send it out [the word], and it always produces fruit. It shall accomplish all I want it to and prosper everywhere I send it." (Isaiah 55:11)

"Go out and tell them whatever I tell you to say. Don't be afraid of them, or else I will make a fool of you in front of them. . . . today I have made you impervious to their attacks. They cannot harm you. You are strong like a fortified city that cannot be captured, like an iron pillar and heavy gates of brass." (Jeremiah 1:17–18a)

"You are to influence them, not let them influence you! They will fight against you like a besieging army against a high city wall. But they will not conquer you, for I am with you to protect and deliver you, says the Lord." (Jeremiah 15:19b–20)

"And those who are wise—the people of God—shall shine as brightly as the sun's brilliance, and those who turn many to righteousness will glitter like stars forever." (Daniel 12:3)

As noted in the verses above, the most important thing is to be certain you know and understand exactly who Jesus is, how much he loves you, and what he did for you in granting you eternal salvation despite your sinful human nature. You must also continue to make an effort throughout your lifetime to know him better and better, thereby allowing yourself to mirror Christ more and more accurately over time to others.

After Christ rose and then ascended to heaven, his plan was and is to continue living tangibly and visibly here in this world through his people, including you. You are to be his transforming hands, feet, voice, and ears to this world, which is so very lost without him. He is the power source, not you or any other person or even church leaders.

So, as you try to be your best to live for Christ, he lives in and through you. As Paul writes, his body is manifested in us. 2 Corinthians 4:10–11 says that we are "always carrying in the body the death of Jesus, so that the life of Jesus may also be manifested in our bodies. For we who live are always being given over to death for Jesus' sake, so that the life of Jesus also may be manifested in our mortal flesh" (ESV). Also, consider Galatians 2:20: "I have been crucified with Christ. It is no longer I who live, but Christ who lives in me. And the life I now live in the flesh I live by faith in the Son of God, who loved me and gave himself for me" (ESV).

***

In trying to reach others, one thing we must remember is to persistently maintain the virtue of humility. We cannot exhibit (although we may feel so) any outwardly visible frustration, agitation, anger, discouragement, prejudice, or belittling of other cultures or belief systems. Christ would never do that.

What helps me here, no matter the situation, is to try to remain acting, speaking, and thinking as I feel Christ would, typically engaging the other person and then allowing first a discussion of their beliefs (or their lack of belief in anything, in the case of some). The discussion always provides multiple points that they have brought up personally that can be examined. Find out what that person's views are on life and what they think happens after we die. Also, get their thoughts on sin. Then you can ask what they base their beliefs on.

Any rational person will admit that such views must be based on a solid foundation if one is going to bet their eternity upon them! You can then discuss Christianity's firm foundation, with its historical, archaeological, eyewitness, scientific, and supernatural components (as we discussed in detail above), which have been verified by non-Christian sources as well as Christian ones!

One thing I like to present is that Jesus said he was the only way (John 14:6). So, this leaves us with only two choices: either he was right, and therefore must be God, or that he was wrong, and therefore must be either a liar or an insanely deranged mental case. Yet, absolutely no evidence for any potential classic psychiatric illness comorbidities are reported anywhere in the chronicles of Jesus's life besides, if you wish to call it such, a possible delusion of grandiosity.

This is extremely important: I will tell you from my experience in dealing with psychiatric patients over my many years in medical practice that you will never see delusional grandeur in isolation. There are typically many, many other concurrent issues in these cases, which cause significant interference with normal social functioning. Nothing like them is mentioned in the reports we have of Jesus, neither in the Scriptures nor the Jewish writings nor the secular Roman reports about him. Therefore, this psychiatric diagnosis clearly does not fit Jesus of Nazareth.

Next, then, it follows that if indeed Jesus Christ is God, he does not, and in fact cannot, ever tell a lie, especially not one about his being divine. Yet, consider the alternative to this position: if he was not God, then how exactly did he do—and how could you explain away—all his miracles, his healings, his prophetic fulfillments? Also, most importantly, how do you then explain away his resurrection and his subsequent appearance to over five hundred eyewitnesses?

One can only explain it by the evident conclusion that Jesus was and is God! This is the only logical conclusion, if we look at all the evidence objectively and without bias, emotion, or prejudice.

***

So, in trying to reach others and to share Jesus's good news, pray with them, befriend them, and invite them to church and to Bible study with you. Be sure also to have the actual gospel discussion with them, describing what Christ has done for us and how they can claim his gift for themselves!

Remember, it is not up to you to win the war; rather, you are his soldier, placed there into that spot for the Holy Spirit to act as your general to guide you into the appropriate action or, at times, the correct inaction. You must first step out. Then give the battle to him. Let him handle it as your commander.

I must reemphasize that one must step out into action. Passivity is very easy, but it bears no reward. Adopting this mindset takes vision. We act now with eternity in view. Do you want a complete and exciting life, full of gusto? Then undertake this task. What could ever be more exciting and fulfilling than positively impacting others for eternity in Christ's kingdom?

***

We have already discussed what to review with nonbelievers: that God's Word is the one evidenced truth. That Christianity is backed up by historical, scientific, archaeological, and legal (eyewitness) evidence. And these make so strong a case that if you examine the evidence openly and honestly, you cannot help but be convinced of its truthfulness above all other creeds.

I again strongly recommend that all people look at these data supporting Christ's divinity themselves rather than blindly accepting a religious leader or family's views, traditions, or cultures or following one's uninvestigated feelings.

I again like to challenge seeking and lost people to read the New Testament. I recommend they read at least one Gospel and preferably all four by doing at least one chapter a day for thirty days. Most people are up for a challenge, and when presented with such, most will agree to do it. I ask them to give it thirty days and then to honestly ask themselves and tell me whether they are positively changed by the experience. Almost every single one admits they have been!

**

Satan again does not waste his time going after false religions, because only the true faith is of any threat to him. This explains the overwhelmingly one-sided persecution of Christians in this world. (Christian persecution is far fiercer than the hatred between Muslims and Hindus or between the Sunni and Shiite Muslim factions.)

Why is no other religion so universally persecuted to the degree that Christianity is? This is because none of them are the true faith. Satan likes having these other paths around to distract and confuse searchers. Finding the truth is then like trying to maneuver through an endless maze of twisting trails in a dark mountain wood with multiple switchbacks, while perils of fierce beasts, pitfalls, deep rivers and swamps, hidden cliffs, quicksand, landslides, and avalanches await.

Satan's primary goal is to keep you from finding the true God. And he will use whatever distraction he can, be it the desires and things of this world or misleading and fraudulent belief systems. And the more distracting options available, the better! If he can keep you blinded within his chains and irons, locked firmly within his trap until you die, you will be his! That is his sole motivation: to keep you away from God and thus get you for himself, and in so doing, dishonoring God your Father.

Many people I speak to about Christianity will say, "Religions are all the same, just different ways to god." Yet, I ask them then to look at the lives of the followers of each creed. What fruits or positive results do they bear, if any at all?

All that these false faiths or non-faiths have is a grasp of non-truths or of half-truths. While many atheists, agnostics, Muslims, Hindus, Buddhists, Witnesses, Mormons, cultists, and the like may have great zeal and, in many cases, good intent, they are nonetheless blinded! No matter how dedicated they are, just like the founders of their respective faiths, their zeal can never convert false beliefs into true facts!

Alternatively, Christians have the true faith. They also possess the true Word of the living God and his Son, Jesus, in the Holy Bible!

***

In John 8:24 Jesus states, "Unless you believe that I am the Messiah, the Son of God, you will die in your sins." So, if we feel that any other path can also potentially save us, we make Christ's blood, which he shed for us, completely worthless. We will die in our sins if we deny his gift to us.

Consider several types of persons. First, there are the self-righteous who say, "I am good enough for heaven," or, "I do more good than bad," or, "I can save myself." If you do not admit that you are a sinner who needs a savior and acknowledge that you can never save yourself by any good works, rituals, church-temple-mosque-hall attendance, or prayers, you will definitively die in your sins.

Second, consider the worldly people who are preoccupied with this physical world and its busy workings. They live only for its goods, its cultures, and its ideologies. Many of those are Satan-devised to distract us from Christ. Remember that Jesus said, if you love the world, you do not love the Father. And he also said, a man cannot serve two masters. A choice must be made. Make yours pro-God, not pro-world.

A third group are deniers, scorners, and scoffers, the unbelievers in Christ. These people are willfully in denial. They are obstinate and ignorantly blind. Jesus answered people like this, some of the Pharisees of his day, in John 8:25–29. Jesus told them that they should have seen God in him, yet they did not. Also, 1 John 2:22 states that the greatest liar is the one who says that Jesus is not the Christ. Other direct quotes from Jesus Christ in the Scriptures that are pertinent here include:

> "I say emphatically that anyone who listens to my message and believes in God who sent me has eternal life, and will never be damned for his sins, but has already passed out of death into life." (John 5:24)

> "For it is my Father's will that everyone who sees his Son and believes on him should have eternal life—that I should raise him at the Last Day." (John 6:40)

> "I am the Way—yes, and the Truth and the Life. No one can get to the Father except by means of me." (John 14:6)

> "I am the one who raises the dead and gives them life again. Anyone who believes in me, even though he dies like anyone else, shall live again. He is given eternal life for believing in me and shall never perish." (John 11:25–26)

As Jesus said, we must realize and believe that we are all sinners and that we need to be saved by our Creator, who is far beyond ourselves and our own control. We must repent of our sins to date, believing that Jesus is the Messiah sent by God his Father to save us, and we must place our faith in him as saving Lord. If we do not, the price is an eternal penalty! Why wouldn't you accept his atonement, which he offers as his free gift for you? Why would you choose to die when you can live?

Important points to make and then to discuss here include:

1) You say you are a good person. So, you think and hope that you'll go to heaven. But are you willing to stake everything on that one little thought you came up with in your own little head? I don't see how you can know this with 100 percent certainty.

2) Just one sin keeps you out of heaven without Christ. He died two thousand years ago to forgive all sins. Yet, in the end, he will forgive only the sins of those who believe on him.

3) God wants each of us to do something great for him. But our lives are racing by. So do it and do it now!

4) Some will say, "I am too old now. I have not believed all these years, and you can't teach an old dog new tricks." My reply here is, "These are not tricks. You are more important to him than any old dog. And God can change anyone." Consider the above-noted legend of Stalin on his death bed. I tell them, "You need to make a commitment to him. Ask him into your life to save you, though a sinner. State your belief in Christ, and in what he did for you. And ask him to help you follow him as his true disciple!"

***

To initially open the discussion of religion and beliefs, some more basic yet very good introductory questions here are:

- Do you go to a church or other place of worship?

- What is God to you?

- How can I pray for you?

- How is your life without Christ going? How is it working for you?

If the person I'm addressing is not a Christian, I like to ask how they came to be in their present faith system. Was it passed through the family since childhood, or was it something they accepted later in life? What were the circumstances?

Again, I like to biblically challenge them, stating, "I have a challenge for you. Let's make a deal. Please read some of the New Testament Gospels, starting with John, at least a chapter per day. Spend some time in this living Word of God with an open mind. Let it speak to you, and ask God to reveal himself as you do so."

I challenge them to do this for thirty days and see at that point whether they feel changed. I hope this will allow for more discussion at that time. With some Muslims, I have even agreed to read the Koran if they will read John's Gospel. I even make the lopsided trade-deal of reading their entire book in exchange for their reading John's twenty-one chapters. This certainly opens the lines for communication and comparison!

***

Once one admits that they are a sinner, a great response is: "Repent, be sorry for your misdeeds against our Lord, and humbly ask his forgiveness." Then, you can pray with them. This was the message and the process of all of the biblical prophets, and this message often accomplished its intent of moving God's people back to him (as well as some entire pagan cities such as Nineveh), whether the speaker was Jonah, Isaiah, Jeremiah, Ezekiel, Elisha, Hosea, Amos, John the Baptist, or any of the host of God's other prophets.

His Word changes hearts by the recognition and repentance of sin and by a restoration of human beings with God. This pattern is what Peter, in the early days of the church, outlined when asked what should be done for salvation. He said that we must repent of sin, return to God, and be baptized for the forgiveness of sins. God's amazing gift of forgiveness will then be granted, a gift that he freely gives to all who seek him.

Regarding this realization of our sin and returning to our Father God, I have developed a pneumonic I refer to as the 4 S's.

SEE YOUR SIN for what it really is!

SORROWFULLY REPENT: formally ask him to forgive you. Then,

SPEED BACK TO GOD. Do not delay, no matter how inadequate or dirty you may feel. He is looking for and waiting on you, and he will clean you up and care for you, just as did the father in the parable of the prodigal son (Luke 15:11–32). Last, as you progress through the remainder of your life,

SEEK always to do continually better, using Christ as your example. Always remember that God promises the following:

> "You will seek me and find me, when you seek me with all your heart." (Jeremiah 29:13 ESV)

> "He rewards those who sincerely look for him." (Hebrews 11:6b)

25. Am I Saved?

We, once again, come back to this ultimate, mandatory question: what have you decided about Jesus? Have you put your trust in God and in our Lord Jesus definitively and absolutely?

Knowing that you are saved is not arrogance. Rather, it is in fact humility, as you realize that you cannot save yourself. You humbly submit your salvation to him alone rather than to something that you either do or do not do.

The slogan of all other world religions and cults, which are all inspired by evil, is just this: save yourself! Christianity's slogan is the only one that is different: Christ has done it all for you already! All you need to do is to believe in your heart and confess with your mouth that Jesus is Lord and God!

Please consider these Scripture references:

"In this man Jesus there is forgiveness for your sins! Everyone who trusts in him is freed from all guilt and declared righteous—something the Jewish law could never do." (Acts 13:38–39)

"For the good works of a righteous man will not save him if he turns to sin; and the sins of an evil man will not destroy him if he repents and turns from his sins." (Ezekiel 33:12)

It is much easier to believe and give up your sins to him than it is to go through your entire life trying to be good, attempting to live a good enough life or to be a good enough person, while remaining forever unsure and anxious about your salvation. Consider:

"This Good News tells us that God makes us ready for heaven—makes us right in God's sight—when we put our faith and trust in Christ to save us. This is accomplished from start to finish by faith. As the Scripture says it, 'The man who finds life will find it through trusting God.'" (Romans 1:17)

"Those who depend on the . . . laws to save them are under God's curse, for the Scriptures point out very clearly, 'Cursed is everyone who at any time breaks a single one of these laws that are written in God's Book of the Law.' Consequently, it is clear that no one can ever win God's favor by trying to keep … laws because God has said that the only way we can be right in his sight is by faith. As the prophet Habakkuk says it, 'The man who finds life will find it through trusting God.' How different from this way of faith is the way of law, which says that a man is saved by obeying every law of God, without one slip. But Christ has bought us out from under the doom of that impossible system by taking the curse for our wrongdoing upon himself. … The only way out is through faith in Jesus Christ; the way of escape is open to all who believe him." (Galatians 3:10–13, 22b)

***

Charles Spurgeon once reportedly said, "The grace that does not change my life cannot save my soul." Christ said if we abide in him, we will bear fruit. Those who follow him, he said, will be those who stay in his Word. And he stated that his followers would know the truth and that it would set them free. Therefore, through knowing him, you will also produce good fruit.

However, regarding those people who do not produce good fruit, Jesus says that they are to be pruned off and burned. In order to avoid this bad ending, he disciplines us if and when we are not appropriately fruitful because we are his children. Remember that he disciplines the ones he loves.

Still, you will often see an unsaved person who is wealthy, healthy, and happy by this world's standards. They outwardly look to be doing very well. Yet, remember that such is only a façade. It is just for the present and not a permanent state. God will eventually, although not always immediately, discipline the devil's kids. Think about yourself. Do you want to discipline the kids of your neighbors or your friends? No. We would rather only discipline our own. It is similar with our Lord!

***

Also, as discussed above, don't waste your life's time by dawdling around thinking that you have forever here:

> "That day of the Lord will come unexpectedly, like a thief in the night. … there will be no place to hide." (1 Thessalonians 5:2–3b)

> "So be on your guard, not asleep like the others. Watch for his return and stay sober. … let us who live in the light keep sober, protected by the armor of faith and love, and wearing as our helmet the happy hope of salvation." (1 Thessalonians 5:6, 8)

Further, consider these verses that demonstrate the importance of a solid faith in our Lord God:

"For only we who believe God can enter into his place of rest. He has said, 'I have sworn in my anger that those who don't believe me will never get in,' even though he has been ready and waiting for them since the world began." (Hebrews 4:3)

"But we have never turned our backs on God and sealed our fate. No, our faith in him assures our souls' salvation." (Hebrews 10:39)

"What is faith? It is the confident assurance that something we want is going to happen. It is the certainty that what we hope for is waiting for us, even though we cannot see it up ahead." (Hebrews 11:1)

"You can never please God without faith, without depending on him. Anyone who wants to come to God must believe that there is a God and that he rewards those who sincerely look for him." (v. 6)

"And how can we be sure that we belong to him? By looking within ourselves: are we really trying to do what he wants us to?" (1 John 2:3)

"Anyone who believes and says that Jesus is the Son of God has God living in him, and he is living with God." (1 John 4:15)

***

But you may ask, what about our failures? Fortunately, Christ does not regard these as the end of our stories, just as the loving father did not in the story of the prodigal son. God knows that his chosen ones, his real children, will in time make their way back to him. The three questions here are how, what, and when. How long will you be away? What will be the means that brings you back? What adverse consequences will befall you as a result of your decisions during the lost time? And when will you realize that your return is inevitable?

Consider the example of Saint Paul, who severely persecuted Christians before his conversion. Or consider the eleven disciples who fled and abandoned Jesus at his arrest in the garden but who yet returned to him and lived out the remainder of their lives for their risen Christ's great glory!

Before you can be saved, you must realize and agree that you and, in fact, all people are lost sinners. Then realize how Christ has already won your salvation for you by his sacrificial death for your sins. He thereby saves all of those who believe and follow him for the rest of their lives!

You need to realize that you need it and then accept it. It's not at all complicated. Once you hear of his sacrifice for you, you have a choice and a responsibility: what are you going to do with this knowledge?

You may accept it in faith and then come to him, thus letting him also come to you as well, with all his blessings and benefits for your life. As great as these are, they still pale in comparison to your now-guaranteed future beyond this world's meager boundaries.

Or, alternatively, you may reject him and continue onward in your blind error, neglect, and ignorance. You push God away, out of your mind and far from your heart. If you are doing so, I would ask you this: Have you ever really tried an honest and sincere investigation of God? Have you studied and researched this enough and heard or read the testimonies of those real Christians who have reaped his blessings here in this life? Can you honestly say, "This is obviously wrong," or, "This is not for me"?

If so, while I respect your choice made of your individual free will, I must say that no other modern-day, educated, mortal mind who ever started this quest, no matter how initially skeptical or bitter or how steadfast or prejudicially driven, has ever been able to disprove the person and claims of Jesus Christ and his church. Most have realized their error and turned in conversion to our one true Lord!

***

Have you ever gotten out into our streets and rubbed elbows with those out there? I meet and interact daily with real humanity, those struggling with the physical and mental craziness of our world. Modern people still need to know, absolutely, of the forgiveness of sin by Jesus's death and of the all-inclusive reality of his gift. God knows that we all have human hearts, and that we thus often feel cheated, and that life is unfair. But if we can move past this attitude, we can receive his many blessings, including his salvation!

Consider the example in Genesis 40:15 in which Joseph, jailed for something that he had not done, told fellow prisoners how he was "kidnapped from my homeland . . . and now this—here I am in jail when I did nothing to deserve it."

This is a very human reaction. The events in Joseph's early life were bitter and unfair. Nevertheless, when Joseph finally got past this human view and gave this up to the Lord, God got him out of jail and mightily blessed him. Joseph became the second most powerful and influential man in all of Egypt. This ultimately led to the saving of the Israelite nation, thereby preserving them for God's later purposes in his divine scheme of salvation for all people.

***

So, let's talk some more about faith. Consider faith the invisible expression of our personal relationship with Christ and with God, our knowledge that they are always with us and are ever guiding us. They, as the Bible describes, provide a light to all around, as their leadership along the trail provides a comforting hope and a good path through this world's darkness.

Hebrews 11:1 states: "Now faith is confidence in what we hope for and assurance about what we do not see" (NIV). Consider how in Genesis 15:5–6, God counted Abraham as worthy solely because of his faith. This was both before he tested him by asking him to sacrifice his son Isaac and even after Abraham showed fear and distrust in God by lying to the Egyptians. Abraham lied and said Sarah was his sister rather than trusting God enough to declare truthfully that she was his wife.

Real faith is a gift from God. And, as Scripture says, "If you tell others with your own mouth that Jesus Christ is your Lord and believe in your own heart that God has raised him from the dead, you will be saved" (Romans 10:9).

Do you believe this? If yes, that is absolutely fantastic! This is the biggest choice that we all are faced with in our lives, and the only positive answer is a resounding yes!

If, however, you still do not believe, I pray that you will, in seeking him, soon receive this gift from the Lord.

However, remember that believing alone is not enough. Scripture again says even the demons believe. Besides a mental acknowledgement, you must confess with your lips, openly and publicly, that Christ is Lord, the Lord of all, and especially that he is the Lord of your life.

Have you done this? If not, can you do so now? Some believe but cannot bring themselves yet, in their lives, to confess him. If this includes you, why are you unable? What is keeping you from doing so? Examine your life and see what you need to eliminate, reduce, or minimize. What things have you made your god or gods, so that they keep you from making Christ, the one true Lord, your personal Lord and your own personal savior?

As Scripture says, if we deny him before men, he will deny us before God. Neglecting to confess him as Lord, a sin of omission (neglect), is as bad as vocally denying him from your mouth loudly to others: you are still rejecting God's free and perfect gift of grace, that of forgiveness for our utterly evil hearts' acts and thoughts. Thus, you are still rejecting the salvation that he so freely offers, that of an ultimate oneness with him! What in this world could ever be so important or any more imperative than this?

***

What about doubt? What about those mysteries that we are uncertain of, as well as all those other questions we have in our minds? As discussed above, we as humans must concede that we will never be fully able to mentally grasp every single concept in this world, no matter how accomplished or expert we may become.

I once again have seen this routinely as the medicine I practice has evolved over the past thirty-plus years. The half-life of what we think we know is quite short, and the changes in diagnostics and treatments continue to evolve. Things we did decades ago are now felt to be useless or less effective and at times even harmfully contraindicated now, compared with our current medical knowledge.

Looking at our minds in this way, how can we presume that we might ever begin to even scratch the surface of the entire wealth of knowledge in our own occupation or niche in life? To believe we could is pure arrogance! Therefore, we can never come close to understanding all of God's mysteries.

However, with Jesus, we can learn to accept his Word on faith. He will help us understand it and allow us to know for certain about his atonement, which God has provided for us. Think of his disciples: After Christ died, they did not understand and were bewildered and devastated by the events of those three dark days. Even after his return and the forty days he then spent with them after rising, it still took the Holy Spirit's coming to fully open their minds to the reality of what they had witnessed over those three years spent at Jesus's side.

As was the case with his disciples, we too cannot even begin to comprehend Christ's mysteries, grace, love, and sacrifice for us, by ourselves alone. If we, however, stay in him and in his Word while asking for his help and understanding, he will assist us and give us understanding day by day in a lifelong, never-ending process. Then, in eternity with him, all these mysteries will finally be made clear.

Thus, we humans are very limited. And we must recognize that we can never see nor understand everything fully. We even will distort what we think that we see and know.

However, we fortunately have God as the source of all wisdom. He is all-knowing, all-seeing, and perfect in all ways. Despite our limits, he is ever there to help us through life's dark woods moments. So, we must not worry or be afraid. He is the source of all true wisdom, and he has given us his guidebook of knowledge, which is immediately accessible at our very fingertips. We simply need to open it, read it, and investigate it, while asking his help in doing so.

We will then allow and nurture God's presence within us to grow, helping us greatly in this life and ultimately rewarding us with heaven. Alternatively, we on the other hand can ignore and reject him of our free will. We, thus, can choose whether to obey and to honor him or not to do so. He does not force himself upon us, nor will he storm in to invade our souls. True love cannot be forced. Imagine forcing your love on a potential spouse or pending friend to make them love you. How strange and perverse does that seem!

Your life will never spiritually grow to its optimal potential unless you first gain the complete assurance that you are definitively saved! If you are not assured, there will be limited or even no growth.

As an example, imagine one hesitant, doubting farmer who is exceedingly worried about potential drought or flood, insects or blight, and who, thus, sows just a handful of seeds. Compare this to another positive, non-worrying farmer who sows an entire truckload. Then, consider the growth difference of each farm, even if some problems do arise!

* * *

In conclusion, how do we know for certain that we are saved? We must believe John 3:16. We must accept the gospel's good news and trust our hopes for heaven on Christ alone. We must believe that he, God's Son, has given us this gift, and then we must accept it. We must not count solely upon that good person we are or the great work that we do. We must realize that such will never help us to gain our salvation.

We must be able to say, by his sacrifice, I am covered by his royal robe of goodness, which he exchanged for the filthy rags of my old sinful self. And no matter what else happens from here on in my life, this cannot and will not never be taken away from me. As 1 John 1:8–10 states:

> "If we say that we have no sin, we are only fooling ourselves and refusing to accept the truth. But if we confess our sins to him, he can be depended on to forgive us and to cleanse us

from every wrong. And it is perfectly proper for God to do this for us because Christ died to wash away our sins. If we claim we have not sinned, we are lying and calling God a liar, for he says we have sinned."

1 John 4:16 also states: "We know how much God loves us because we have felt his love and because we believe him when he tells us that he loves us dearly." And 1 John 5:13 also states: "I have written this to you who believe in the Son of God so that you may know you have eternal life."

Again, we must all remember that merely being good will not get any of us into heaven. Heaven is not for good people but for forgiven people, saved people. We, by ourselves, cannot do it all. We need Christ for our salvation. He took God's punishment for us and exchanged his blamelessly clean royal robes for our dirty sinner's rags.

If we are not in him when we die, we will become forever separated from God by being hurled into an eternal judgment in hell! Earlier, we discussed how a loving God can make a hell and how he can send people there to eternal punishment. Again, as we reviewed, our God is very loving and merciful, yet he is not solely a loving God. He is also a just and a perfectly holy God. Therefore, we must be forgiven of our sins in order to be able to come into his presence. He cannot be in the presence of sin, ever, given his holiness. Tolerating sin would compromise his holiness, which our unchanging God can never do.

He originally made hell not for us but for the devil and the bad angels. He doesn't want even one person to go there. His love and mercy are why he then sent his Son to give us an open door, he who is in fact the only door to God's heaven, this eternally blissful lifetime with him.

Christ died in our place in the ultimate act of love. His is the greatest sacrificial love-act our world has ever known. And if we believe in him and accept him as our Savior, we can never be judged or sent to an eternal punishment. Make the correct choice today!

> "Listen! I stand at the door and knock. If anyone hears My voice and opens the door, I will come in to him and have dinner with him, and he with Me." (Revelation 3:20 HCSB)

> "Turn from your sins . . . turn to God . . . for the Kingdom of Heaven is coming soon." (Matthew 3:2)

> "Right now God is ready to welcome you. Today he is ready to save you." (2 Corinthians 6:2b)

Conclusion

The bottom-line question is this: why in the world would one want to seek, let alone follow, the one true God? There are several reasons.

The first is that he made you and puts each continuing breath into your lungs. He has you here for a purpose. So, if you do not know him, how is your life going without him? Can you honestly say that you feel at peace, fully joyful, and completely fulfilled? Are you in absolutely no need of being rescued from the craziness of our world? Do you ever lie awake nights, tossing and turning, wrestling with these questions?

Second, God sent his Son here. And the definitive historical documentation of Jesus's life, death, and rising are hard facts that are not evident in any other religion born of men upon this planet. Therefore, one cannot dismiss, without researching for oneself, the eyewitness reports of so many honest men, including Christians and the Jewish and secular Roman historians of Jesus's day.

Third, do you really think that this life is all that there is? Does that proposition seem at all likely to you, as you see and experience all his amazing creations? Can you truly chalk these all up to science or to evolution, with its presumed-yet-suspect natural selection, or even to random chance? Doesn't it seem more likely that there is a grand designer and Creator? Further, if there is one Creator, does it not seem that he would likely have more plans for us than just our living here for a bit and then dying without any further activity, goals, or extension of life thereafter?

Fourth, if God loves us enough to keep us breathing and supply us with blessings such as food, clothes, shelter, family, and jobs (the sorts of things he grants even to those who ignore and deny him), why wouldn't he develop a grand rescue plan in order to save any and all who will commit to him, through his redemption with Christ's innocent blood? Doesn't it seem logical that he would do so?

Fifth, don't let others determine your future and your eternity. Check it out for yourself! Please consider and undertake the thirty-day Gospel reading challenge while praying and asking for assistance and insightful wisdom from him. Did some so-called Christians in a church or elsewhere bother you, ignore you, or act arrogantly or even harmfully toward you? Were they contentious, rude or pushy, or did they even betray or hurt you? Christ is very sorry if they did, as am I. You must realize, however, that those people are not Christ himself. They did not act as his true ministers and followers should. Do not let them continue to drag you down as well! Remember, all people are sinners and make mistakes. No one can ever fully and consistently represent the goodness of Christ. We are all pitiful sinners.

***

Paul C. Buechel, M.D.

So, in conclusion, why do we need to choose Christ? We should do so for his peace, his joy, our fulfillment, and his rescue. By rescuing us, he forgives our sins. He changes our perspectives and our lives. And he grants us eternal life in heaven with himself, once our worldly time is finished! What greater achievement or goal could we ever strive for in our lifetimes? Can anything whatsoever compare to such blessings?

No matter who we are or who we know or what our position is in this world, we are all moving toward a specific individual moment in which our entire lifetimes, including everything we have ever done or not done, said or not said, and achieved or failed at, comes down to a singular and specific focal point. At that time, everything will converge into one specific question: what did you do about our one Lord and Savior, Jesus Christ?

If you did not know Christ, everything that occurred in your life will be gone, and that will be your end if you hold an atheistic viewpoint, assuming for the moment that your belief is true, that there is nothing else after this world. But if you are incorrect, you will endure an eternity separated from God. You will be extremely unhappy, as he is the only thing that can satisfy that deep yet unmet need you have sought to fill throughout your lifetime. You now will unfortunately possess it for all eternity. Without him, you will never have true joy, satisfaction, completeness, peace, or rescue.

Now consider the great contrast for those who do know him! The lesser things we spend so much time on in this life will seem meaningless to us on our dying day. The important thing will be that all our efforts, events, and activities, both good and bad, will have forged each of us into a person, and into a soul, who knows Christ. Therefore, we will go directly to our loving Father into a blissful, heavenly eternity with him. Our every need will be forever met, and we will know the pure happiness of being in his presence forevermore!

Rise and Soar

***

Therefore, why not be certain? Why not check this out for yourself, as I have described above? Look at this open-mindedly. I can make arguments and debate apologetics for decades, but if you will not open your human mind to even consider the possibility of Jesus Christ as Messiah and to see what he has already done for all of us, such talk will never change you.

Trust your gifts of perception, intelligence, conscience, and understanding. God gave you all of them. Employ these to explore his truth, which he gives us in his Word. And ask him for wisdom. Ask him to reveal himself to you! This, above all else, is what he desires for you.

In all truthfulness, he is our greatest need, not more money, a better job or nicer family, the perfect mate, more technology, or a great vacation. Our greatest need is just this: a savior! And only our loving Father above can provide this perfect love that we all seek, whether we realize it or not.

His is not a romantic love or a friendship type of love. It is the perfect love, one that can be found only in him. Perhaps the most famous verse in the entire Bible is John 3:16, which states, "For God loved the world so much that he gave his only Son so that anyone who believes in him shall not perish but have eternal life."

So you see, we must investigate this option and possibility or risk missing it forever!

The best description of God we have is that of a loving and patient Father, waiting anxiously for his lost children to return. Do not disappoint him. No matter who you are or what you have believed or done up to this point, he will forgive you and then gladly take you back into his arms.

He promises this to us in his Word, his Holy Bible. And, as we have shown above, his Word remains steadfast and true, standing firmly forever.

Therefore, escape and transcend this world's dark woods. Achieve, through Jesus Christ, the life you were meant to live! Let God's holy Word guide you first to your rising and then to your sustained soaring! Let it be the mighty wind beneath your wings. This is my continuing prayer for you and for all who read this message. Amen! Come, Lord Jesus!

Notes

1. Robert D. Wilson, *Scientific Investigation of the Old Testament* (Chicago: IL, Moody Press, 1959).

2. William Albright, *Archeology and the Religion of Israel*, 3rd ed. (Baltimore: MD, Johns Hopkins Press, 1953), 176.

3. John MacArthur, *Twelve Ordinary Men*, (Nashville: TN, Thomas Nelson, 2002), 94, 105—106.

4. Amanda Borschel-Dan, "2,000-year-old 'Pilate' ring just might have belonged to notorious Jesus judge," *The Times of Israel*, November 29, 2018, https://www.time-sofisrael.com/2000-year-old-ring-engraved-with-pilate-may-have-belonged-to-notorious-ruler/.

5. Sir William Ramsay, *St. Paul the Traveler and Roman Citizen* (Grand Rapids: MI, Baker Book House, 1949).

6. J. Warner Wallace, *Cold Case Christianity* (Colorado Springs: CO, David C. Cook, 2013).

7. Ibid., 99—108.

8. Ibid., 161—252.

9. Ibid.

10. Francis Collins, *The Language of God* (London, Simon & Schuster, 2008).

11. Fred Hoyle, *Mathematics of Evolution* (Clinton: TN, Acorn Enterprises, 1999).

12. Peter W. Stoner, *Science Speaks* (Chicago, Moody Press, 1963), 5, 97—110.

13. Ibid.

14. "United States Population," Worldometers, accessed February 4, 2020, https://www.worldometers.info/world-population/us-population/.

15. Charles H. Spurgeon, *The Autobiography of Charles H. Spurgeon* (Philadelphia, American Baptist Publication Society, 1899-1900), 177.

16. Sabina Wurmbrand, *The Pastor's Wife* (Bartlesville: OK, VOM Books, 2013), 147.

17. Ibid., 104.

Scripture Index

New Testament